SOLA SCRIPTURA
TOPICAL BIBLE™

®

SEVEN SYMBOLS
OF JESUS

SOLA SCRIPTURA
TOPICAL BIBLE™

SEVEN SYMBOLS
OF JESUS

Featuring the text of the **New American Standard Bible (NASB)**

Compiled by:

Daniel John

Smart Publishing Ltd.

solascriptura.ca

Sola Scriptura Topical Bible:
Seven Symbols of Jesus

Paperback Edition
ISBN 978-1-77885-019-6

Copyright © 2009, 2017, 2022

Smart Publishing Ltd.
Surrey, British Columbia   Canada
solascriptura.ca

Compiled by: Daniel John

Cover by: Daniel John

Printed by Amazon.

*   *   *   *   *

Other editions of this publication,

Sola Scriptura Topical Bible: *Seven Symbols of Jesus*

Kindle: ISBN 978-1-77885-021-9   ePub: ISBN 978-1-77885-022-6
PDF: ISBN 978-1-77885-023-3   Hard Cover: ISBN 978-1-77885-020-2

Sola Scriptura Topical Bible: *Seven Symbols of Healing*

Kindle: ISBN 978-1-77885-35-6   ePub: ISBN 978-1-77885-031-8
PDF: ISBN 978-1-77885-032-5
Paperback: ISBN 978-1-77885-033-2   Hard Cover: ISBN 978-1-77885-034-9

Editions of: **Sola Scriptura Topical Bible**: *Top 20 Spiritual Symbols*

Kindle: ISBN 978-1-988271-14-9   ePub: ISBN 978-1-988271-13-2
PDF: ISBN 978-1-988271-12-5
Paperback: ISBN 978-1-988271-86-6   Hard Cover: ISBN 978-1-988271-87-3

are available at: solascriptura.ca

TABLE OF CONTENTS

*The fear of the Lord is the beginning of **wisdom**,*

*and the **knowledge** of the Holy One*

*is **understanding**.*   Proverbs 9:10

All Scripture is given by inspiration of God,

and is profitable for doctrine, for reproof, for correction,

for instruction in righteousness;

that the man of God may be complete,

thoroughly equipped for every good work.

2 Timothy 3:16-17

Dedicated To All Who Love The Word of God.

FOREWORD

Welcome, to a powerful, new way to understand the spiritual message and meaning of *The Holy Bible*.

As God has used the words of the Old and New Testaments to teach a message of wisdom and salvation to humanity, the **Sola Scriptura Topical Bible** is an expanded Concordance that lists all of the verses that mention some of the most important spiritual symbols and topical themes that are used in *The Bible* to tell that story.

To show the full context of how a spiritual keyword is being used, and to better understand its meaning within a verse of Scripture, additional verses have been provided before and after the verse that contains the **keyword**, which is highlighted in **bold** font.

As reading all of the verses that relate to a spiritual topic is the only way to know everything that *The Bible* itself says about it, reading all of the related verses in order provides a unique understanding of how the meaning of the topical symbol changes, and sometimes becomes even more spiritual, as the story progresses from the books of the Old Testament to its conclusion in the New Testament.

This book in the **Sola Scriptura Topical Bible** series contains the Biblical verses of seven important related spiritual topics, which were chosen as being among the most valuable for gaining a basic knowledge and understanding about Jesus Christ.

This work was created so that every person can more easily read the important words of *The Bible* for themselves, and be able to more fully contemplate the meaning of the spiritual message of God's Holy Word.

As **Sola Scriptura** means *"the Scriptures alone"*, because *"each person must be fully convinced in his own mind"* (*Romans 14:5*), a verse by verse Commentary on the meaning of the spiritual themes and topical keywords of the Chapters of this book is not included in this text, and is left for a future work. Until then, other resources can be consulted for additional information and meanings, such as a *Bible Dictionary*, *Bible Commentary*, or a *Concordance*.

INTRODUCTION

Since our beginning, humanity has searched for the meaning of this physical, earthly life. Many people believe that God has created mankind on the earth to know Him, and to worship Him. God is Spirit (*John 4:24*), and as an educator of humanity, He has communicated a spiritual message to us, using the physical things of this world as symbols, that our human minds can understand. Many people also believe that God's guidance to us, can be found within the Scriptures of the Holy *Bible*.

"You search the Scriptures, for in them you think you have eternal life..."

~ *Jesus Christ (John 5:39)*

Understanding *The Bible* (Latin: *biblios* - meaning "little books") can be challenging because *The Bible* is actually two different covenants, in two sets of books, that have been bound together as a single volume, for almost two millennia.

The Latin word *testament* means *covenant*, and these two covenants are known as the Hebrew **Tanakh**, or the **Old Testament**, and the **New Testament**, or the Christian covenant. In most modern translations of *The Bible*, there are 39 little books in the Old Testament, and 27 books in the New, for a total of 66 books in a standard Protestant *Bible*.

Together, the 66 *little books* of *The Bible* were written by some forty men, over a period of more than 1,600 years, in three different languages (Hebrew, Aramaic & Greek). So what do the one thousand plus pages of *The Bible* say? How can the meaning of its message be understood?

One way to understand something about the message that is contained within the words of *The Bible* is to study the topics and themes that it uses. To see what *The Bible* says about something, it is necessary to read all of the Scriptures that mention the topic. For this purpose, a Concordance is useful to show the location (Chapter & Verse) of all of the occurrences of a topical theme word, such as *angel* or *gospel*.

However, a Concordance only lists the chapter and verse of where the topic word is found, and the reader must then flip through *The Bible* to find and read the exact verse that contains the topical keyword. In order to understand the context of how the topical keyword is used in the verse, and therefore what it might mean, it is usually necessary to also read the verses that appear immediately before and after the verse that contains the keyword itself; and this process can be time-consuming and confusing to find the beginning and end of the meaningful context.

So that one can quickly and easily read for themselves all of the related words of God on a given topic, this book attempts to display all of the verses mentioning various important spiritual themes in full their context, so that reading a topical Chapter would show everything that *The Bible* itself says about the subject. *The Bible* does not say anything more or less about a topic or theme than everything that it says about it;

from both the Old and the New Testaments.

To quickly see all of the verses that relate to a given topic, this book presents the power of a contextually expanded Concordance, in the easy-to-read format of a novel. The verses provided in each topical Chapter are comprehensive, and include every relevant reference from both the Old and the New Testaments. Reading all of the Scriptures that relate to a topic in sequence allows the mind to be able to quickly see all of the related information, and to arrive at a point of personal truth and understanding, about the underlying spiritual message that is contained within of the word of God.

> *"...line upon line, line upon line, here a little, there a little."*
> *~ Isaiah 28:10 & 13*

As each topical theme becomes understood, it can be seen how their spiritual symbols are interwoven to provide a storyline, which is the meaning, purpose, and message of *The Bible*. In many of these topical Chapters, the meaning of a symbol can be seen to become less physical, and more spiritual, or even purely symbolic, as the storyline progresses from the Old Testament, to its fulfillment in the New Testament.

Reading the Old Testament is necessary to understand how the symbols of the topical themes are later presented and used by Jesus Christ, and the writers of the New Testament.

While not all of the Scriptures provided within each Chapter of this book may be necessary to understand the meaning of a topical theme, they are all included, so that the references for each topic is complete. As a study tool, the reader can mark or highlight for future reference, those passages that are of most importance and interest.

As for the title of this work, *Sola Scriptura* is a Latin term that means "the Scriptures alone" or, "only the Scriptures". *Sola Scriptura* was one of the *solae*, or *solas*, which were among the primary foundational doctrines of the reformers of the medieval Catholic Church, and were popularized by the German priest, Martin Luther, in the early 16th century.

The other important *solas* of the Reformation are *Sola Fide* - Faith alone (that salvation is through faith in Jesus Christ alone), and *Sola Gratia* - Grace alone (that salvation is by the grace of God alone). The later additions of *Solus Christus* - Christ alone (Jesus Christ alone is our Lord, Savior, and King) and *Soli Deo Gloria* - to the Glory of God alone (that we live for the glory of God alone), brought the number of fundamental *Solas* to five.

Sola Scriptura means that the Scripture of *The Bible* alone is the highest and final authority on all matters that deal with salvation. For the reformers, this meant that each person should read the words of God for themselves, and in their own language (and not in Latin, by either necessity or force) to see what *The Bible* itself says, and to be inspired by God for the meaning of those words, and not unduly influenced or completely controlled by the theological doctrines and traditions of men, or of any particular church, denomination or group.

As *Sola Scriptura* means by *the Scriptures alone,* the Scriptures included within the Chapters of this book are presented without comment, and in the same order as they appear within a standard *Bible.*

As this work is intended as a reference, and contains only the verses and words of the Scriptures, other resources should be consulted to gain a deeper understanding of what each topical symbol means. This search should begin with an examination of the origins of the keyword in the original language(s), through the use of an original language *Lexicon, Interlinear* and *Dictionary,* although some basic meanings and definitions have been provided for the topical keywords.

Other resources that help to give a fuller knowledge and understanding of the symbolic keywords of the spiritual symbols include a topical *Bible Concordance* (as *Strong's* or *Young's*), a *Bible Commentary,* and an *Encyclopedia.*

As for the meaning of the spiritual message of *The Bible,* the more that the topical Chapters of this book are read, the greater your understanding of the Word of God will grow to be.

May the Holy Spirit of God guide us to understand His Holy Word.

Daniel John

2009

NOTES ON READING THIS BOOK

This book contains seven topical Chapters, each of which focuses on a different important spiritual topic or theme.

All quoted verses are from the **New American Standard Bible (NASB)** version of the Scriptures. For more information, visit the Lockman Foundation at *lockman.org*.

This section of notes provides the methodology that was used to define the topical theme of each Chapter, and provides information on how the selection of included verses was made.

In these notes the following terms are used:

Keyword	A word that identifies a topical theme. *(see page ix)*
Keyword Phrase	A **keyword** that consists of two or more words.

Verse	A verse from *The Bible*; a line of Scripture.
Concordant Text	A verse, or series of consecutive verses, from a book of *The Bible*, that usually includes a topical **keyword** or **keyword phrase**. "Concordant" is used in the sense that all of the provided texts are discussing the same topical symbol or spiritual theme.
	Most **Concordant Texts** include additional lines of Scripture, before and/or after the verse that includes a **keyword**. These additional verses help to provide sufficient context to understand the use and meaning of the topical keyword within the Scriptures.

For more information about the features of this book,
please see the following sections of Notes:

1. READING THE CONCORDANT TEXTS

A *Concordant Text* is a verse, or a series of consecutive verses, from a book of *The Holy Bible*, that usually contains a topical **keyword** or **keyword phrase**. The Concordant Texts provided in each Chapter of this book are all related to the same spiritual topic or theme.

Where possible, every scriptural occurrence of a topical keyword has been included within the Concordant Texts of each Chapter. Also included are any other keywords that have the same meaning, along with any related keywords, which may include derivatives of a keyword's English root, such as nouns, verbs, adjectives, and adverbs, etc. For example, the Chapter titled **Believe** includes the tertiary keywords *believes*, *believing*, and *believed*. For more information on the types of keywords (main, secondary, tertiary) see page *ix*.

In a few topical Chapters, some scriptural occurrences of a listed keyword were not included within the provided set of Concordant Texts. For more information on the two types of "Inclusion Exceptions" see page *xi*.

In a few Chapters, verses from *The Bible* were included as a Concordant Text even though they do not contain one of the Chapter's listed keywords. While not always directly mentioning a topical keyword, any additional included verses contribute to understanding the spiritual theme of the Chapter.

The seven spiritual topics are presented as Chapters in alphabetical order, and the verses that they contain are presented in the order in which they appear in a standard or NASB edition of *The Bible*.

1. The Concordant Texts of each topical Chapter appear in the same order as most *Bibles*, beginning with the *Book of Genesis* in the Old Testament, and ending with the *Book of Revelation* in the New Testament.

2. *The Bible* chapter and verse reference for each set of Concordant Texts is listed at the end of the set of included verses. Use this reference to locate the full story in a standard *Bible*.

3. For easy identification, the keywords that appear within the Concordant Texts of each topical Chapter are highlighted in **bold** font.

4. The length of the included Scriptures in each set of Concordant Texts has been edited to provide sufficient context to understand the use and the meaning of the topical keyword or keyword phrase. For additional context, use the Scripture reference at the end of each set of concordant verses to find the original verse(s) in a standard *Bible*.

5. Quotation marks are used to attribute words to a specific speaker only if a speaker is identified within the provided set of Concordant Texts.

6. "Selah" and other Hebrew liturgical terms and musical expressions (as found in the books of *Psalms* and *Habakkuk)* have been omitted.

SYMBOLS USED within The CONCORDANT TEXTS:

~   Indicates that the end of a long *Bible* verse has been omitted because it does not contribute to the spiritual understanding of the symbolic theme of the topical Chapter. The omitted portion of a verse is cut off after either a comma, a colon, a semi-colon, a dash, or a period.

He ordered them to be **baptized** in the name of Jesus Christ. ~   *Acts 10:48~*

...   Indicates that the middle part of a long series of verses has been omitted from the provided Concordant Texts because the verses do not directly contribute to the spiritual understanding of the topical theme of the Chapter.

      The missing verses are indicated by ...   ... within the Concordant Texts, and by ... within the scriptural reference which is located at the end of the Concordant Set. Use this reference to locate the omitted verses in a *Bible*.

They cast lots, and the lot fell on Jonah. ...
... So they picked up Jonah and threw him into the sea, and the sea ceased from its raging.   *Jonah 1:7...15*

<list>   Indicates that the middle of a series of verses that form a long list has been omitted from the provided Concordant Texts.

      The missing verses are indicated by ..<list>.. and the miss-

>   ing part of the list is indicated by **>** within the scriptural reference for the Concordant Set. Use this reference to locate the omitted verses in a standard *Bible*.

The book of the genealogy of Jesus **Christ**, the son of David, the son of Abraham: Abraham begot Isaac, Isaac begot Jacob, and Jacob begot Judah and his brothers.

      Judah begot Perez and Zerah by Tamar, Perez begot Hezron, and Hezron begot Ram.   **..<list>..**   Eliud begot Eleazar, Eleazar begot Matthan, and Matthan begot Jacob.   *Matthew 1:1-3 > 15-16*

[ ]   Square brackets indicate that the verse(s) does not appear in all translations of *The Bible*, but is included in the NASB edition.

As they went along the road they came to some water; and the eunuch said, "Look! Water! What prevents me from being **baptized**?" [And Philip said, "If you believe with all your heart, you may." And he answered and said, "I believe that Jesus Christ is the Son of God."]   *Acts 8:36-38*

2. CHAPTER HEADER

Each Chapter in this book begins with a header that details some basic information about the topical theme of the Chapter.

The header of each Chapter has three parts:

Title Block

TITHE
/ TITHES / TITHING + TENTH*

Definitions

Definitions

Tithe
1. The tenth part of goods or income, usually a voluntary contribution, paid as a tax for the support of the temple or church etc.
2. To give or pay a tithe of goods or money.
3. To give tithes to, or to pay tithes on, as income.
4. To levy or impose a tithe on, as money.
5. Any tax, levy or tribute, especially of one-tenth.
6. To exact or collect a tithe.
7. A tenth part (or small part) of something.

1. <u>**Title Block**</u>

The Title Block identifies the spiritual or topical theme of the Chapter. It lists all of the keywords and keyword phrases that have been included within the provided Concordant Texts of the Chapter. For more information on the Chapter Title Block, and the different types of keywords, see the following page.

2. <u>**Definitions**</u>

The definition section provides basic word definitions and meanings for some of the spiritual and symbolic keywords that are included within the topical Chapter. Generally, only those definitions of a key-word that are relevant and applicable to the topical theme of the Chapter have been included. While several definitions are provided, even including some modern or secular meanings, additional meanings and definitions can be found in a standard dictionary, *Bible Dictionary*, *Concordance* (as *Strong's* or *Young's* etc.) or *Bible Commentary*.

3. TITLE BLOCK

The first part of each **Chapter Header** features a **Title Block** that identifies the topical **keywords** and **keyword phrases** that have been included within the Concordant Texts of the current Chapter, along with any omissions (see *Inclusion Exception* on the following page) and/or any *Keyword Phrase Variations (see page xi).*

KEYWORD TYPES:

1. **Main Keyword**   (*Chapter Title*)

   This **keyword** or **keyword phrase** is the title of the Chapter, and it defines the starting point for the list of topically related keywords.

2. **Secondary Keyword**   *Symbol:* **+**

   This keyword or keyword phrase is closely related or similar in meaning to the **main keyword**, but it does not share its root in English.

3. **Tertiary Keyword**   *Symbol:* **/**

   A **tertiary keyword** shares the same English root as the keyword that proceeds it in the list of keywords in the Title Block. **Tertiary keywords** are other forms of the **main** or **secondary** keyword that proceeds it in the list, and can include nouns, verbs, adjectives, adverbs, etc.

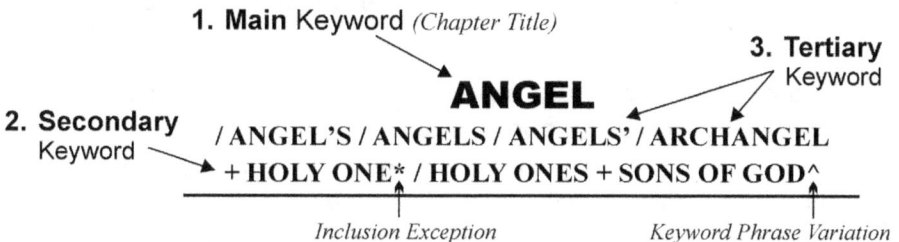

---

1. Main Keyword *(Chapter Title)*

3. Tertiary Keyword

ANGEL

2. Secondary Keyword

/ ANGEL'S / ANGELS / ANGELS' / ARCHANGEL

+ HOLY ONE* / HOLY ONES + SONS OF GOD^

Inclusion Exception   *Keyword Phrase Variation*

Inclusion Exception   *Symbol:* *****

Indicates that not all occurrences of the keyword or keyword phrase have been included. See section *3 A.* on the following page.

Keyword Phrase Variation   *Symbol:* **^**

The words that make up a keyword phrase may appear in a variety of arrangements, and/or may include additional words. See section *3 B.*

3 A. INCLUSION EXCEPTION   Symbol: *

An **inclusion exception** is a term that identifies a topical keyword or keyword phrase in the Title Block for which every scriptural occurrence has not been included within the Concordant Texts of the current Chapter. If the keyword or keyword phrase does not have an asterisk * to the right of it, then all of the related Scriptures containing the keyword, as found within the NASB version of the Old and New Testaments of *The Bible*, have been included in the Concordant Texts of the Chapter.

In some Chapters an explanation for the inclusion exception may be noted as the last line of the Title Block (and sometimes specified by a reference number [1.] to the right of the keyword).

There are two types of inclusion exceptions:

1. The keyword has two (or more) different meanings

Some topical keywords and keyword phrases have more than one distinct meaning. In such cases, only those occurrences of the keyword as found in the Scriptures that are topically related to the symbolic theme of the current Chapter have been included within the Concordant Texts of the Chapter. An example is in the Chapter titled **Fasting** (not included in this book) which includes the keyword "fast". The word "fast" can refer to quickness and speed, or to hold something firmly (*to hold fast*), as well as the abstinence from eating food, as in *to fast* or *fasting*. For the purposes of this book, only those Scriptural occurrences of the word "fast", as in fasting - to abstain from food - have been included in the Concordant Texts of the Chapter titled **Fasting** (which includes **Fast***).

2. The keyword has both a physical meaning and also a spiritually symbolic connotation

Some keywords have both a literal, physical, earthly or secular meaning, and also a distinctly different spiritual or symbolic meaning and use, where the word refers to something of God, either in the spiritual realm or as a metaphor for God or Heaven.

Generally, where a keyword can represent something that is both physical and also something purely symbolic or spiritual, only those occurrences of the keyword that are of spiritual significance to the symbolic theme have been included within the Chapter.

An example is the Chapter titled **Kingdom***. The word "kingdom" is used in *The Bible* with reference to both the physical kingdoms that are the countries, nations and empires of the earth (as Israel, Judah, Assyria etc.), and also to the spiritual "Kingdom" that represents God, Heaven, or even the Church. For the purposes of this book, references to the physical nations of the earth, such as the kingdoms of Israel, Judah, Babylon, and Assyria, etc. were not included within the provided Concordant Texts of the topical Chapter titled **Kingdom***.

3B. KEYWORD PHRASE VARIATION   Symbol: ^

Sometimes in Scripture the group of words that form a keyword phrase can include additional words that provide further descriptive meaning, context or content. An example is the Chapter titled **Son of God^**, which includes other variations of the keyword phrase, such as the "**Son of** the living **God**", "**Son of** the Most High **God**", "His only begotten **Son**", etc.

In a few cases, the sequence of the individual words that comprise a keyword phrase can also appear in a rearranged or different order, such as "**God's Son**".

Where a keyword phrase has a variety of possible word additions and/or arrangements, all combinations and forms of the keyword phrase, as found in the NASB translation of the Scriptures, have generally been included within the Concordant Texts of the topical Chapter, although not all of the additional derivatives and combinations of the keyword ^ phrase have been specifically listed in the Title Block of the Chapter.

The presence of multiple word combinations and variations of a keyword phrase in the Concordant Texts of a Chapter is indicated by a ^ to the right of the listing of the keyword phrase in the Title Block, as in **Son of God^**.

~ End of Notes ~

THE BOOKS OF THE BIBLE

OLD TESTAMENT

The HEBREW COVENANT / TANAKH

1	Genesis	14	II Chronicles	27	Daniel
2	Exodus	15	Ezra	28	Hosea
3	Leviticus	16	Nehemiah	29	Joel
4	Numbers	17	Esther	30	Amos
5	Deuteronomy	18	Job	31	Obadiah
6	Joshua	19	Psalms	32	Jonah
7	Judges	20	Proverbs	33	Micah
8	Ruth	21	Ecclesiastes	34	Nahum
9	I Samuel	22	Song of Solomon	35	Habakkuk
10	II Samuel	23	Isaiah	36	Zephaniah
11	I Kings	24	Jeremiah	37	Haggai
12	II Kings	25	Lamentations	38	Zechariah
13	I Chronicles	26	Ezekiel	39	Malachi

NEW TESTAMENT

The CHRISTIAN COVENANT

1	Matthew	10	Ephesians	19	Hebrews
2	Mark	11	Philippians	20	James
3	Luke	12	Colossians	21	I Peter
4	John	13	I Thessalonians	22	II Peter
5	Acts	14	II Thessalonians	23	I John
6	Romans	15	I Timothy	24	II John
7	I Corinthians	16	II Timothy	25	III John
8	II Corinthians	17	Titus	26	Jude
9	Galatians	18	Philemon	27	Revelation

The

CONCORDANT

TEXTS

of SEVEN IMPORTANT
SPIRITUAL SYMBOLS
about JESUS CHRIST

CHRIST

/ CHRIST'S / CHRISTS + MESSIAH + EXPECTED ONE

Definitions

Messiah   1. From the Hebrew word *mashiach* meaning "anointed", or "anointed one".

            2. The expected king and deliverer of the Jewish people.

            3. Jesus Christ, regarded by Christians as fulfilling this Old Testament promise and expectation.

            4. Any expected deliverer or savior.

Christ   1. From the Greek *Khristos (Christos)* meaning "anointed", the Greek translation of the Hebrew word *mashiach*.

            2. Jesus of Nazareth, held by Christians to be the fulfillment of prophecies in the Old Testament regarding the coming Messiah.

            3. Someone regarded as resembling or similar to Jesus of Nazareth.

OLD TESTAMENT

While I was speaking and praying, and confessing my sin and the sin of my people Israel, and presenting my supplication before the Lord my God in behalf of the holy mountain of my God, while I was still speaking in prayer, then the man Gabriel, whom I had seen in the vision previously, came to me in my extreme weariness about the time of the evening offering.

He gave me instruction and talked with me and said, "O Daniel, I have now come forth to give you insight with understanding.

"At the beginning of your supplications the command was issued, and I have come to tell you, for you are highly esteemed; so give heed to the message and gain understanding of the vision.

"Seventy weeks have been decreed for your people and your holy city, to finish the transgression, to make an end of sin, to make atonement for iniquity, to bring in everlasting righteousness, to seal up vision and prophecy and to anoint the most holy place.

"So you are to know and discern that from the issuing of a decree to restore and rebuild Jerusalem until **Messiah** the Prince there will be seven weeks and sixty-two weeks; it will be built again, with plaza and moat, even in times of distress.

"Then after the sixty-two weeks the **Messiah** will be cut off and have nothing, and the people of the prince who is to come will destroy the city and the sanctuary. And its end will come with a flood; even to the end there will be war; desolations are determined.

"And he will make a firm covenant with the many for one week, but in the middle of the week he will put a stop to sacrifice and grain offering; and on the wing of abominations will come one who makes desolate, even until a complete destruction, one that is decreed, is poured out on the one who makes desolate."

Daniel 9:20-27

NEW TESTAMENT

The record of the genealogy of Jesus the **Messiah**, the son of David, the son of Abraham: Abraham was the father of Isaac, Isaac the father of Jacob, and Jacob the father of Judah and his brothers.

Judah was the father of Perez and Zerah by Tamar, Perez was the father of Hezron, and Hezron the father of Ram. ..<list>..

Eliud was the father of Eleazar, Eleazar the father of Matthan, and Matthan the father of Jacob. Jacob was the father of Joseph the husband of Mary, by whom Jesus was born, who is called the **Messiah**.

So all the generations from Abraham to David are fourteen generations; from David to the deportation to Babylon, fourteen generations; and from the deportation to Babylon to the **Messiah**, fourteen generations.

Now the birth of Jesus **Christ** was as follows: when His mother Mary had been betrothed to Joseph, before they came together she was found to be with child by the Holy Spirit.

And Joseph her husband, being a righteous man and not wanting to disgrace her, planned to send her away secretly.

But when he had considered this, behold, an angel of the Lord appeared to him in a dream, saying, "Joseph, son of David, do not be afraid to take Mary as your wife; for the Child who has been conceived in her is of the Holy Spirit. She will bear a Son; and you shall call His name Jesus, for He will save His people from their sins."

Now all this took place to fulfill what was spoken by the Lord through the prophet: "Behold, the virgin shall be with child and shall bear a Son, and they shall call His name Immanuel," which translated means, "God with us."

And Joseph awoke from his sleep and did as the angel of the Lord commanded him, and took Mary as his wife, but kept her a virgin until she gave birth to a Son; and he called His name Jesus.

Now after Jesus was born in Bethlehem of Judea in the days of Herod the king, magi from the east arrived in Jerusalem, saying, "Where is He who has been born King of the Jews? For we saw His star in the east and have come to worship Him."

When Herod the king heard this, he was troubled, and all Jerusalem with him. Gathering together all the chief priests and scribes of the people, he inquired of them where the **Messiah** was to be born.

They said to him, "In Bethlehem of Judea; for this is what has been written by the prophet: 'And you, Bethlehem, land of Judah, are by no means least among the leaders of Judah; for out of you shall come forth a Ruler who will shepherd My people Israel.' " *Matthew 1:1-3 > 15 - 2:6*

When John, while imprisoned, heard of the works of **Christ**, he sent word by his disciples and said to Him, "Are You the **Expected One**, or shall we look for someone else?"

Jesus answered and said to them, "Go and report to John what you hear and see: the blind receive sight and the lame walk, the lepers are cleansed and the deaf hear, the dead are raised up, and the poor have the gospel preached to them.

"And blessed is he who does not take offense at Me." *Matthew 11:2-6*

When Jesus came into the district of Caesarea Philippi, He was asking His disciples, "Who do people say that the Son of Man is?"

And they said, "Some say John the Baptist; and others, Elijah; but still others, Jeremiah, or one of the prophets."

He said to them, "But who do you say that I am?"

Simon Peter answered, "You are the **Christ**, the Son of the living God."

And Jesus said to him, "Blessed are you, Simon Barjona, because flesh and blood did not reveal this to you, but My Father who is in heaven.

"I also say to you that you are Peter, and upon this rock I will build My church; and the gates of Hades will not overpower it. I will give you the keys of the kingdom of heaven; and whatever you bind on earth shall have been bound in heaven, and whatever you loose on earth shall have been loosed in heaven."

Then He warned the disciples that they should tell no one that He was the **Christ**.

From that time Jesus began to show His disciples that He must go to Jerusalem, and suffer many things from the elders and chief priests and scribes, and be killed, and be raised up on the third day.

Matthew 16:13-21

While the Pharisees were gathered together, Jesus asked them a question: "What do you think about the **Christ**, whose son is He?" They said to Him, "The son of David."

He said to them, "Then how does David in the Spirit call Him 'Lord,' saying, 'The Lord said to my Lord, "Sit at My right hand, until I put Your enemies beneath Your feet" '?

"If David then calls Him 'Lord,' how is He his son?"

No one was able to answer Him a word, nor did anyone dare from that day on to ask Him another question.

Matthew 22:41-46

Do not be called Rabbi; for One is your Teacher, and you are all brothers.

Do not call anyone on earth your father; for One is your Father, He who is in heaven.

Do not be called leaders; for One is your Leader, that is, **Christ**.

But the greatest among you shall be your servant. Whoever exalts himself shall be humbled; and whoever humbles himself shall be exalted. *Matthew 23:8-12*

As He was sitting on the Mount of Olives, the disciples came to Him privately, saying, "Tell us, when will these things happen, and what will be the sign of Your coming, and of the end of the age?"

And Jesus answered and said to them, "See to it that no one misleads you. For many will come in My name, saying, 'I am the **Christ**,' and will mislead many. You will be hearing of wars and rumors of wars.

See that you are not frightened, for those things must take place, but that is not yet the end." *Matthew 24:3-6*

Unless those days had been cut short, no life would have been saved; but for the sake of the elect those days will be cut short.

Then if anyone says to you, "Behold, here is the **Christ**," or "There He is," do not believe him. For false **Christs** and false prophets will arise and will show great signs and wonders, so as to mislead, if possible, even the elect.

So if they say to you, "Behold, He is in the wilderness," do not go out, or, "Behold, He is in the inner rooms," do not believe them. For just as the lightning comes from the east and flashes even to the west, so will the coming of the Son of Man be." *Matthew 24:22-27*

The chief priests and the whole Council kept trying to obtain false testimony against Jesus, so that they might put Him to death. They did not find any, even though many false witnesses came forward.

But later on two came forward, and said, "This man stated, 'I am able to destroy the temple of God and to rebuild it in three days.' "

The high priest stood up and said to Him, "Do You not answer? What is it that these men are testifying against You?" But Jesus kept silent.

And the high priest said to Him, "I adjure You by the living God, that You tell us whether You are the **Christ**, the Son of God."

Jesus said to him, "You have said it yourself; nevertheless I tell you, hereafter you will see the Son of Man sitting at the right hand of Power, and coming on the clouds of heaven."

Then the high priest tore his robes and said, "He has blasphemed! What further need do we have of witnesses? Behold, you have now heard the blasphemy; do you think?"

They answered, "He deserves death!"

Then they spat in His face and beat Him with their fists; and others slapped Him, and said, "Prophesy to us, You **Christ**; who is the one who hit You?"

Matthew 26:59-68

Jesus stood before the governor, and the governor questioned Him, saying, "Are You the King of the Jews?"

And Jesus said to him, "It is as you say." And while He was being accused by the chief priests and elders, He did not answer.

Then Pilate said to Him, "Do You not hear how many things they testify against You?" And He did not answer him with regard to even a single charge, so the governor was quite amazed.

Now at the feast the governor was accustomed to release for the people any one prisoner whom they wanted. At that time they were holding a notorious prisoner, called Barabbas.

So when the people gathered together, Pilate said to them, "Whom do you want me to release for you? Barabbas, or Jesus who is called **Christ**?" For he knew that because of envy they had handed Him over.

While he was sitting on the judgment seat, his wife sent him a message, saying, "Have nothing to do with that righteous Man; for last night I suffered greatly in a dream because of Him."

But the chief priests and the elders persuaded the crowds to ask for Barabbas and to put Jesus to death.

But the governor said to them, "Which of the two do you want me to release for you?" And they said, "Barabbas."

Pilate said to them, "Then what shall I do with Jesus who is called **Christ**?" They all said, "Crucify Him!"

And he said, "Why, what evil has He done?" But they kept shouting all the more, saying, "Crucify Him!"

When Pilate saw that he was accomplishing nothing, but rather that a riot was starting, he took water and washed his hands in front of the crowd, saying, "I am innocent of this Man's blood; see to that yourselves."

And all the people said, "His blood shall be on us and on our children!"

Then he released Barabbas for them; but after having Jesus scourged, he handed Him over to be crucified.

Matthew 27:11-26

The beginning of the gospel of Jesus **Christ**, the Son of God.

As it is written in Isaiah the prophet: "Behold, I send My messenger ahead of You, who will prepare Your way; the voice of one crying in the wilderness, 'Make ready the way of the Lord, make His paths straight.'"

Mark 1:1-3

Jesus went out, along with His disciples, to the villages of Caesarea Philippi; and on the way He questioned His disciples, saying to them, "Who do people say that I am?"

They told Him, saying, "John the Baptist; and others say Elijah; but others, one of the prophets."

And He continued by questioning them, "But who do you say that I am?"

Peter answered and said to Him, "You are the **Christ**."

And He warned them to tell no one about Him.

Mark 8:27-30

John said to Him, "Teacher, we saw someone casting out demons in Your name, and we tried to prevent him because he was not following us."

But Jesus said, "Do not hinder him, for there is no one who will perform a miracle in My name, and be able soon afterward to speak evil of Me. For he who is not against us is for us. For whoever gives you a cup of water to drink because of your name as followers of **Christ**, truly I say to you, he will not lose his reward."

Mark 9:38-41

Jesus began to say, as He taught in the temple, "How is it that the scribes say that the **Christ** is the son of David? David himself said in the Holy Spirit, 'The Lord said to my Lord, "Sit at My right hand, until I put Your enemies beneath Your feet." '

"David himself calls Him 'Lord'; so in what sense is He his son?"

And the large crowd enjoyed listening to Him. *Mark 12:35-37*

Those days will be a time of tribulation such as has not occurred since the beginning of the creation which God created until now, and never will. Unless the Lord had shortened those days, no life would have been saved; but for the sake of the elect, whom He chose, He shortened the days.

And then if anyone says to you, "Behold, here is the **Christ**"; or, "Behold, He is there"; do not believe him; for false **Christs** and false prophets will arise, and will show signs and wonders, in order to lead astray, if possible, the elect.

But take heed; behold, I have told you everything in advance. *Mark 13:19-23*

The high priest stood up and came forward and questioned Jesus, saying, "Do You not answer? What is it that these men are testifying against You?" But He kept silent and did not answer.

Again the high priest was questioning Him, and saying to Him, "Are You the **Christ**, the Son of the Blessed One?"

And Jesus said, "I am; and you shall see the Son of Man sitting at the right hand of Power, and coming with the clouds of heaven."

Tearing his clothes, the high priest said, "What further need do we have of witnesses? You have heard the blasphemy; how does it seem to you?"

And they all condemned Him to be deserving of death. *Mark 14:60-64*

They crucified two robbers with Him, one on His right and one on His left. [And the Scripture was fulfilled which says, "And He was numbered with transgressors."]

Those passing by were hurling abuse at Him, wagging their heads, and saying, "Ha! You who are going to destroy the temple and rebuild it in three days, save Yourself, and come down from the cross!"

In the same way the chief priests also, along with the scribes, were mocking Him among themselves and saying, "He saved others; He cannot save Himself. Let this **Christ**, the King of Israel, now come down from the cross, so that we may see and believe!"

Those who were crucified with Him were also insulting Him. *Mark 15:27-32*

In the same region there were some shepherds staying out in the fields and keeping watch over their flock by night.

And an angel of the Lord suddenly stood before them, and the glory of the Lord shone around them; and they were terribly frightened.

But the angel said to them, "Do not be afraid; for behold, I bring you good news of great joy which will be for all the people; for today in the city of David there has been born for you a Savior, who is **Christ** the Lord.

"This will be a sign for you: you will find a baby wrapped in cloths and lying in a manger."

And suddenly there appeared with the angel a multitude of the heavenly host praising God and saying, "Glory to God in the highest, and on earth peace among men with whom He is pleased." *Luke 2:8-14*

There was a man in Jerusalem whose name was Simeon; and this man was righteous and devout, looking for the consolation of Israel; and the Holy Spirit was upon him. And it had been revealed to him by the Holy Spirit that he would not see death before he had seen the Lord's **Christ**.

And he came in the Spirit into the temple; and when the parents brought in the child Jesus, to carry out for Him the custom of the Law, then he took Him into his arms, and blessed God, and said, "Now Lord, You are releasing Your bondservant to depart in peace, according to

Your word; for my eyes have seen Your salvation, which You have prepared in the presence of all peoples, a Light of revelation to the Gentiles, and the glory of Your people Israel."

And His father and mother were amazed at the things which were being said about Him.

And Simeon blessed them and said to Mary His mother, "Behold, this Child is appointed for the fall and rise of many in Israel, and for a sign to be opposed - and a sword will pierce even your own soul - to the end that thoughts from many hearts may be revealed."   *Luke 2:25-35*

While the people were in a state of expectation and all were wondering in their hearts about John, as to whether he was the **Christ**, John answered and said to them all, "As for me, I baptize you with water; but One is coming who is mightier than I, and I am not fit to untie the thong of His sandals; He will baptize you with the Holy Spirit and fire.

"His winnowing fork is in His hand to thoroughly clear His threshing floor, and to gather the wheat into His barn; but He will burn up the chaff with unquenchable fire."   *Luke 3:15-17*

While the sun was setting, all those who had any who were sick with various diseases brought them to Him; and laying His hands on each one of them, He was healing them.

Demons also were coming out of many, shouting, "You are the Son of God!"

But rebuking them, He would not allow them to speak, because they knew Him to be the **Christ**.   *Luke 4:40-41*

As He approached the gate of the city, a dead man was being carried out, the only son of his mother, and she was a widow; and a sizeable crowd from the city was with her.

When the Lord saw her, He felt compassion for her, and said to her, "Do not weep." And He came up and touched the coffin; and the bearers came to a halt.

And He said, "Young man, I say to you, arise!"

The dead man sat up and began to speak. And Jesus gave him back to his mother.

Fear gripped them all, and they began glorifying God, saying, "A great prophet has arisen among us!" and, "God has visited His people!" This report concerning Him went out all over Judea and in all the surrounding district.

The disciples of John reported to him about all these things. Summoning two of his disciples, John sent them to the Lord, saying, "Are You the **Expected One**, or do we look for someone else?"

When the men came to Him, they said, "John the Baptist has sent us to You, to ask, 'Are You the **Expected One**, or do we look for someone else?' "

At that very time He cured many people of diseases and afflictions and evil spirits; and He gave sight to many who were blind.

And He answered and said to them, "Go and report to John what you have seen and heard: the blind receive sight, the lame walk, the lepers are cleansed, and the deaf hear, the dead are raised up, the poor have the gospel preached to them.

"Blessed is he who does not take offense at Me."   *Luke 7:12-23*

It happened that while He was praying alone, the disciples were with Him, and He questioned them, saying, "Who do the people say that I am?"

They answered and said, "John the Baptist, and others say Elijah; but others, that one of the prophets of old has risen again."

And He said to them, "But who do you say that I am?"

And Peter answered and said, "The **Christ** of God."

But He warned them and instructed them not to tell this to anyone, saying, "The Son of Man must suffer many things and be rejected by the elders and chief priests and scribes, and be killed and be raised up on the third day."   *Luke 9:18-22*

He said to them, "How is it that they say the **Christ** is David's son? For David himself says in the book of Psalm, 'The Lord said to my Lord, "Sit at My right hand, until I make Your enemies a footstool for Your feet." '

"Therefore David calls Him 'Lord,' and how is He his son?" *Luke 20:41-44*

When it was day, the Council of elders of the people assembled, both chief priests and scribes, and they led Him away to their council chamber, saying, "If You are the **Christ**, tell us."

But He said to them, "If I tell you, you will not believe; and if I ask a question, you will not answer. But from now on the Son of Man will be seated at the right hand of the power of God."

And they all said, "Are You the Son of God, then?"

And He said to them, "Yes, I am."

Then they said, "What further need do we have of testimony? For we have heard it ourselves from His own mouth."

Then the whole body of them got up and brought Him before Pilate. And they began to accuse Him, saying, "We found this man misleading our nation and forbidding to pay taxes to Caesar, and saying that He Himself is **Christ**, a King."

So Pilate asked Him, saying, "Are You the King of the Jews?"

And He answered him and said, "It is as you say."

Then Pilate said to the chief priests and the crowds, "I find no guilt in this man."

But they kept on insisting, saying, "He stirs up the people, teaching all over Judea, starting from Galilee even as far as this place." *Luke 22:66 - 23:5*

Two others also, who were criminals, were being led away to be put to death with Him.

When they came to the place called The Skull, there they crucified Him and the criminals, one on the right and the other on the left.

But Jesus was saying, "Father, forgive them; for they do not know what they are doing."

And they cast lots, dividing up His garments among themselves.

And the people stood by, looking on. And even the rulers were sneering at Him, saying, "He saved others; let Him save Himself if this is the **Christ** of God, His Chosen One."

The soldiers also mocked Him, coming up to Him, offering Him sour wine, and saying, "If You are the King of the Jews, save Yourself!"

Now there was also an inscription above Him, "THIS IS THE KING OF THE JEWS."

One of the criminals who were hanged there was hurling abuse at Him, saying, "Are You not the **Christ**? Save Yourself and us!"

But the other answered, and rebuking him said, "Do you not even fear God, since you are under the same sentence of condemnation? And we indeed are suffering justly, for we are receiving what we deserve for our deeds; but this man has done nothing wrong." *Luke 23:32-41*

He said to them, "O foolish men and slow of heart to believe in all that the prophets have spoken! Was it not necessary for the **Christ** to suffer these things and to enter into His glory?"

Then beginning with Moses and with all the prophets, He explained to them the things concerning Himself in all the Scriptures. *Luke 24:25-27*

He said to them, "These are My words which I spoke to you while I was still with you, that all things which are written about Me in the Law of Moses and the Prophets and the Psalm must be fulfilled."

Then He opened their minds to understand the Scriptures, and He said to them, "Thus it is written, that the **Christ** would suffer and rise again from the dead the third day, and that repentance for forgiveness of sins would be proclaimed in His name to all the nations, beginning from Jerusalem." *Luke 24:44-47*

The Word became flesh, and dwelt among us, and we saw His glory, glory as of the only begotten from the Father, full of grace and truth.

John testified about Him and cried out, saying, "This was He of whom I said, 'He who comes after me has a higher rank than I, for He existed before me.' "

For of His fullness we have all received, and grace upon grace. For the Law was given through Moses; grace and truth were realized through Jesus **Christ**.

No one has seen God at any time; the only begotten God who is in the bosom of the Father, He has explained Him.

This is the testimony of John, when the Jews sent to him priests and Levites from Jerusalem to ask him, "Who are you?"

And he confessed and did not deny, but confessed, "I am not the **Christ**."

They asked him, "What then? Are you Elijah?"

And he said, "I am not."

"Are you the Prophet?"

And he answered, "No."

Then they said to him, "Who are you, so that we may give an answer to those who sent us? What do you say about yourself?"

He said, "I am a voice of one crying in the wilderness, 'Make straight the way of the Lord,' as Isaiah the prophet said."

Now they had been sent from the Pharisees. They asked him, and said to him, "Why then are you baptizing, if you are not the **Christ**, nor Elijah, nor the Prophet?"

John answered them saying, "I baptize in water, but among you stands One whom you do not know. It is He who comes after me, the thong of whose sandal I am not worthy to untie."

These things took place in Bethany beyond the Jordan, where John was baptizing.   *John 1:14-28*

One of the two who heard John speak and followed Him, was Andrew, Simon Peter's brother. He found first his own brother Simon and said to him, "We have found the **Messiah**" (which translated means **Christ**).

He brought him to Jesus. Jesus looked at him and said, "You are Simon the son of John; you shall be called Cephas" (which is translated Peter).
John 1:40-42

They came to John and said to him, "Rabbi, He who was with you beyond the Jordan, to whom you have testified, behold, He is baptizing and all are coming to Him."

John answered and said, "A man can receive nothing unless it has been given him from heaven. You yourselves are my witnesses that I said, 'I am not the **Christ**,' but, 'I have been sent ahead of Him.'

"He who has the bride is the bridegroom; but the friend of the bridegroom, who stands and hears him, rejoices greatly because of the bridegroom's voice. So this joy of mine has been made full.

"He must increase, but I must decrease."   *John 3:26-30*

He said to her, "Go, call your husband and come here."

The woman answered and said, "I have no husband."

Jesus said to her, "You have correctly said, 'I have no husband'; for you have had five husbands, and the one whom you now have is not your husband; this you have said truly."

The woman said to Him, "Sir, I perceive that You are a prophet. Our fathers worshiped in this mountain, and you people say that in Jerusalem is the place where men ought to worship."

Jesus said to her, "Woman, believe Me, an hour is coming when neither in this mountain nor in Jerusalem will you worship the Father. You worship what you do not know; we worship what we know, for salvation is from the Jews.

"But an hour is coming, and now is, when the true worshipers will worship the Father in spirit and truth; for such people the Father seeks to be His worshipers. God is spirit, and those who worship Him must worship in spirit and truth."

The woman said to Him, "I know that **Messiah** is coming (He who is called **Christ**); when that One comes, He will declare all things to us."

Jesus said to her, "I who speak to you am He."

At this point His disciples came, and they were amazed that He had been speaking with a woman, yet no one said, "What do You seek?" or, "Why do You speak with her?"

So the woman left her waterpot, and went into the city and said to the men, "Come, see a man who told me all the things that I have done; this is not the **Christ**, is it?"

They went out of the city, and were coming to Him.   *John 4:16-30*

"Do not judge according to appearance, but judge with righteous judgment."

So some of the people of Jerusalem were saying, "Is this not the man whom they are seeking to kill? Look, He is speaking publicly, and they are saying nothing to Him.

"The rulers do not really know that this is the **Christ**, do they? However, we know where this man is from; but whenever the **Christ** may come, no one knows where He is from."

Then Jesus cried out in the temple, teaching and saying, "You both know Me and know where I am from; and I have not come of Myself, but He who sent Me is true, whom you do not know. I know Him, because I am from Him, and He sent Me."

So they were seeking to seize Him; and no man laid his hand on Him, because His hour had not yet come. But many of the crowd believed in Him; and they were saying, "When the **Christ** comes, He will not perform more signs than those which this man has, will He?"
                              John 7:24-31

On the last day, the great day of the feast, Jesus stood and cried out, saying, "If anyone is thirsty, let him come to Me and drink. He who believes in Me, as the Scripture said, 'From his innermost being

will flow rivers of living water.' "

But this He spoke of the Spirit, whom those who believed in Him were to receive; for the Spirit was not yet given, because Jesus was not yet glorified.

Some of the people therefore, when they heard these words, were saying, "This certainly is the Prophet."

Others were saying, "This is the **Christ**." Still others were saying, "Surely the **Christ** is not going to come from Galilee, is He? Has not the Scripture said that the **Christ** comes from the descendants of David, and from Bethlehem, the village where David was?"

So a division occurred in the crowd because of Him. Some of them wanted to seize Him, but no one laid hands on Him.
                              John 7:37-44

They said to the blind man again, "What do you say about Him, since He opened your eyes?"

And he said, "He is a prophet."

The Jews then did not believe it of him, that he had been blind and had received sight, until they called the parents of the very one who had received his sight, and questioned them, saying, "Is this your son, who you say was born blind? Then how does he now see?"

His parents answered them and said, "We know that this is our son, and that he was born blind; but how he now sees, we do not know; or who opened his eyes, we do not know. Ask him; he is of age, he will speak for himself."

His parents said this because they were afraid of the Jews; for the Jews had already agreed that if anyone confessed Him to be **Christ**, he was to be put out of the synagogue. For this reason his parents said, "He is of age; ask him."
                              John 9:18-23

The Feast of the Dedication took place at Jerusalem; it was winter, and Jesus was walking in the temple in the portico of Solomon.

The Jews then gathered around Him, and were saying to Him, "How long will You keep us in suspense? If You are the

Christ, tell us plainly."

Jesus answered them, "I told you, and you do not believe; the works that I do in My Father's name, these testify of Me. But you do not believe because you are not of My sheep.

"My sheep hear My voice, and I know them, and they follow Me; and I give eternal life to them, and they will never perish; and no one will snatch them out of My hand.

"My Father, who has given them to Me, is greater than all; and no one is able to snatch them out of the Father's hand. I and the Father are one."

The Jews picked up stones again to stone Him.

Jesus answered them, "I showed you many good works from the Father; for which of them are you stoning Me?"

The Jews answered Him, "For a good work we do not stone You, but for blasphemy; and because You, being a man, make Yourself out to be God."

John 10:22-33

Martha said to Jesus, "Lord, if You had been here, my brother would not have died. Even now I know that whatever You ask of God, God will give You."

Jesus said to her, "Your brother will rise again."

Martha said to Him, "I know that he will rise again in the resurrection on the last day."

Jesus said to her, "I am the resurrection and the life; he who believes in Me will live even if he dies, and everyone who lives and believes in Me will never die. Do you believe this?"

She said to Him, "Yes, Lord; I have believed that You are the Christ, the Son of God, even He who comes into the world."

John 11:21-27

"Now judgment is upon this world; now the ruler of this world will be cast out. And I, if I am lifted up from the earth, will draw all men to Myself."

But He was saying this to indicate the kind of death by which He was to die.

The crowd then answered Him, "We have heard out of the Law that the Christ is to remain forever; and how can You say, 'The Son of Man must be lifted up'? Who is this Son of Man?"

So Jesus said to them, "For a little while longer the Light is among you. Walk while you have the Light, so that darkness will not overtake you; he who walks in the darkness does not know where he goes. While you have the Light, believe in the Light, so that you may become sons of Light."

These things Jesus spoke, and He went away and hid Himself from them.

John 12:31-36

"These things I have spoken to you, so that in Me you may have peace. In the world you have tribulation, but take courage; I have overcome the world."

Jesus spoke these things; and lifting up His eyes to heaven, He said, "Father, the hour has come; glorify Your Son, that the Son may glorify You, even as You gave Him authority over all flesh, that to all whom You have given Him, He may give eternal life.

"This is eternal life, that they may know You, the only true God, and Jesus Christ whom You have sent. I glorified You on the earth, having accomplished the work which You have given Me to do.

"Now, Father, glorify Me together with Yourself, with the glory which I had with You before the world was. I have manifested Your name to the men whom You gave Me out of the world; they were Yours and You gave them to Me, and they have kept Your word.

"Now they have come to know that everything You have given Me is from You; for the words which You gave Me I have given to them; and they received them and truly understood that I came forth from You, and they believed that You sent Me."

John 16:33 - 17:8

There are many other signs Jesus also performed in the presence of the disciples, which are not written in this book; but these have been written so that you may believe that Jesus is the Christ, the

Son of God; and that believing you may have life in His name. *John 20:30-31*

"Brethren, I may confidently say to you regarding the patriarch David that he both died and was buried, and his tomb is with us to this day. And so, because he was a prophet and knew that God had sworn to him with an oath to seat one of his descendants on his throne, he looked ahead and spoke of the resurrection of the **Christ**, that He was neither abandoned to Hades, nor did His flesh suffer decay.

"This Jesus God raised up again, to which we are all witnesses.

"Therefore having been exalted to the right hand of God, and having received from the Father the promise of the Holy Spirit, He has poured forth this which you both see and hear. For it was not David who ascended into heaven, but he himself says: 'The Lord said to my Lord, "Sit at My right hand, until I make Your enemies a footstool for Your feet." '

"Therefore let all the house of Israel know for certain that God has made Him both Lord and **Christ** - this Jesus whom you crucified."

Now when they heard this, they were pierced to the heart, and said to Peter and the rest of the apostles, "Brethren, what shall we do?"

Peter said to them, "Repent, and each of you be baptized in the name of Jesus **Christ** for the forgiveness of your sins; and you will receive the gift of the Holy Spirit. For the promise is for you and your children and for all who are far off, as many as the Lord our God will call to Himself."

And with many other words he solemnly testified and kept on exhorting them, saying, "Be saved from this perverse generation!"

So then, those who had received his word were baptized; and that day there were added about three thousand souls. *Acts 2:29-41*

Peter and John were going up to the temple at the ninth hour, the hour of prayer.

And a man who had been lame from his mother's womb was being carried along, whom they used to set down every day at the gate of the temple which is called Beautiful, in order to beg alms of those who were entering the temple.

When he saw Peter and John about to go into the temple, he began asking to receive alms. But Peter, along with John, fixed his gaze on him and said, "Look at us!"

And he began to give them his attention, expecting to receive something from them.

But Peter said, "I do not possess silver and gold, but what I do have I give to you: In the name of Jesus **Christ** the Nazarene - walk!"

And seizing him by the right hand, he raised him up; and immediately his feet and his ankles were strengthened.

With a leap he stood upright and began to walk; and he entered the temple with them, walking and leaping and praising God. *Acts 3:1-8*

Brethren, I know that you acted in ignorance, just as your rulers did also. But the things which God announced beforehand by the mouth of all the prophets, that His **Christ** would suffer, He has thus fulfilled.

Therefore repent and return, so that your sins may be wiped away, in order that times of refreshing may come from the presence of the Lord; and that He may send Jesus, the **Christ** appointed for you, whom heaven must receive until the period of restoration of all things about which God spoke by the mouth of His holy prophets from ancient time.

Moses said, "The Lord God will raise up for you a prophet like me from your brethren; to Him you shall give heed to everything He says to you. And it will be that every soul that does not heed that prophet shall be utterly destroyed from among the people. And likewise, all the prophets who have spoken, from Samuel and his successors onward, also announced these days.

"It is you who are the sons of the prophets and of the covenant which God made with your fathers, saying to Abraham, 'And in your seed all the families of the earth shall be blessed.' For you first, God raised up His Servant and sent Him to bless you by turning every one of you from your wicked ways." *Acts 3:17-26*

When they had placed them in the center, they began to inquire, "By what power, or in what name, have you done this?"

Then Peter, filled with the Holy Spirit, said to them, "Rulers and elders of the people, if we are on trial today for a benefit done to a sick man, as to how this man has been made well, let it be known to all of you and to all the people of Israel, that by the name of Jesus **Christ** the Nazarene, whom you crucified, whom God raised from the dead - by this name this man stands here before you in good health.

"He is the stone which was rejected by you, the builders, but which became the chief corner stone.

"And there is salvation in no one else; for there is no other name under heaven that has been given among men by which we must be saved." *Acts 4:7-12*

When they had been released, they went to their own companions and reported all that the chief priests and the elders had said to them.

And when they heard this, they lifted their voices to God with one accord and said, "O Lord, it is You who made the heaven and the earth and the sea, and all that is in them, who by the Holy Spirit, through the mouth of our father David Your servant, said, 'Why did the Gentiles rage, and the peoples devise futile things? The kings of the earth took their stand, and the rulers were gathered together against the Lord and against His **Christ**.'

"For truly in this city there were gathered together against Your holy servant Jesus, whom You anointed, both Herod and Pontius Pilate, along with the Gentiles and the peoples of Israel, to do whatever Your hand and Your purpose pre-

destined to occur." *Acts 4:23-28*

He said to them, "Men of Israel, take care what you propose to do with these men. For some time ago Theudas rose up, claiming to be somebody, and a group of about four hundred men joined up with him. But he was killed, and all who followed him were dispersed and came to nothing.

"After this man, Judas of Galilee rose up in the days of the census and drew away some people after him; he too perished, and all those who followed him were scattered.

"So in the present case, I say to you, stay away from these men and let them alone, for if this plan or action is of men, it will be overthrown; but if it is of God, you will not be able to overthrow them; or else you may even be found fighting against God."

They took his advice; and after calling the apostles in, they flogged them and ordered them not to speak in the name of Jesus, and then released them.

So they went on their way from the presence of the Council, rejoicing that they had been considered worthy to suffer shame for His name. And every day, in the temple and from house to house, they kept right on teaching and preaching Jesus as the **Christ**. *Acts 5:35-42*

Philip went down to the city of Samaria and began proclaiming **Christ** to them. The crowds with one accord were giving attention to what was said by Philip, as they heard and saw the signs which he was performing. For in the case of many who had unclean spirits, they were coming out of them shouting with a loud voice; and many who had been paralyzed and lame were healed. So there was much rejoicing in that city.

Now there was a man named Simon, who formerly was practicing magic in the city and astonishing the people of Samaria, claiming to be someone great; and they all, from smallest to greatest, were giving attention to him, saying, "This man is what is called the Great Power of God."

And they were giving him attention because he had for a long time astonished them with his magic arts.

But when they believed Philip preaching the good news about the kingdom of God and the name of Jesus **Christ**, they were being baptized, men and women alike.

Even Simon himself believed; and after being baptized, he continued on with Philip, and as he observed signs and great miracles taking place, he was constantly amazed.   *Acts 8:5-13*

Philip opened his mouth, and beginning from this Scripture he preached Jesus to him. As they went along the road they came to some water; and the eunuch said, "Look! Water! What prevents me from being baptized?"

And Philip said, "If you believe with all your heart, you may."

And he answered and said, "I believe that Jesus **Christ** is the Son of God."]

And he ordered the chariot to stop; and they both went down into the water, Philip as well as the eunuch, and he baptized him.   *Acts 8:35-38*

Ananias departed and entered the house, and after laying his hands on him said, "Brother Saul, the Lord Jesus, who appeared to you on the road by which you were coming, has sent me so that you may regain your sight and be filled with the Holy Spirit."

And immediately there fell from his eyes something like scales, and he regained his sight, and he got up and was baptized; and he took food and was strengthened.

Now for several days he was with the disciples who were at Damascus, and immediately he began to proclaim Jesus in the synagogues, saying, "He is the Son of God."

All those hearing him continued to be amazed, and were saying, "Is this not he who in Jerusalem destroyed those who called on this name, and who had come here for the purpose of bringing them bound before the chief priests?"

But Saul kept increasing in strength and confounding the Jews who lived at Damascus by proving that this Jesus is the **Christ**.   *Acts 9:17-22*

As Peter was traveling through all those regions, he came down also to the saints who lived at Lydda. There he found a man named Aeneas, who had been bedridden eight years, for he was paralyzed.

Peter said to him, "Aeneas, Jesus **Christ** heals you; get up and make your bed." Immediately he got up.

And all who lived at Lydda and Sharon saw him, and they turned to the Lord.
Acts 9:32-35

Opening his mouth, Peter said: "I most certainly understand now that God is not one to show partiality, but in every nation the man who fears Him and does what is right is welcome to Him.

"The word which He sent to the sons of Israel, preaching peace through Jesus **Christ** (He is Lord of all) - you yourselves know the thing which took place throughout all Judea, starting from Galilee, after the baptism which John proclaimed.

"You know of Jesus of Nazareth, how God anointed Him with the Holy Spirit and with power, and how He went about doing good and healing all who were oppressed by the devil, for God was with Him. We are witnesses of all the things He did both in the land of the Jews and in Jerusalem. They also put Him to death by hanging Him on a cross.

"God raised Him up on the third day and granted that He become visible, not to all the people, but to witnesses who were chosen beforehand by God, that is, to us who ate and drank with Him after He arose from the dead.

"And He ordered us to preach to the people, and solemnly to testify that this is the One who has been appointed by God as Judge of the living and the dead. Of Him all the prophets bear witness that through His name everyone who believes in Him receives forgiveness of sins."

While Peter was still speaking these words, the Holy Spirit fell upon all those who were listening to the message.

All the circumcised believers who came with Peter were amazed, because the gift of the Holy Spirit had been poured out on the Gentiles also. For they were hearing them speaking with tongues and exalting God.

Then Peter answered, "Surely no one can refuse the water for these to be baptized who have received the Holy Spirit just as we did, can he?"

And he ordered them to be baptized in the name of Jesus **Christ**. ~

Acts 10:34-48

"As I began to speak, the Holy Spirit fell upon them just as He did upon us at the beginning. And I remembered the word of the Lord, how He used to say, 'John baptized with water, but you will be baptized with the Holy Spirit.'

"Therefore if God gave to them the same gift as He gave to us also after believing in the Lord Jesus **Christ**, who was I that I could stand in God's way?"

When they heard this, they quieted down and glorified God, saying, "Well then, God has granted to the Gentiles also the repentance that leads to life."

Acts 11:15-18

Since we have heard that some of our number to whom we gave no instruction have disturbed you with their words, unsettling your souls, it seemed good to us, having become of one mind, to select men to send to you with our beloved Barnabas and Paul, men who have risked their lives for the name of our Lord Jesus **Christ**.

Acts 15:24-26

It happened that as we were going to the place of prayer, a slave-girl having a spirit of divination met us, who was bringing her masters much profit by fortune-telling. Following after Paul and us, she kept crying out, saying, "These men are bond-servants of the Most High God, who are proclaiming to you the way of salvation." She continued doing this for many days.

But Paul was greatly annoyed, and turned and said to the spirit, "I command

you in the name of Jesus **Christ** to come out of her!" And it came out at that very moment.

Acts 16:16-18

When they had traveled through Amphipolis and Apollonia, they came to Thessalonica, where there was a synagogue of the Jews. And according to Paul's custom, he went to them, and for three Sabbaths reasoned with them from the Scriptures, explaining and giving evidence that the **Christ** had to suffer and rise again from the dead, and saying, "This Jesus whom I am proclaiming to you is the **Christ**."

And some of them were persuaded and joined Paul and Silas, along with a large number of the God-fearing Greeks and a number of the leading women.

Acts 17:1-4

When Silas and Timothy came down from Macedonia, Paul began devoting himself completely to the word, solemnly testifying to the Jews that Jesus was the **Christ**. But when they resisted and blasphemed, he shook out his garments and said to them, "Your blood be on your own heads! I am clean. From now on I will go to the Gentiles."

Acts 18:5-6

When he wanted to go across to Achaia, the brethren encouraged him and wrote to the disciples to welcome him; and when he had arrived, he greatly helped those who had believed through grace, for he powerfully refuted the Jews in public, demonstrating by the Scriptures that Jesus was the **Christ**.

Acts 18:27-28

Paul had decided to sail past Ephesus so that he would not have to spend time in Asia; for he was hurrying to be in Jerusalem, if possible, on the day of Pentecost. From Miletus he sent to Ephesus and called to him the elders of the church.

And when they had come to him, he said to them, "You yourselves know, from the first day that I set foot in Asia, how I was with you the whole time, serving the Lord with all humility and with tears and with trials which came upon me through the plots of the Jews; how I did not shrink from declaring to you anything that was profitable, and teaching you publicly and from house to house, solemnly testifying to both Jews and Greeks of repentance toward God and faith in our Lord Jesus **Christ**." *Acts 20:16-21*

Some days later Felix arrived with Drusilla, his wife who was a Jewess, and sent for Paul and heard him speak about faith in **Christ** Jesus.

But as he was discussing righteousness, self-control and the judgment to come, Felix became frightened and said, "Go away for the present, and when I find time I will summon you." *Acts 24:24-25*

Having obtained help from God, I stand to this day testifying both to small and great, stating nothing but what the Prophets and Moses said was going to take place; that the **Christ** was to suffer, and that by reason of His resurrection from the dead He would be the first to proclaim light both to the Jewish people and to the Gentiles. *Acts 26:22-23*

He stayed two full years in his own rented quarters and was welcoming all who came to him, preaching the kingdom of God and teaching concerning the Lord Jesus **Christ** with all openness, unhindered. *Acts 28:30-31*

Paul, a bond-servant of **Christ** Jesus, called as an apostle, set apart for the gospel of God, which He promised beforehand through His prophets in the holy Scriptures, concerning His Son, who was born of a descendant of David according to the flesh, who was declared the Son of God with power by the resurrection from the dead, according to the Spirit of holiness, Jesus **Christ** our Lord, through whom we have received grace and apostleship to bring about the obedience of faith among all the Gentiles for His name's sake, among whom you also are the called of Jesus **Christ**; to all who are beloved of God in Rome, called as saints: Grace to you and peace from God our Father and the Lord Jesus **Christ**.

First, I thank my God through Jesus **Christ** for you all, because your faith is being proclaimed throughout the whole world. *Romans 1:1-8*

There will be tribulation and distress for every soul of man who does evil, of the Jew first and also of the Greek, but glory and honor and peace to everyone who does good, to the Jew first and also to the Greek.

For there is no partiality with God. For all who have sinned without the Law will also perish without the Law, and all who have sinned under the Law will be judged by the Law; for it is not the hearers of the Law who are just before God, but the doers of the Law will be justified.

For when Gentiles who do not have the Law do instinctively the things of the Law, these, not having the Law, are a law to themselves, in that they show the work of the Law written in their hearts, their conscience bearing witness and their thoughts alternately accusing or else defending them, on the day when, according to my gospel, God will judge the secrets of men through **Christ** Jesus. *Romans 2:9-16*

We know that whatever the Law says, it speaks to those who are under the Law, so that every mouth may be closed and all the world may become accountable to God; because by the works of the Law no flesh will be justified in His sight; for through the Law comes the knowledge of sin.

But apart from the Law the righteousness of God has been manifested, being witnessed by the Law and the Prophets, even the righteousness of God through faith in Jesus **Christ** for all those who believe; for there is no distinction; for all have sinned and fall short of the glory of God, being justified as a gift by His grace through the redemption which is in **Christ** Jesus; whom God displayed publicly as a propitiation in His blood through faith.

This was to demonstrate His righteousness, because in the forbearance of

God He passed over the sins previously committed; for the demonstration, I say, of His righteousness at the present time, so that He would be just and the justifier of the one who has faith in Jesus.

Romans 3:19-26

Having been justified by faith, we have peace with God through our Lord Jesus **Christ**, through whom also we have obtained our introduction by faith into this grace in which we stand; and we exult in hope of the glory of God.

And not only this, but we also exult in our tribulations, knowing that tribulation brings about perseverance; and perseverance, proven character; and proven character, hope; and hope does not disappoint, because the love of God has been poured out within our hearts through the Holy Spirit who was given to us. For while we were still helpless, at the right time **Christ** died for the ungodly.

For one will hardly die for a righteous man; though perhaps for the good man someone would dare even to die. But God demonstrates His own love toward us, in that while we were yet sinners, **Christ** died for us.

Much more then, having now been justified by His blood, we shall be saved from the wrath of God through Him. For if while we were enemies we were reconciled to God through the death of His Son, much more, having been reconciled, we shall be saved by His life. And not only this, but we also exult in God through our Lord Jesus **Christ**, through whom we have now received the reconciliation.

Therefore, just as through one man sin entered into the world, and death through sin, and so death spread to all men, because all sinned - for until the Law sin was in the world, but sin is not imputed when there is no law.

Nevertheless death reigned from Adam until Moses, even over those who had not sinned in the likeness of the offense of Adam, who is a type of Him who was to come.

But the free gift is not like the transgression. For if by the transgression of the one the many died, much more did the grace of God and the gift by the grace of the one Man, Jesus **Christ**, abound to the many.

The gift is not like that which came through the one who sinned; for on the one hand the judgment arose from one transgression resulting in condemnation, but on the other hand the free gift arose from many transgressions resulting in justification.

For if by the transgression of the one, death reigned through the one, much more those who receive the abundance of grace and of the gift of righteousness will reign in life through the One, Jesus **Christ**.

So then as through one transgression there resulted condemnation to all men, even so through one act of righteousness there resulted justification of life to all men. For as through the one man's disobedience the many were made sinners, even so through the obedience of the One the many will be made righteous.

The Law came in so that the transgression would increase; but where sin increased, grace abounded all the more, so that, as sin reigned in death, even so grace would reign through righteousness to eternal life through Jesus **Christ** our Lord.

What shall we say then? Are we to continue in sin so that grace may increase? May it never be! How shall we who died to sin still live in it? Or do you not know that all of us who have been baptized into **Christ** Jesus have been baptized into His death?

Therefore we have been buried with Him through baptism into death, so that as **Christ** was raised from the dead through the glory of the Father, so we too might walk in newness of life.

For if we have become united with Him in the likeness of His death, certainly we shall also be in the likeness of His resurrection, knowing this, that our old self was crucified with Him, in order that our body of sin might be done away with, so that we would no longer be slaves to sin; for he who has died is freed from sin.

Now if we have died with **Christ**, we believe that we shall also live with Him, knowing that **Christ**, having been raised from the dead, is never to die again; death no longer is master over Him. For the death that He died, He died to sin once for all; but the life that He lives, He lives to God.

Even so consider yourselves to be dead to sin, but alive to God in **Christ** Jesus.

Therefore do not let sin reign in your mortal body so that you obey its lusts, and do not go on presenting the members of your body to sin as instruments of un-righteousness; but present yourselves to God as those alive from the dead, and your members as instruments of right-eousness to God.

For sin shall not be master over you, for you are not under law but under grace.

Romans 5:1 - 6:14

Having been freed from sin and enslaved to God, you derive your benefit, resulting in sanctification, and the outcome, eternal life.

For the wages of sin is death, but the free gift of God is eternal life in **Christ** Jesus our Lord. Or do you not know, brethren (for I am speaking to those who know the law), that the law has jurisdic-tion over a person as long as he lives?

For the married woman is bound by law to her husband while he is living; but if her husband dies, she is released from the law concerning the husband.

So then, if while her husband is living she is joined to another man, she shall be called an adulteress; but if her husband dies, she is free from the law, so that she is not an adulteress though she is joined to another man.

Therefore, my brethren, you also were made to die to the Law through the body of **Christ**, so that you might be joined to another, to Him who was raised from the dead, in order that we might bear fruit for God. For while we were in the flesh, the sinful passions, which were aroused by the Law, were at work in the members of our body to bear fruit for

death.

But now we have been released from the Law, having died to that by which we were bound, so that we serve in newness of the Spirit and not in oldness of the let-ter.

Romans 6:22 - 7:6

I joyfully concur with the law of God in the inner man, but I see a different law in the members of my body, waging war against the law of my mind and making me a prisoner of the law of sin which is in my members.

Wretched man that I am! Who will set me free from the body of this death? Thanks be to God through Jesus **Christ** our Lord!

So then, on the one hand I myself with my mind am serving the law of God, but on the other, with my flesh the law of sin. Therefore there is now no condem-nation for those who are in **Christ** Jesus. For the law of the Spirit of life in **Christ** Jesus has set you free from the law of sin and of death.

For what the Law could not do, weak as it was through the flesh, God did: sending His own Son in the likeness of sinful flesh and as an offering for sin, He condemned sin in the flesh, so that the requirement of the Law might be fulfilled in us, who do not walk according to the flesh but according to the Spirit.

For those who are according to the flesh set their minds on the things of the flesh, but those who are according to the Spirit, the things of the Spirit.

For the mind set on the flesh is death, but the mind set on the Spirit is life and peace, because the mind set on the flesh is hostile toward God; for it does not sub-ject itself to the law of God, for it is not even able to do so, and those who are in the flesh cannot please God.

However, you are not in the flesh but in the Spirit, if indeed the Spirit of God dwells in you. But if anyone does not have the Spirit of **Christ**, he does not belong to Him. If **Christ** is in you, though the body is dead because of sin, yet the spirit is alive because of righteousness.

But if the Spirit of Him who raised

Jesus from the dead dwells in you, He who raised **Christ** Jesus from the dead will also give life to your mortal bodies through His Spirit who dwells in you.

So then, brethren, we are under obligation, not to the flesh, to live according to the flesh - for if you are living according to the flesh, you must die; but if by the Spirit you are putting to death the deeds of the body, you will live. For all who are being led by the Spirit of God, these are sons of God.

For you have not received a spirit of slavery leading to fear again, but you have received a spirit of adoption as sons by which we cry out, "Abba! Father!"

The Spirit Himself testifies with our spirit that we are children of God, and if children, heirs also, heirs of God and fellow heirs with **Christ**, if indeed we suffer with Him so that we may also be glorified with Him. *Romans 7:22 - 8:17*

He who did not spare His own Son, but delivered Him over for us all, how will He not also with Him freely give us all things? Who will bring a charge against God's elect? God is the one who justifies; who is the one who condemns? **Christ** Jesus is He who died, yes, rather who was raised, who is at the right hand of God, who also intercedes for us.

Who will separate us from the love of **Christ**? Will tribulation, or distress, or persecution, or famine, or nakedness, or peril, or sword? Just as it is written, "For Your sake we are being put to death all day long; we were considered as sheep to be slaughtered." But in all these things we overwhelmingly conquer through Him who loved us.

For I am convinced that neither death, nor life, nor angels, nor principalities, nor things present, nor things to come, nor powers, nor height, nor depth, nor any other created thing, will be able to separate us from the love of God, which is in **Christ** Jesus our Lord.

I am telling the truth in **Christ**, I am not lying, my conscience testifies with me in the Holy Spirit, that I have great sorrow and unceasing grief in my heart. For I

could wish that I myself were accursed, separated from **Christ** for the sake of my brethren, my kinsmen according to the flesh, who are Israelites, to whom belongs the adoption as sons, and the glory and the covenants and the giving of the Law and the temple service and the promises, whose are the fathers, and from whom is the **Christ** according to the flesh, who is over all, God blessed forever. Amen. *Romans 8:32 - 9:5*

What shall we say then? That Gentiles, who did not pursue righteousness, attained righteousness, even the righteousness which is by faith; but Israel, pursuing a law of righteousness, did not arrive at that law. Why?

Because they did not pursue it by faith, but as though it were by works. They stumbled over the stumbling stone, just as it is written, "Behold, I lay in Zion a stone of stumbling and a rock of offense, and he who believes in Him will not be disappointed."

Brethren, my heart's desire and my prayer to God for them is for their salvation. For I testify about them that they have a zeal for God, but not in accordance with knowledge.

For not knowing about God's righteousness and seeking to establish their own, they did not subject themselves to the righteousness of God. For **Christ** is the end of the law for righteousness to everyone who believes. For Moses writes that the man who practices the righteousness which is based on law shall live by that righteousness.

But the righteousness based on faith speaks as follows: "Do not say in your heart, 'Who will ascend into heaven?' (that is, to bring **Christ** down), or 'Who will descend into the abyss? ' (that is, to bring **Christ** up from the dead)."

But what does it say? "The word is near you, in your mouth and in your heart" - that is, the word of faith which we are preaching, that if you confess with your mouth Jesus as Lord, and believe in your heart that God raised Him from the dead, you will be saved; for with the heart a person believes, resulting in righteousness, and with the mouth he confesses, resulting in salvation.

For the Scripture says, "Whoever believes in Him will not be disappointed." For there is no distinction between Jew and Greek; for the same Lord is Lord of all, abounding in riches for all who call on Him; for "Whoever will call on the name of the Lord will be saved."

How then will they call on Him in whom they have not believed? How will they believe in Him whom they have not heard? And how will they hear without a preacher? How will they preach unless they are sent? Just as it is written, "How beautiful are the feet of those who bring good news of good things!"

However, they did not all heed the good news; for Isaiah says, "Lord, who has believed our report?"

So faith comes from hearing, and hearing by the word of **Christ**.

Romans 9:30 - 10:17

Just as we have many members in one body and all the members do not have the same function, so we, who are many, are one body in **Christ**, and individually members one of another. *Romans 12:4-5*

The night is almost gone, and the day is near. Therefore let us lay aside the deeds of darkness and put on the armor of light. Let us behave properly as in the day, not in carousing and drunkenness, not in sexual promiscuity and sensuality, not in strife and jealousy.

But put on the Lord Jesus **Christ**, and make no provision for the flesh in regard to its lusts. *Romans 13:12-14*

Not one of us lives for himself, and not one dies for himself; for if we live, we live for the Lord, or if we die, we die for the Lord; therefore whether we live or die, we are the Lord's.

For to this end **Christ** died and lived again, that He might be Lord both of the dead and of the living. *Romans 14:7-9*

I know and am convinced in the Lord Jesus that nothing is unclean in itself; but to him who thinks anything to be unclean, to him it is unclean. For if because of food your brother is hurt, you are no longer walking according to love. Do not destroy with your food him for whom **Christ** died.

Therefore do not let what is for you a good thing be spoken of as evil; for the kingdom of God is not eating and drinking, but righteousness and peace and joy in the Holy Spirit. For he who in this way serves **Christ** is acceptable to God and approved by men.

So then we pursue the things which make for peace and the building up of one another. *Romans 14:14-19*

We who are strong ought to bear the weaknesses of those without strength and not just please ourselves.

Each of us is to please his neighbor for his good, to his edification. For even **Christ** did not please Himself; but as it is written, "The reproaches of those who reproached You fell on Me."

For whatever was written in earlier times was written for our instruction, so that through perseverance and the encouragement of the Scriptures we might have hope.

Now may the God who gives perseverance and encouragement grant you to be of the same mind with one another according to **Christ** Jesus, so that with one accord you may with one voice glorify the God and Father of our Lord Jesus **Christ**. Therefore, accept one another, just as **Christ** also accepted us to the glory of God.

For I say that **Christ** has become a servant to the circumcision on behalf of the truth of God to confirm the promises given to the fathers, and for the Gentiles to glorify God for His mercy; as it is written, "Therefore I will give praise to You among the Gentiles, and I will sing to Your name." *Romans 15:1-9*

Concerning you, my brethren, I myself also am convinced that you yourselves are full of goodness, filled with all knowledge and able also to admonish one another. But I have written very boldly to you on some points so as to remind you again, because of the grace that was given me from God, to be a minister of **Christ** Jesus to the Gentiles, ministering as a priest the gospel of God, so that my offering of the Gentiles may become acceptable, sanctified by the Holy Spirit.

Therefore in **Christ** Jesus I have found reason for boasting in things pertaining to God. For I will not presume to speak of anything except what **Christ** has accomplished through me, resulting in the obedience of the Gentiles by word and deed, in the power of signs and wonders, in the power of the Spirit; so that from Jerusalem and round about as far as Illyricum I have fully preached the gospel of **Christ**.

And thus I aspired to preach the gospel, not where **Christ** was already named, so that I would not build on another man's foundation; but as it is written, "They who had no news of Him shall see, and they who have not heard shall understand." *Romans 15:14-21*

I know that when I come to you, I will come in the fullness of the blessing of **Christ**. Now I urge you, brethren, by our Lord Jesus **Christ** and by the love of the Spirit, to strive together with me in your prayers to God for me, that I may be rescued from those who are disobedient in Judea, and that my service for Jerusalem may prove acceptable to the saints; so that I may come to you in joy by the will of God and find refreshing rest in your company. Now the God of peace be with you all. Amen. *Romans 15:29-33*

Greet Prisca and Aquila, my fellow workers in **Christ** Jesus, who for my life risked their own necks, to whom not only do I give thanks, but also all the churches of the Gentiles; greet the church that is in their house.

Greet Epaenetus, my beloved, who is the first convert to **Christ** from Asia. Greet Mary, who has worked hard for you. Greet Andronicus and Junias, my kinsmen and my fellow prisoners, who are outstanding among the apostles, who also were in **Christ** before me.

Greet Ampliatus, my beloved in the Lord. Greet Urbanus, our fellow worker in **Christ**, and Stachys my beloved. Greet Apelles, the approved in **Christ**. Greet those who are of the household of Aristobulus. *Romans 16:3-10*

Greet one another with a holy kiss. All the churches of **Christ** greet you.

Now I urge you, brethren, keep your eye on those who cause dissensions and hindrances contrary to the teaching which you learned, and turn away from them. For such men are slaves, not of our Lord **Christ** but of their own appetites; and by their smooth and flattering speech they deceive the hearts of the unsuspecting. *Romans 16:16-18*

[The grace of our Lord Jesus **Christ** be with you all. Amen.]

Now to Him who is able to establish you according to my gospel and the preaching of Jesus **Christ**, according to the revelation of the mystery which has been kept secret for long ages past, but now is manifested, and by the Scriptures of the prophets, according to the commandment of the eternal God, has been made known to all the nations, leading to obedience of faith; to the only wise God, through Jesus **Christ**, be the glory forever. Amen. *Romans 16:24-27*

Paul, called as an apostle of Jesus **Christ** by the will of God, and Sosthenes our brother, to the church of God which is at Corinth, to those who have been sanctified in **Christ** Jesus, saints by calling, with all who in every place call on the name of our Lord Jesus **Christ**, their Lord and ours: Grace to you and peace from God our Father and the Lord Jesus **Christ**.

I thank my God always concerning you for the grace of God which was given you in **Christ** Jesus, that in everything you were enriched in Him, in all speech and all knowledge, even as the testimony concerning **Christ** was confirmed in you, so that you are not lacking in any gift, awaiting eagerly the revelation of our Lord Jesus **Christ**, who will also confirm you to the end, blameless in the day of our Lord Jesus **Christ**. God is faithful, through whom you were called into fellowship with His Son, Jesus **Christ** our Lord.

Now I exhort you, brethren, by the name of our Lord Jesus **Christ**, that you all agree and that there be no divisions among you, but that you be made complete in the same mind and in the same judgment. For I have been informed concerning you, my brethren, by Chloe's people, that there are quarrels among you.

Now I mean this, that each one of you is saying, "I am of Paul," and "I of Apollos," and "I of Cephas," and "I of **Christ**." Has **Christ** been divided? Paul was not crucified for you, was he? Or were you baptized in the name of Paul?

I thank God that I baptized none of you except Crispus and Gaius, so that no one would say you were baptized in my name. Now I did baptize also the household of Stephanas; beyond that, I do not know whether I baptized any other.

For **Christ** did not send me to baptize, but to preach the gospel, not in cleverness of speech, so that the cross of **Christ** would not be made void. For the word of the cross is foolishness to those who are perishing, but to us who are being saved it is the power of God.

For it is written, "I will destroy the wisdom of the wise, and the cleverness of the clever I will set aside." Where is the wise man? Where is the scribe? Where is the debater of this age? Has not God made foolish the wisdom of the world?

For since in the wisdom of God the world through its wisdom did not come to know God, God was well-pleased through the foolishness of the message preached to save those who believe.

For indeed Jews ask for signs and Greeks search for wisdom; but we preach **Christ** crucified, to Jews a stumbling block and to Gentiles foolishness, but to those who are the called, both Jews and Greeks, **Christ** the power of God and the

wisdom of God. Because the foolishness of God is wiser than men, and the weakness of God is stronger than men.

For consider your calling, brethren, that there were not many wise according to the flesh, not many mighty, not many noble; but God has chosen the foolish things of the world to shame the wise, and God has chosen the weak things of the world to shame the things which are strong, and the base things of the world and the despised God has chosen, the things that are not, so that He may nullify the things that are, so that no man may boast before God.

But by His doing you are in **Christ** Jesus, who became to us wisdom from God, and righteousness and sanctification, and redemption, so that, just as it is written, "Let him who boasts, boast in the Lord."

And when I came to you, brethren, I did not come with superiority of speech or of wisdom, proclaiming to you the testimony of God. For I determined to know nothing among you except Jesus **Christ**, and Him crucified.   *1 Corinthians 1:1 - 2:2*

We have received, not the spirit of the world, but the Spirit who is from God, so that we may know the things freely given to us by God, which things we also speak, not in words taught by human wisdom, but in those taught by the Spirit, combining spiritual thoughts with spiritual words.

But a natural man does not accept the things of the Spirit of God, for they are foolishness to him; and he cannot understand them, because they are spiritually appraised. But he who is spiritual appraises all things, yet he himself is appraised by no one.

For who has known the mind of the Lord, that he will instruct Him? But we have the mind of **Christ**.

And I, brethren, could not speak to you as to spiritual men, but as to men of flesh, as to infants in **Christ**.

I gave you milk to drink, not solid food; for you were not yet able to receive it. Indeed, even now you are not yet able, for you are still fleshly. For since there is jealousy and strife among you, are you not fleshly, and are you not walking like mere men?   *1 Corinthians 2:12 - 3:3*

According to the grace of God which was given to me, like a wise master builder I laid a foundation, and another is building on it.

But each man must be careful how he builds on it. For no man can lay a foundation other than the one which is laid, which is Jesus **Christ**.   *1 Corinthians 3:10-11*

Let no one boast in men. For all things belong to you, whether Paul or Apollos or Cephas or the world or life or death or things present or things to come; all things belong to you, and you belong to **Christ**; and **Christ** belongs to God.

Let a man regard us in this manner, as servants of **Christ** and stewards of the mysteries of God. In this case, moreover, it is required of stewards that one be found trustworthy.   *1 Corinthians 3:21 - 4:2*

For, I think, God has exhibited us apostles last of all, as men condemned to death; because we have become a spectacle to the world, both to angels and to men. We are fools for **Christ's** sake, but you are prudent in **Christ**; we are weak, but you are strong; you are distinguished, but we are without honor.

To this present hour we are both hungry and thirsty, and are poorly clothed, and are roughly treated, and are homeless; and we toil, working with our own hands; when we are reviled, we bless; when we are persecuted, we endure; when we are slandered, we try to conciliate; we have become as the scum of the world, the dregs of all things, even until now.

I do not write these things to shame you, but to admonish you as my beloved children. For if you were to have countless tutors in **Christ**, yet you would not have many fathers, for in **Christ** Jesus I became your father through the gospel.

Therefore I exhort you, be imitators of me. For this reason I have sent to you Timothy, who is my beloved and faithful child in the Lord, and he will remind you of my ways which are in **Christ**, just as I teach everywhere in every church.
1 Corinthians 4:9-17

Your boasting is not good. Do you not know that a little leaven leavens the whole lump of dough? Clean out the old leaven so that you may be a new lump, just as you are in fact unleavened.

For **Christ** our Passover also has been sacrificed. Therefore let us celebrate the feast, not with old leaven, nor with the leaven of malice and wickedness, but with the unleavened bread of sincerity and truth.   *1 Corinthians 5:6-8*

Do you not know that the unrighteous will not inherit the kingdom of God? Do not be deceived; neither fornicators, nor idolaters, nor adulterers, nor effeminate, nor homosexuals, nor thieves, nor the covetous, nor drunkards, nor revilers, nor swindlers, will inherit the kingdom of God.

Such were some of you; but you were washed, but you were sanctified, but you were justified in the name of the Lord Jesus **Christ** and in the Spirit of our God.
1 Corinthians 6:9-11

God has not only raised the Lord, but will also raise us up through His power. Do you not know that your bodies are members of **Christ**? Shall I then take away the members of **Christ** and make them members of a prostitute? May it never be!

Or do you not know that the one who joins himself to a prostitute is one body with her? For He says, "The two shall become one flesh."

But the one who joins himself to the Lord is one spirit with Him.
1 Corinthians 6:14-17

Circumcision is nothing, and uncircumcision is nothing, but what matters is the keeping of the commandments of God. Each man must remain in that condition in which he was called.

Were you called while a slave? Do not worry about it; but if you are able also to become free, rather do that. For he who was called in the Lord while a slave, is the Lord's freedman; likewise he who was called while free, is **Christ's** slave.

You were bought with a price; do not become slaves of men. *1 Corinthians 7:19-23*

Concerning the eating of things sacrificed to idols, we know that there is no such thing as an idol in the world, and that there is no God but one.

For even if there are so-called gods whether in heaven or on earth, as indeed there are many gods and many lords, yet for us there is but one God, the Father, from whom are all things and we exist for Him; and one Lord, Jesus **Christ**, by whom are all things, and we exist through Him.

However not all men have this knowledge; but some, being accustomed to the idol until now, eat food as if it were sacrificed to an idol; and their conscience being weak is defiled.

But food will not commend us to God; we are neither the worse if we do not eat, nor the better if we do eat.

But take care that this liberty of yours does not somehow become a stumbling block to the weak. For if someone sees you, who have knowledge, dining in an idol's temple, will not his conscience, if he is weak, be strengthened to eat things sacrificed to idols?

For through your knowledge he who is weak is ruined, the brother for whose sake **Christ** died. And so, by sinning against the brethren and wounding their conscience when it is weak, you sin against **Christ**.

Therefore, if food causes my brother to stumble, I will never eat meat again, so that I will not cause my brother to stumble. *1 Corinthians 8:4-13*

If we sowed spiritual things in you, is it too much if we reap material things from you? If others share the right over you, do we not more? Nevertheless, we did not use this right, but we endure all things so that we will cause no hindrance to the gospel of **Christ**.

Do you not know that those who per-form sacred services eat the food of the temple, and those who attend regularly to the altar have their share from the altar? So also the Lord directed those who proclaim the gospel to get their living from the gospel. *1 Corinthians 9:11-14*

What then is my reward? That, when I preach the gospel, I may offer the gospel without charge, so as not to make full use of my right in the gospel.

For though I am free from all men, I have made myself a slave to all, so that I may win more.

To the Jews I became as a Jew, so that I might win Jews; to those who are under the Law, as under the Law though not being myself under the Law, so that I might win those who are under the Law; to those who are without law, as without law, though not being without the law of God but under the law of **Christ**, so that I might win those who are without law.

To the weak I became weak, that I might win the weak; I have become all things to all men, so that I may by all means save some. *1 Corinthians 9:18-22*

I do not want you to be unaware, brethren, that our fathers were all under the cloud and all passed through the sea; and all were baptized into Moses in the cloud and in the sea; and all ate the same spiritual food; and all drank the same spiritual drink, for they were drinking from a spiritual rock which followed them; and the rock was **Christ**. Nevertheless, with most of them God was not well-pleased; for they were laid low in the wilderness.

Now these things happened as examples for us, so that we would not crave evil things as they also craved.

Do not be idolaters, as some of them were; ~ *1 Corinthians 10:1-7*

Is not the cup of blessing which we bless a sharing in the blood of **Christ**? Is not the bread which we break a sharing in the body of **Christ**? Since there is one bread, we who are many are one body; for we all partake of the one bread.

1 Corinthians 10:16-17

Be imitators of me, just as I also am of **Christ**.

Now I praise you because you remember me in everything and hold firmly to the traditions, just as I delivered them to you.

But I want you to understand that **Christ** is the head of every man, and the man is the head of a woman, and God is the head of **Christ**. *1 Corinthians 11:1-3*

There are varieties of gifts, but the same Spirit. And there are varieties of ministries, and the same Lord.

There are varieties of effects, but the same God who works all things in all persons. But to each one is given the manifestation of the Spirit for the common good.

For to one is given the word of wisdom through the Spirit, and to another the word of knowledge according to the same Spirit; to another faith by the same Spirit, and to another gifts of healing by the one Spirit, and to another the effecting of miracles, and to another prophecy, and to another the distinguishing of spirits, to another various kinds of tongues, and to another the interpretation of tongues.

But one and the same Spirit works all these things, distributing to each one individually just as He wills. For even as the body is one and yet has many members, and all the members of the body, though they are many, are one body, so also is **Christ**.

For by one Spirit we were all baptized into one body, whether Jews or Greeks, whether slaves or free, and we were all made to drink of one Spirit. For the body is not one member, but many.
1 Corinthians 12:4-14

If one member suffers, all the members suffer with it; if one member is honored, all the members rejoice with it.

Now you are **Christ's** body, and individually members of it.
1 Corinthians 12:26-27

I make known to you, brethren, the gospel which I preached to you, which also you received, in which also you stand, by which also you are saved, if you hold fast the word which I preached to you, unless you believed in vain. For I delivered to you as of first importance what I also received, that **Christ** died for our sins according to the Scriptures, and that He was buried, and that He was raised on the third day according to the Scriptures, and that He appeared to Cephas, then to the twelve.

After that He appeared to more than five hundred brethren at one time, most of whom remain until now, but some have fallen asleep; then He appeared to James, then to all the apostles; and last of all, as to one untimely born, He appeared to me also. For I am the least of the apostles, and not fit to be called an apostle, because I persecuted the church of God.

But by the grace of God I am what I am, and His grace toward me did not prove vain; but I labored even more than all of them, yet not I, but the grace of God with me. Whether then it was I or they, so we preach and so you believed.

Now if **Christ** is preached, that He has been raised from the dead, how do some among you say that there is no resurrection of the dead?

But if there is no resurrection of the dead, not even **Christ** has been raised; and if **Christ** has not been raised, then our preaching is vain, your faith also is vain.

Moreover we are even found to be false witnesses of God, because we testified against God that He raised **Christ**, whom He did not raise, if in fact the dead are not raised.

For if the dead are not raised, not even **Christ** has been raised; and if **Christ** has not been raised, your faith is worthless; you are still in your sins. Then those also who have fallen asleep in **Christ** have perished. If we have hoped in **Christ** in this life only, we are of all men most to be pitied.

But now **Christ** has been raised from the dead, the first fruits of those who are asleep. For since by a man came death, by a man also came the resurrection of the dead. For as in Adam all die, so also in **Christ** all will be made alive.

But each in his own order: **Christ** the first fruits, after that those who are **Christ's** at His coming, then comes the end, when He hands over the kingdom to the God and Father, when He has abolished all rule and all authority and power.

For He must reign until He has put all His enemies under His feet.

The last enemy that will be abolished is death. For He has put all things in subjection under His feet. But when He says, "All things are put in subjection," it is evident that He is excepted who put all things in subjection to Him.

When all things are subjected to Him, then the Son Himself also will be subjected to the One who subjected all things to Him, so that God may be all in all.

Otherwise, what will those do who are baptized for the dead? If the dead are not raised at all, why then are they baptized for them? Why are we also in danger every hour? I affirm, brethren, by the boasting in you which I have in **Christ** Jesus our Lord, I die daily.

1 Corinthians 15:1-31

"O death, where is your victory? O death, where is your sting?"

The sting of death is sin, and the power of sin is the law; but thanks be to God, who gives us the victory through our Lord Jesus **Christ**.

Therefore, my beloved brethren, be steadfast, immovable, always abounding in the work of the Lord, knowing that your toil is not in vain in the Lord.

1 Corinthians 15:55-58

The grace of the Lord Jesus be with you. My love be with you all in **Christ** Jesus. Amen.   *1 Corinthians 16:23-24*

Paul, an apostle of **Christ** Jesus by the will of God, and Timothy our brother, to the church of God which is at Corinth with all the saints who are throughout Achaia: Grace to you and peace from God our Father and the Lord Jesus **Christ**.

Blessed be the God and Father of our Lord Jesus **Christ**, the Father of mercies and God of all comfort, who comforts us in all our affliction so that we will be able to comfort those who are in any affliction with the comfort with which we ourselves are comforted by God. For just as the sufferings of **Christ** are ours in abundance, so also our comfort is abundant through **Christ**.   *2 Corinthians 1:1-5*

The Son of God, **Christ** Jesus, who was preached among you by us - by me and Silvanus and Timothy - was not yes and no, but is yes in Him. For as many as are the promises of God, in Him they are yes; therefore also through Him is our Amen to the glory of God through us.

Now He who establishes us with you in **Christ** and anointed us is God, who also sealed us and gave us the Spirit in our hearts as a pledge. *2 Corinthians 1:19-22*

I also wrote so that I might put you to the test, whether you are obedient in all things.

But one whom you forgive anything, I forgive also; for indeed what I have forgiven, if I have forgiven anything, I did it for your sakes in the presence of **Christ**, so that no advantage would be taken of us by Satan, for we are not ignorant of his schemes.

Now when I came to Troas for the gospel of **Christ** and when a door was opened for me in the Lord, I had no rest for my spirit, not finding Titus my brother; but taking my leave of them, I went on to Macedonia.

But thanks be to God, who always leads us in triumph in **Christ**, and manifests through us the sweet aroma of the knowledge of Him in every place. For we are a fragrance of **Christ** to God among those who are being saved and among those who are perishing; to the one an aroma from death to death, to the other an aroma from life to life.

And who is adequate for these things? For we are not like many, peddling the word of God, but as from sincerity, but as from God, we speak in **Christ** in the sight of God. Are we beginning to commend ourselves again? Or do we need, as some, letters of commendation to you or from you?

You are our letter, written in our hearts, known and read by all men; being manifested that you are a letter of **Christ**, cared for by us, written not with ink but with the Spirit of the living God, not on tablets of stone but on tablets of human hearts. Such confidence we have through **Christ** toward God.

Not that we are adequate in ourselves to consider anything as coming from ourselves, but our adequacy is from God, who also made us adequate as servants of a new covenant, not of the letter but of the Spirit; for the letter kills, but the Spirit gives life. *2 Corinthians 2:9 - 3:6*

Having such a hope, we use great boldness in our speech, and are not like Moses, who used to put a veil over his face so that the sons of Israel would not look intently at the end of what was fading away. But their minds were hardened; for until this very day at the reading of the old covenant the same veil remains unlifted, because it is removed in **Christ**. But to this day whenever Moses is read, a veil lies over their heart; but whenever a person turns to the Lord, the veil is taken away.

Now the Lord is the Spirit, and where the Spirit of the Lord is, there is liberty. But we all, with unveiled face, beholding as in a mirror the glory of the Lord, are being transformed into the same image from glory to glory, just as from the Lord, the Spirit. *2 Corinthians 3:12-18*

If our gospel is veiled, it is veiled to those who are perishing, in whose case the god of this world has blinded the minds of the unbelieving so that they might not see the light of the gospel of the glory of **Christ**, who is the image of God. For we do not preach ourselves but **Christ** Jesus as Lord, and ourselves as your bond-servants for Jesus' sake.

For God, who said, "Light shall shine out of darkness," is the One who has shone in our hearts to give the Light of the knowledge of the glory of God in the face of **Christ**. *2 Corinthians 4:3-6*

Being always of good courage, and knowing that while we are at home in the body we are absent from the Lord - for we walk by faith, not by sight - we are of good courage, I say, and prefer rather to be absent from the body and to be at home with the Lord. Therefore we also have as our ambition, whether at home or absent, to be pleasing to Him.

For we must all appear before the judgment seat of **Christ**, so that each one may be recompensed for his deeds in the body, according to what he has done, whether good or bad. *2 Corinthians 5:6-10*

The love of **Christ** controls us, having concluded this, that one died for all, therefore all died; and He died for all, so that they who live might no longer live for themselves, but for Him who died and rose again on their behalf.

Therefore from now on we recognize no one according to the flesh; even though we have known **Christ** according to the flesh, yet now we know Him in this way no longer.

Therefore if anyone is in **Christ**, he is a new creature; the old things passed away; behold, new things have come.

Now all these things are from God, who reconciled us to Himself through **Christ** and gave us the ministry of reconciliation, namely, that God was in **Christ** reconciling the world to Himself, not counting their trespasses against them, and He has committed to us the word of reconciliation.

Therefore, we are ambassadors for **Christ**, as though God were making an appeal through us; we beg you on behalf of **Christ**, be reconciled to God. He made Him who knew no sin to be sin on our behalf, so that we might become the righteousness of God in Him.
2 Corinthians 5:14-21

Do not be bound together with unbelievers; for what partnership have righteousness and lawlessness, or what fellowship has light with darkness? Or what harmony has **Christ** with Belial, or what has a believer in common with an unbeliever? Or what agreement has the temple of God with idols?

For we are the temple of the living God; just as God said, "I will dwell in them and walk among them; and I will be their God, and they shall be My people. Therefore, come out from their midst and be separate," says the Lord. "And do not touch what is unclean; and I will welcome you. And I will be a father to you, and you shall be sons and daughters to Me," says the Lord Almighty.   *2 Corinthians 6:14-18*

You know the grace of our Lord Jesus **Christ**, that though He was rich, yet for your sake He became poor, so that you through His poverty might become rich.
    2 Corinthians 8:9

As for Titus, he is my partner and fellow worker among you; as for our brethren, they are messengers of the churches, a glory to **Christ**. Therefore openly before the churches, show them the proof of your love and of our reason for boasting about you.   *2 Corinthians 8:23-24*

Because of the proof given by this ministry, they will glorify God for your obedience to your confession of the gospel of **Christ** and for the liberality of your contribution to them and to all, while they also, by prayer on your behalf, yearn for you because of the surpassing grace of God in you. Thanks be to God for His indescribable gift!

Now I, Paul, myself urge you by the meekness and gentleness of **Christ** - I who am meek when face to face with you, but bold toward you when absent!
    2 Corinthians 9:13 - 10:1

Though we walk in the flesh, we do not war according to the flesh, for the weapons of our warfare are not of the flesh, but divinely powerful for the destruction of fortresses.

We are destroying speculations and every lofty thing raised up against the knowledge of God, and we are taking every thought captive to the obedience of **Christ**, and we are ready to punish all disobedience, whenever your obedience is complete.

You are looking at things as they are outwardly. If anyone is confident in himself that he is **Christ's**, let him consider this again within himself, that just as he is **Christ's**, so also are we.
    2 Corinthians 10:3-7

We will not boast beyond our measure, but within the measure of the sphere which God apportioned to us as a measure, to reach even as far as you. For we are not overextending ourselves, as if we did not reach to you, for we were the first to come even as far as you in the gospel of **Christ**; not boasting beyond our measure, that is, in other men's labors, but with the hope that as your faith grows, we will be, within our sphere, enlarged even more by you, so as to preach the gospel even to the regions beyond you, and not to boast in what has been accomplished in the sphere of another.

But he who boasts is to boast in the Lord. For it is not he who commends himself that is approved, but he whom the Lord commends.

I wish that you would bear with me in a little foolishness; but indeed you are bearing with me. For I am jealous for you with a godly jealousy; for I betrothed you to one husband, so that to **Christ** I might present you as a pure virgin.

But I am afraid that, as the serpent deceived Eve by his craftiness, your minds will be led astray from the simplicity and purity of devotion to **Christ**.
    2 Corinthians 10:14 - 11:3

As the truth of **Christ** is in me, this boasting of mine will not be stopped in the regions of Achaia. Why? Because I do not love you? God knows I do!

But what I am doing I will continue to do, so that I may cut off opportunity from those who desire an opportunity to be regarded just as we are in the matter about which they are boasting. For such men are false apostles, deceitful workers, disguising themselves as apostles of **Christ**.

No wonder, for even Satan disguises himself as an angel of light. Therefore it is not surprising if his servants also disguise themselves as servants of righteousness, whose end will be according to their deeds.   *2 Corinthians 11:10-15*

Are they Hebrews? So am I. Are they Israelites? So am I. Are they descendants of Abraham? So am I. Are they servants of **Christ**? - I speak as if insane - I more so; in far more labors, in far more imprisonments, beaten times without number, often in danger of death.
                    2 Corinthians 11:22-23

I know a man in **Christ** who fourteen years ago - whether in the body I do not know, or out of the body I do not know, God knows - such a man was caught up to the third heaven.

And I know how such a man - whether in the body or apart from the body I do not know, God knows - was caught up into Paradise and heard inexpressible words, which a man is not permitted to speak.

On behalf of such a man I will boast; but on my own behalf I will not boast, except in regard to my weaknesses. For if I do wish to boast I will not be foolish, for I will be speaking the truth; but I refrain from this, so that no one will credit me with more than he sees in me or hears from me.

Because of the surpassing greatness of the revelations, for this reason, to keep me from exalting myself, there was given me a thorn in the flesh, a messenger of Satan to torment me - to keep me from exalting myself!

Concerning this I implored the Lord three times that it might leave me. And He has said to me, "My grace is sufficient for you, for power is perfected in weakness."

Most gladly, therefore, I will rather boast about my weaknesses, so that the power of **Christ** may dwell in me.

Therefore I am well content with weaknesses, with insults, with distresses, with persecutions, with difficulties, for **Christ's** sake; for when I am weak, then I am strong.   *2 Corinthians 12:2-10*

All this time you have been thinking that we are defending ourselves to you. Actually, it is in the sight of God that we have been speaking in **Christ**; and all for your upbuilding, beloved.   *2 Corinthians 12:19*

I have previously said when present the second time, and though now absent I say in advance to those who have sinned in the past and to all the rest as well, that if I come again I will not spare anyone, since you are seeking for proof of the **Christ** who speaks in me, and who is not weak toward you, but mighty in you.

For indeed He was crucified because of weakness, yet He lives because of the power of God. For we also are weak in Him, yet we will live with Him because of the power of God directed toward you.

Test yourselves to see if you are in the faith; examine yourselves! Or do you not recognize this about yourselves, that Jesus **Christ** is in you - unless indeed you fail the test?   *2 Corinthians 13:2-5*

Finally, brethren, rejoice, be made complete, be comforted, be like-minded, live in peace; and the God of love and peace will be with you. Greet one another with a holy kiss. All the saints greet you.

The grace of the Lord Jesus **Christ**, and the love of God, and the fellowship of the Holy Spirit, be with you all.
                    2 Corinthians 13:13-14

Paul, an apostle (not sent from men nor through the agency of man, but through Jesus **Christ** and God the Father, who raised Him from the dead), and all the brethren who are with me, to the churches of Galatia: Grace to you and peace from God our Father and the Lord Jesus **Christ**, who gave Himself for our sins so that He might rescue us from this present evil age, according to the will of our God and Father, to whom be the glory forevermore. Amen.

I am amazed that you are so quickly deserting Him who called you by the grace of **Christ**, for a different gospel; which is really not another; only there are some who are disturbing you and want to distort the gospel of **Christ**. But even if we, or an angel from heaven, should preach to you a gospel contrary to what we have preached to you, he is to be accursed!

As we have said before, so I say again now, if any man is preaching to you a gospel contrary to what you received, he is to be accursed! For am I now seeking the favor of men, or of God? Or am I striving to please men? If I were still trying to please men, I would not be a bond-servant of **Christ**.

For I would have you know, brethren, that the gospel which was preached by me is not according to man. For I neither received it from man, nor was I taught it, but I received it through a revelation of Jesus **Christ**. *Galatians 1:1-12*

I went into the regions of Syria and Cilicia. I was still unknown by sight to the churches of Judea which were in **Christ**; but only, they kept hearing, "He who once persecuted us is now preaching the faith which he once tried to destroy." And they were glorifying God because of me.

Then after an interval of fourteen years I went up again to Jerusalem with Barnabas, taking Titus along also. It was because of a revelation that I went up; and I submitted to them the gospel which I preach among the Gentiles, but I did so in private to those who were of reputation, for fear that I might be running, or had run, in vain.

But not even Titus, who was with me, though he was a Greek, was compelled to be circumcised. But it was because of the false brethren secretly brought in, who had sneaked in to spy out our liberty which we have in **Christ** Jesus, in order to bring us into bondage.

But we did not yield in subjection to them for even an hour, so that the truth of the gospel would remain with you. *Galatians 1:21 - 2:5*

We are Jews by nature and not sinners from among the Gentiles; nevertheless knowing that a man is not justified by the works of the Law but through faith in **Christ** Jesus, even we have believed in **Christ** Jesus, so that we may be justified by faith in **Christ** and not by the works of the Law; since by the works of the Law no flesh will be justified.

But if, while seeking to be justified in **Christ**, we ourselves have also been found sinners, is **Christ** then a minister of sin? May it never be! For if I rebuild what I have once destroyed, I prove myself to be a transgressor.

For through the Law I died to the Law, so that I might live to God. I have been crucified with **Christ**; and it is no longer I who live, but **Christ** lives in me; and the life which I now live in the flesh I live by faith in the Son of God, who loved me and gave Himself up for me.

I do not nullify the grace of God, for if righteousness comes through the Law, then **Christ** died needlessly. You foolish Galatians, who has bewitched you, before whose eyes Jesus **Christ** was publicly portrayed as crucified?

This is the only thing I want to find out from you: Did you receive the Spirit by the works of the Law, or by hearing with faith? Are you so foolish? Having begun by the Spirit, are you now being perfected by the flesh? Did you suffer so many things in vain - if indeed it was in vain? *Galatians 2:15 - 3:4*

That no one is justified by the Law before God is evident; for, "The righteous man shall live by faith." However, the Law is not of faith; on the contrary, "He who practices them shall live by them."

Christ redeemed us from the curse of the Law, having become a curse for us - for it is written, "Cursed is everyone who hangs on a tree" - in order that in **Christ** Jesus the blessing of Abraham might come to the Gentiles, so that we would receive the promise of the Spirit through faith.

Brethren, I speak in terms of human relations: even though it is only a man's covenant, yet when it has been ratified, no one sets it aside or adds conditions to it.

Now the promises were spoken to Abraham and to his seed. He does not say, "And to seeds," as referring to many, but rather to one, "And to your seed," that is, **Christ**.

What I am saying is this: The Law, which came four hundred and thirty years later, does not invalidate a covenant previously ratified by God, so as to nullify the promise. For if the inheritance is based on law, it is no longer based on a promise; but God has granted it to Abraham by means of a promise.

Why the Law then? It was added because of transgressions, having been ordained through angels by the agency of a mediator, until the seed would come to whom the promise had been made. Now a mediator is not for one party only; whereas God is only one.

Is the Law then contrary to the promises of God? May it never be! For if a law had been given which was able to impart life, then righteousness would indeed have been based on law. But the Scripture has shut up everyone under sin, so that the promise by faith in Jesus **Christ** might be given to those who believe.

But before faith came, we were kept in custody under the law, being shut up to the faith which was later to be revealed.

Therefore the Law has become our tutor to lead us to **Christ**, so that we may be justified by faith. But now that faith has come, we are no longer under a tutor. For you are all sons of God through faith in **Christ** Jesus.

For all of you who were baptized into **Christ** have clothed yourselves with **Christ**. There is neither Jew nor Greek, there is neither slave nor free man, there is neither male nor female; for you are all one in **Christ** Jesus.

And if you belong to **Christ**, then you are Abraham's descendants, heirs according to promise. *Galatians 3:11-29*

I beg of you, brethren, become as I am, for I also have become as you are. You have done me no wrong; but you know that it was because of a bodily illness that I preached the gospel to you the first time; and that which was a trial to you in my bodily condition you did not despise or loathe, but you received me as an angel of God, as **Christ** Jesus Himself.

Where then is that sense of blessing you had? For I bear you witness that, if possible, you would have plucked out your eyes and given them to me.
Galatians 4:12-15

My children, with whom I am again in labor until **Christ** is formed in you - but I could wish to be present with you now and to change my tone, for I am perplexed about you. Tell me, you who want to be under law, do you not listen to the law? *Galatians 4:19-21*

It was for freedom that **Christ** set us free; therefore keep standing firm and do not be subject again to a yoke of slavery.

Behold I, Paul, say to you that if you receive circumcision, **Christ** will be of no benefit to you.

And I testify again to every man who receives circumcision, that he is under obligation to keep the whole Law.

You have been severed from **Christ**, you who are seeking to be justified by law; you have fallen from grace. For we through the Spirit, by faith, are waiting for the hope of righteousness. For in **Christ** Jesus neither circumcision nor uncircumcision means anything, but faith working through love. *Galatians 5:1-6*

Those who belong to **Christ** Jesus have crucified the flesh with its passions and desires. If we live by the Spirit, let us also walk by the Spirit. Let us not become boastful, challenging one another, envying one another.

Brethren, even if anyone is caught in any trespass, you who are spiritual, restore such a one in a spirit of gentleness; each one looking to yourself, so that you too will not be tempted.

Bear one another's burdens, and thereby fulfill the law of **Christ**.

Galatians 5:24 - 6:2

Those who desire to make a good showing in the flesh try to compel you to be circumcised, simply so that they will not be persecuted for the cross of **Christ**.

For those who are circumcised do not even keep the Law themselves, but they desire to have you circumcised so that they may boast in your flesh. But may it never be that I would boast, except in the cross of our Lord Jesus **Christ**, through which the world has been crucified to me, and I to the world. For neither is circumcision anything, nor uncircumcision, but a new creation. And those who will walk by this rule, peace and mercy be upon them, and upon the Israel of God.

From now on let no one cause trouble for me, for I bear on my body the brand-marks of Jesus.

The grace of our Lord Jesus **Christ** be with your spirit, brethren. Amen.

Galatians 6:12-18

Paul, an apostle of **Christ** Jesus by the will of God, to the saints who are at Ephesus and who are faithful in **Christ** Jesus: Grace to you and peace from God our Father and the Lord Jesus **Christ**.

Blessed be the God and Father of our Lord Jesus **Christ**, who has blessed us with every spiritual blessing in the heavenly places in **Christ**, just as He chose us in Him before the foundation of the world, that we would be holy and blameless before Him.

In love He predestined us to adoption as sons through Jesus **Christ** to Himself, according to the kind intention of His will, to the praise of the glory of His grace, which He freely bestowed on us in the Beloved. In Him we have redemption through His blood, the forgiveness of our trespasses, according to the riches of His grace which He lavished on us.

In all wisdom and insight He made known to us the mystery of His will, according to His kind intention which He purposed in Him with a view to an administration suitable to the fullness of the times, that is, the summing up of all things in **Christ**, things in the heavens and things on the earth.

In Him also we have obtained an inheritance, having been predestined according to His purpose who works all things after the counsel of His will, to the end that we who were the first to hope in **Christ** would be to the praise of His glory.

In Him, you also, after listening to the message of truth, the gospel of your salvation - having also believed, you were sealed in Him with the Holy Spirit of promise, who is given as a pledge of our inheritance, with a view to the redemption of God's own possession, to the praise of His glory.

For this reason I too, having heard of the faith in the Lord Jesus which exists among you and your love for all the saints, do not cease giving thanks for you, while making mention of you in my prayers; that the God of our Lord Jesus **Christ**, the Father of glory, may give to you a spirit of wisdom and of revelation in the knowledge of Him.

I pray that the eyes of your heart may be enlightened, so that you will know what is the hope of His calling, what are the riches of the glory of His inheritance in the saints, and what is the surpassing greatness of His power toward us who believe.

These are in accordance with the working of the strength of His might which He brought about in **Christ**, when He raised Him from the dead and seated Him at His right hand in the heavenly places, far above all rule and authority and power and dominion, and every name that is named, not only in this age but also in the one to come.

And He put all things in subjection under His feet, and gave Him as head over all things to the church, which is His body, the fullness of Him who fills all in all.

And you were dead in your trespasses and sins, in which you formerly walked according to the course of this world, according to the prince of the power of the air, of the spirit that is now working in the sons of disobedience.

Among them we too all formerly lived in the lusts of our flesh, indulging the desires of the flesh and of the mind, and were by nature children of wrath, even as the rest.

But God, being rich in mercy, because of His great love with which He loved us, even when we were dead in our transgressions, made us alive together with **Christ** (by grace you have been saved), and raised us up with Him, and seated us with Him in the heavenly places in **Christ** Jesus, so that in the ages to come He might show the surpassing riches of His grace in kindness toward us in **Christ** Jesus.

For by grace you have been saved through faith; and that not of yourselves, it is the gift of God; not as a result of works, so that no one may boast. For we are His workmanship, created in **Christ** Jesus for good works, which God prepared beforehand so that we would walk in them.

Therefore remember that formerly you, the Gentiles in the flesh, who are called "Uncircumcision" by the so-called "Circumcision," which is performed in the flesh by human hands - remember that you were at that time separate from **Christ**, excluded from the commonwealth of Israel, and strangers to the covenants of promise, having no hope and without God in the world. But now in **Christ** Jesus you who formerly were far off have been brought near by the blood of **Christ**.

For He Himself is our peace, who made both groups into one and broke down the barrier of the dividing wall, by abolishing in His flesh the enmity, which is the Law of commandments contained in ordinances, so that in Himself He might make the two into one new man, thus establishing peace, and might reconcile them both in one body to God through the cross, by it having put to death the enmity.

And He came and preached peace to you who were far away, and peace to those who were near; for through Him we both have our access in one Spirit to the Father.

So then you are no longer strangers and aliens, but you are fellow citizens with the saints, and are of God's household, having been built on the foundation of the apostles and prophets, **Christ** Jesus Himself being the corner stone, in whom the whole building, being fitted together, is growing into a holy temple in the Lord, in whom you also are being built together into a dwelling of God in the Spirit

For this reason I, Paul, the prisoner of **Christ** Jesus for the sake of you Gentiles - if indeed you have heard of the stewardship of God's grace which was given to me for you; that by revelation there was made known to me the mystery, as I wrote before in brief.

By referring to this, when you read you can understand my insight into the mystery of **Christ**, which in other generations was not made known to the sons of men, as it has now been revealed to His holy apostles and prophets in the Spirit; to be specific, that the Gentiles are fellow heirs and fellow members of the body, and fellow partakers of the promise in **Christ** Jesus through the gospel, of which I was made a minister, according to the gift of God's grace which was given to me according to the working of His power.

To me, the very least of all saints, this grace was given, to preach to the Gentiles the unfathomable riches of **Christ**, and to bring to light what is the administration of the mystery which for ages has been hidden in God who created all things; so that the manifold wisdom of God might now be made known through the church to the rulers and the authorities in the heavenly places.

This was in accordance with the eternal purpose which He carried out in **Christ** Jesus our Lord, in whom we have boldness and confident access through faith in Him. Therefore I ask you not to lose heart at my tribulations on your behalf, for they are your glory.

For this reason I bow my knees before the Father, from whom every family in heaven and on earth derives its name, that He would grant you, according to the riches of His glory, to be strengthened with power through His Spirit in the inner man, so that **Christ** may dwell in your hearts through faith; and that you, being rooted and grounded in love, may be able to comprehend with all the saints what is the breadth and length and height and depth, and to know the love of **Christ** which surpasses knowledge, that you may be filled up to all the fullness of God.

Now to Him who is able to do far more abundantly beyond all that we ask or think, according to the power that works within us, to Him be the glory in the church and in **Christ** Jesus to all generations forever and ever. Amen.

Ephesians 1:1 - 3:21

I, the prisoner of the Lord, implore you to walk in a manner worthy of the calling with which you have been called, with all humility and gentleness, with patience, showing tolerance for one another in love, being diligent to preserve the unity of the Spirit in the bond of peace.

There is one body and one Spirit, just as also you were called in one hope of your calling; one Lord, one faith, one baptism, one God and Father of all who is over all and through all and in all. But to each one of us grace was given according to the measure of **Christ's** gift. Therefore it says, "When He ascended on high, He led captive a host of captives, and He gave gifts to men."

(Now this expression, "He ascended," what does it mean except that He also had descended into the lower parts of the earth? He who descended is Himself also He who ascended far above all the heavens, so that He might fill all things.)

And He gave some as apostles, and some as prophets, and some as evangelists, and some as pastors and teachers, for the equipping of the saints for the work of service, to the building up of the body of **Christ**; until we all attain to the unity of the faith, and of the knowledge of the Son of God, to a mature man, to the measure of the stature which belongs to the fullness of **Christ**.

As a result, we are no longer to be children, tossed here and there by waves and carried about by every wind of doctrine, by the trickery of men, by craftiness in deceitful scheming; but speaking the truth in love, we are to grow up in all aspects into Him who is the head, even **Christ**, from whom the whole body, being fitted and held together by what every joint supplies, according to the proper working of each individual part, causes the growth of the body for the building up of itself in love.

So this I say, and affirm together with the Lord, that you walk no longer just as the Gentiles also walk, in the futility of their mind, being darkened in their understanding, excluded from the life of God because of the ignorance that is in them, because of the hardness of their heart; and they, having become callous, have given themselves over to sensuality for the practice of every kind of impurity with greediness.

But you did not learn **Christ** in this way, if indeed you have heard Him and have been taught in Him, just as truth is in Jesus, that, in reference to your former manner of life, you lay aside the old self, which is being corrupted in accordance with the lusts of deceit, and that you be renewed in the spirit of your mind, and put on the new self, which in the likeness of God has been created in righteousness and holiness of the truth.   *Ephesians 4:1-24*

Let all bitterness and wrath and anger and clamor and slander be put away from you, along with all malice. Be kind to one another, tender-hearted, forgiving each other, just as God in **Christ** also has forgiven you.

Therefore be imitators of God, as beloved children; and walk in love, just as **Christ** also loved you and gave Himself up for us, an offering and a sacrifice to God as a fragrant aroma.

But immorality or any impurity or greed must not even be named among you, as is proper among saints; and there must be no filthiness and silly talk, or coarse jesting, which are not fitting, but rather giving of thanks.

For this you know with certainty, that no immoral or impure person or covetous man, who is an idolater, has an inheritance in the kingdom of **Christ** and God.

Let no one deceive you with empty words, for because of these things the wrath of God comes upon the sons of disobedience. Therefore do not be partakers with them; for you were formerly darkness, but now you are Light in the Lord; walk as children of Light (for the fruit of the Light consists in all goodness and righteousness and truth), trying to learn what is pleasing to the Lord.

Do not participate in the unfruitful deeds of darkness, but instead even expose them; for it is disgraceful even to speak of the things which are done by them in secret. But all things become visible when they are exposed by the light, for everything that becomes visible is light.

For this reason it says, "Awake, sleeper, and arise from the dead, and **Christ** will shine on you."

Therefore be careful how you walk, not as unwise men but as wise, making the most of your time, because the days are evil. So then do not be foolish, but understand what the will of the Lord is.

And do not get drunk with wine, for that is dissipation, but be filled with the Spirit, speaking to one another in Psalm and hymns and spiritual songs, singing and making melody with your heart to the Lord; always giving thanks for all things in the name of our Lord Jesus **Christ** to God, even the Father; and be subject to one another in the fear of **Christ**.

Wives, be subject to your own husbands, as to the Lord. For the husband is the head of the wife, as **Christ** also is the head of the church, He Himself being the Savior of the body. But as the church is subject to **Christ**, so also the wives ought to be to their husbands in everything.

Husbands, love your wives, just as **Christ** also loved the church and gave Himself up for her, so that He might sanctify her, having cleansed her by the washing of water with the word, that He might present to Himself the church in all her glory, having no spot or wrinkle or any such thing; but that she would be holy and blameless.

So husbands ought also to love their own wives as their own bodies. He who loves his own wife loves himself; for no one ever hated his own flesh, but nourishes and cherishes it, just as **Christ** also does the church, because we are members of His body. For this reason a man shall leave his father and mother and shall be joined to his wife, and the two shall become one flesh.

This mystery is great; but I am speaking with reference to **Christ** and the church. Nevertheless, each individual among you also is to love his own wife even as himself, and the wife must see to it that she respects her husband.

Ephesians 4:31 - 5:33

Slaves, be obedient to those who are your masters according to the flesh, with fear and trembling, in the sincerity of your heart, as to **Christ**; not by way of eyeservice, as men-pleasers, but as slaves of **Christ**, doing the will of God from the heart.

With good will render service, as to the Lord, and not to men, knowing that whatever good thing each one does, this he will receive back from the Lord, whether slave or free.

And masters, do the same things to them, and give up threatening, knowing that both their Master and yours is in heaven, and there is no partiality with Him.

Ephesians 6:5-9

Peace be to the brethren, and love with faith, from God the Father and the Lord Jesus **Christ**.

Grace be with all those who love our Lord Jesus **Christ** with incorruptible love.

Ephesians 6:23-24

Paul and Timothy, bond-servants of **Christ** Jesus, to all the saints in **Christ** Jesus who are in Philippi, including the overseers and deacons: Grace to you and peace from God our Father and the Lord Jesus **Christ**.

I thank my God in all my remembrance of you, always offering prayer with joy in my every prayer for you all, in view of your participation in the gospel from the first day until now. For I am confident of this very thing, that He who began a good work in you will perfect it until the day of **Christ** Jesus.

For it is only right for me to feel this way about you all, because I have you in my heart, since both in my imprisonment and in the defense and confirmation of the gospel, you all are partakers of grace with me. For God is my witness, how I long for you all with the affection of **Christ** Jesus.

And this I pray, that your love may abound still more and more in real knowledge and all discernment, so that you may approve the things that are excellent, in order to be sincere and blameless until the day of **Christ**; having been filled with the fruit of righteousness which comes through Jesus **Christ**, to the glory and praise of God.

Now I want you to know, brethren, that my circumstances have turned out for the greater progress of the gospel, so that my imprisonment in the cause of **Christ** has become well known throughout the whole praetorian guard and to everyone else, and that most of the brethren, trusting in the Lord because of my imprisonment, have far more courage to speak the word of God without fear.

Some, to be sure, are preaching **Christ** even from envy and strife, but some also from good will; the latter do it out of love, knowing that I am appointed for the defense of the gospel; the former proclaim **Christ** out of selfish ambition rather than from pure motives, thinking to cause me distress in my imprisonment. What then? Only that in every way, whether in pretense or in truth, **Christ** is proclaimed; and in this I rejoice.

Yes, and I will rejoice, for I know that this will turn out for my deliverance through your prayers and the provision of the Spirit of Jesus **Christ**, according to my earnest expectation and hope, that I will not be put to shame in anything, but

that with all boldness, **Christ** will even now, as always, be exalted in my body, whether by life or by death. For to me, to live is **Christ** and to die is gain.

But if I am to live on in the flesh, this will mean fruitful labor for me; and I do not know which to choose. But I am hard-pressed from both directions, having the desire to depart and be with **Christ**, for that is very much better; yet to remain on in the flesh is more necessary for your sake.

Convinced of this, I know that I will remain and continue with you all for your progress and joy in the faith, so that your proud confidence in me may abound in **Christ** Jesus through my coming to you again.

Only conduct yourselves in a manner worthy of the gospel of **Christ**, so that whether I come and see you or remain absent, I will hear of you that you are standing firm in one spirit, with one mind striving together for the faith of the gospel; in no way alarmed by your opponents - which is a sign of destruction for them, but of salvation for you, and that too, from God. For to you it has been granted for **Christ's** sake, not only to believe in Him, but also to suffer for His sake, experiencing the same conflict which you saw in me, and now hear to be in me.

Therefore if there is any encouragement in **Christ**, if there is any consolation of love, if there is any fellowship of the Spirit, if any affection and compassion, make my joy complete by being of the same mind, maintaining the same love, united in spirit, intent on one purpose.

Do nothing from selfishness or empty conceit, but with humility of mind regard one another as more important than yourselves; do not merely look out for your own personal interests, but also for the interests of others.

Have this attitude in yourselves which was also in **Christ** Jesus, who, although He existed in the form of God, did not regard equality with God a thing to be grasped, but emptied Himself, taking the form of a bond-servant, and being made in the likeness of men. Being found in appearance as a man, He humbled Himself by becoming obedient to the point of death, even death on a cross.

For this reason also, God highly exalted Him, and bestowed on Him the name which is above every name, so that at the name of Jesus every knee will bow, of those who are in heaven and on earth and under the earth, and that every tongue will confess that Jesus **Christ** is Lord, to the glory of God the Father.

So then, my beloved, just as you have always obeyed, not as in my presence only, but now much more in my absence, work out your salvation with fear and trembling; for it is God who is at work in you, both to will and to work for His good pleasure.

Do all things without grumbling or disputing; so that you will prove yourselves to be blameless and innocent, children of God above reproach in the midst of a crooked and perverse generation, among whom you appear as lights in the world, holding fast the word of life, so that in the day of **Christ** I will have reason to glory because I did not run in vain nor toil in vain.

But even if I am being poured out as a drink offering upon the sacrifice and service of your faith, I rejoice and share my joy with you all. You too, I urge you, rejoice in the same way and share your joy with me.

But I hope in the Lord Jesus to send Timothy to you shortly, so that I also may be encouraged when I learn of your condition. For I have no one else of kindred spirit who will genuinely be concerned for your welfare. For they all seek after their own interests, not those of **Christ** Jesus.

Philippians 1:1 - 2:21

Receive him then in the Lord with all joy, and hold men like him in high regard; because he came close to death for the work of **Christ**, risking his life to complete what was deficient in your service to me. Finally, my brethren, rejoice in the Lord. To write the same things again is no trouble to me, and it is a safeguard for you.

Beware of the dogs, beware of the evil workers, beware of the false circumcision; for we are the true circumcision, who worship in the Spirit of God and glory in **Christ** Jesus and put no confidence in the flesh, although I myself might have confidence even in the flesh.

If anyone else has a mind to put confidence in the flesh, I far more: although I myself might have confidence even in the flesh.

If anyone else has a mind to put confidence in the flesh, I far more: circumcised the eighth day, of the nation of Israel, of the tribe of Benjamin, a Hebrew of Hebrews; as to the Law, a Pharisee; as to zeal, a persecutor of the church; as to the righteousness which is in the Law, found blameless.

But whatever things were gain to me, those things I have counted as loss for the sake of **Christ**. More than that, I count all things to be loss in view of the surpassing value of knowing **Christ** Jesus my Lord, for whom I have suffered the loss of all things, and count them but rubbish so that I may gain **Christ**, and may be found in Him, not having a righteousness of my own derived from the Law, but that which is through faith in **Christ**, the righteousness which comes from God on the basis of faith, that I may know Him and the power of His resurrection and the fellowship of His sufferings, being conformed to His death; in order that I may attain to the resurrection from the dead.

Not that I have already obtained it or have already become perfect, but I press on so that I may lay hold of that for which also I was laid hold of by **Christ** Jesus.

Brethren, I do not regard myself as having laid hold of it yet; but one thing I do: forgetting what lies behind and reaching forward to what lies ahead, I press on toward the goal for the prize of the upward call of God in **Christ** Jesus.

Let us therefore, as many as are perfect, have this attitude; and if in anything you have a different attitude, God will reveal that also to you; however, let us keep living by that same standard to which we have attained.

Brethren, join in following my example, and observe those who walk according to the pattern you have in us. For many walk, of whom I often told you, and now tell you even weeping, that they are enemies of the cross of **Christ**, whose end is destruction, whose god is their appetite, and whose glory is in their shame, who set their minds on earthly things.

For our citizenship is in heaven, from which also we eagerly wait for a Savior, the Lord Jesus **Christ**; who will transform the body of our humble state into conformity with the body of His glory, by the exertion of the power that He has even to subject all things to Himself.

Philippians 2:29 - 3:21

Rejoice in the Lord always; again I will say, rejoice! Be anxious for nothing, but in everything by prayer and supplication with thanksgiving let your requests be made known to God.

And the peace of God, which surpasses all comprehension, will guard your hearts and your minds in **Christ** Jesus.

Philippians 4:4-7

I have received everything in full and have an abundance; I am amply supplied, having received from Epaphroditus what you have sent, a fragrant aroma, an acceptable sacrifice, well-pleasing to God. And my God will supply all your needs according to His riches in glory in **Christ** Jesus.

Now to our God and Father be the glory forever and ever. Amen.

Greet every saint in **Christ** Jesus. The brethren who are with me greet you. All the saints greet you, especially those of Caesar's household.

The grace of the Lord Jesus **Christ** be with your spirit.   *Philippians 4:18-23*

Paul, an apostle of Jesus **Christ** by the will of God, and Timothy our brother, to the saints and faithful brethren in **Christ** who are at Colossae: Grace to you and peace from God our Father.

We give thanks to God, the Father of our Lord Jesus **Christ**, praying always for you, since we heard of your faith in **Christ**

Jesus and the love which you have for all the saints; because of the hope laid up for you in heaven, of which you previously heard in the word of truth, the gospel which has come to you, just as in all the world also it is constantly bearing fruit and increasing, even as it has been doing in you also since the day you heard of it and understood the grace of God in truth; just as you learned it from Epaphras, our beloved fellow bond-servant, who is a faithful servant of **Christ** on our behalf, and he also informed us of your love in the Spirit.

Colossians 1:1-8

I rejoice in my sufferings for your sake, and in my flesh I do my share on behalf of His body, which is the church, in filling up what is lacking in **Christ's** afflictions.

Of this church I was made a minister according to the stewardship from God bestowed on me for your benefit, so that I might fully carry out the preaching of the word of God, that is, the mystery which has been hidden from the past ages and generations, but has now been manifested to His saints, to whom God willed to make known what is the riches of the glory of this mystery among the Gentiles, which is **Christ** in you, the hope of glory.

We proclaim Him, admonishing every man and teaching every man with all wisdom, so that we may present every man complete in **Christ**. For this purpose also I labor, striving according to His power, which mightily works within me.

For I want you to know how great a struggle I have on your behalf and for those who are at Laodicea, and for all those who have not personally seen my face, that their hearts may be encouraged, having been knit together in love, and attaining to all the wealth that comes from the full assurance of understanding, resulting in a true knowledge of God's mystery, that is, **Christ** Himself, in whom are hidden all the treasures of wisdom and knowledge.

I say this so that no one will delude you with persuasive argument. For even though I am absent in body, nevertheless I am with you in spirit, rejoicing to see your good discipline and the stability of your faith in **Christ**.

Therefore as you have received **Christ** Jesus the Lord, so walk in Him, having been firmly rooted and now being built up in Him and established in your faith, just as you were instructed, and overflowing with gratitude. See to it that no one takes you captive through philosophy and empty deception, according to the tradition of men, according to the elementary principles of the world, rather than according to **Christ**.

For in Him all the fullness of Deity dwells in bodily form, and in Him you have been made complete, and He is the head over all rule and authority; and in Him you were also circumcised with a circumcision made without hands, in the removal of the body of the flesh by the circumcision of **Christ**; having been buried with Him in baptism, in which you were also raised up with Him through faith in the working of God, who raised Him from the dead.

When you were dead in your transgressions and the uncircumcision of your flesh, He made you alive together with Him, having forgiven us all our transgressions, having canceled out the certificate of debt consisting of decrees against us, which was hostile to us; and He has taken it out of the way, having nailed it to the cross.

When He had disarmed the rulers and authorities, He made a public display of them, having triumphed over them through Him. Therefore no one is to act as your judge in regard to food or drink or in respect to a festival or a new moon or a Sabbath day - things which are a mere shadow of what is to come; but the substance belongs to **Christ**.

Let no one keep defrauding you of your prize by delighting in self-abasement and the worship of the angels, taking his stand on visions he has seen, inflated without cause by his fleshly mind, and not holding fast to the head, from whom the entire body, being supplied and held together by the joints and ligaments, grows with a growth which is from God.

If you have died with **Christ** to the elementary principles of the world, why, as if you were living in the world, do you submit yourself to decrees, such as, "Do not handle, do not taste, do not touch!" (which all refer to things destined to perish with use) - in accordance with the commandments and teachings of men?

These are matters which have, to be sure, the appearance of wisdom in self-made religion and self-abasement and severe treatment of the body, but are of no value against fleshly indulgence.

Therefore if you have been raised up with **Christ**, keep seeking the things above, where **Christ** is, seated at the right hand of God. Set your mind on the things above, not on the things that are on earth. For you have died and your life is hidden with **Christ** in God.

When **Christ**, who is our life, is revealed, then you also will be revealed with Him in glory. Therefore consider the members of your earthly body as dead to immorality, impurity, passion, evil desire, and greed, which amounts to idolatry. For it is because of these things that the wrath of God will come upon the sons of disobedience, and in them you also once walked, when you were living in them.

But now you also, put them all aside: anger, wrath, malice, slander, and abusive speech from your mouth.

Do not lie to one another, since you laid aside the old self with its evil practices, and have put on the new self who is being renewed to a true knowledge according to the image of the One who created him - a renewal in which there is no distinction between Greek and Jew, circumcised and uncircumcised, barbarian, Scythian, slave and freeman, but **Christ** is all, and in all.

So, as those who have been chosen of God, holy and beloved, put on a heart of compassion, kindness, humility, gentleness and patience; bearing with one another, and forgiving each other, whoever has a complaint against anyone; just as the Lord forgave you, so also should you.

Beyond all these things put on love,

which is the perfect bond of unity. Let the peace of **Christ** rule in your hearts, to which indeed you were called in one body; and be thankful.

Let the word of **Christ** richly dwell within you, with all wisdom teaching and admonishing one another with Psalm and hymns and spiritual songs, singing with thankfulness in your hearts to God. Whatever you do in word or deed, do all in the name of the Lord Jesus, giving thanks through Him to God the Father.

Colossians 1:24 - 3:17

Whatever you do, do your work heartily, as for the Lord rather than for men, knowing that from the Lord you will receive the reward of the inheritance. It is the Lord **Christ** whom you serve.

For he who does wrong will receive the consequences of the wrong which he has done, and that without partiality.

Masters, grant to your slaves justice and fairness, knowing that you too have a Master in heaven.

Devote yourselves to prayer, keeping alert in it with an attitude of thanksgiving; praying at the same time for us as well, that God will open up to us a door for the word, so that we may speak forth the mystery of **Christ**, for which I have also been imprisoned; that I may make it clear in the way I ought to speak.

Conduct yourselves with wisdom toward outsiders, making the most of the opportunity.

Let your speech always be with grace, as though seasoned with salt, so that you will know how you should respond to each person. *Colossians 3:23 - 4:6*

Epaphras, who is one of your number, a bond-slave of Jesus **Christ**, sends you his greetings, always laboring earnestly for you in his prayers, that you may stand perfect and fully assured in all the will of God. *Colossians 4:12*

Paul and Silvanus and Timothy, to the church of the Thessalonians in God the Father and the Lord Jesus **Christ**: Grace to you and peace.

We give thanks to God always for all of you, making mention of you in our prayers; constantly bearing in mind your work of faith and labor of love and steadfastness of hope in our Lord Jesus **Christ** in the presence of our God and Father, knowing, brethren beloved by God, His choice of you; for our gospel did not come to you in word only, but also in power and in the Holy Spirit and with full conviction; just as you know what kind of men we proved to be among you for your sake.

You also became imitators of us and of the Lord, having received the word in much tribulation with the joy of the Holy Spirit, so that you became an example to all the believers in Macedonia and in Achaia. *1 Thessalonians 1:1-7*

We never came with flattering speech, as you know, nor with a pretext for greed - God is witness - nor did we seek glory from men, either from you or from others, even though as apostles of **Christ** we might have asserted our authority. But we proved to be gentle among you, as a nursing mother tenderly cares for her own children. *1 Thessalonians 2:5-7*

You, brethren, became imitators of the churches of God in **Christ** Jesus that are in Judea, for you also endured the same sufferings at the hands of your own countrymen, even as they did from the Jews, who both killed the Lord Jesus and the prophets, and drove us out.

They are not pleasing to God, but hostile to all men, hindering us from speaking to the Gentiles so that they may be saved; with the result that they always fill up the measure of their sins. But wrath has come upon them to the utmost.

1 Thessalonians 2:14-16

When we could endure it no longer, we thought it best to be left behind at Athens alone, and we sent Timothy, our brother and God's fellow worker in the gospel of **Christ**, to strengthen and encourage you as to your faith, so that no one would be disturbed by these afflictions; for you yourselves know that we have been destined for this.

For indeed when we were with you, we kept telling you in advance that we were going to suffer affliction; and so it came to pass, as you know.

1 Thessalonians 3:1-4

We do not want you to be uninformed, brethren, about those who are asleep, so that you will not grieve as do the rest who have no hope. For if we believe that Jesus died and rose again, even so God will bring with Him those who have fallen asleep in Jesus.

For this we say to you by the word of the Lord, that we who are alive and remain until the coming of the Lord, will not precede those who have fallen asleep.

For the Lord Himself will descend from heaven with a shout, with the voice of the archangel and with the trumpet of God, and the dead in **Christ** will rise first. Then we who are alive and remain will be caught up together with them in the clouds to meet the Lord in the air, and so we shall always be with the Lord. Therefore comfort one another with these words.

1 Thessalonians 4:13-18

Those who sleep do their sleeping at night, and those who get drunk get drunk at night. But since we are of the day, let us be sober, having put on the breastplate of faith and love, and as a helmet, the hope of salvation.

For God has not destined us for wrath, but for obtaining salvation through our Lord Jesus **Christ**, who died for us, so that whether we are awake or asleep, we will live together with Him.

Therefore encourage one another and build up one another, just as you also are doing.

1 Thessalonians 5:7-11

Rejoice always; pray without ceasing; in everything give thanks; for this is God's will for you in **Christ** Jesus.

Do not quench the Spirit; do not despise prophetic utterances. But examine everything carefully; hold fast to that which is good; abstain from every form of evil.

Now may the God of peace Himself sanctify you entirely; and may your spirit and soul and body be preserved complete, without blame at the coming of our Lord Jesus **Christ**. Faithful is He who calls you, and He also will bring it to pass.

Brethren, pray for us. Greet all the brethren with a holy kiss. I adjure you by the Lord to have this letter read to all the brethren. The grace of our Lord Jesus **Christ** be with you.

1 Thessalonians 5:16-28

Paul and Silvanus and Timothy, to the church of the Thessalonians in God our Father and the Lord Jesus **Christ**: Grace to you and peace from God the Father and the Lord Jesus **Christ**.

2 Thessalonians 1:1-2

We pray for you always, that our God will count you worthy of your calling, and fulfill every desire for goodness and the work of faith with power, so that the name of our Lord Jesus will be glorified in you, and you in Him, according to the grace of our God and the Lord Jesus **Christ**.

Now we request you, brethren, with regard to the coming of our Lord Jesus **Christ** and our gathering together to Him, that you not be quickly shaken from your composure or be disturbed either by a spirit or a message or a letter as if from us, to the effect that the day of the Lord has come.

Let no one in any way deceive you, for it will not come unless the apostasy comes first, and the man of lawlessness is revealed, the son of destruction, who opposes and exalts himself above every so-called god or object of worship, so that he takes his seat in the temple of God, displaying himself as being God.

2 Thessalonians 1:11 - 2:4

We should always give thanks to God for you, brethren beloved by the Lord, because God has chosen you from the beginning for salvation through sanctification by the Spirit and faith in the truth. It was for this He called you through our gospel, that you may gain the glory of our Lord Jesus **Christ**.

So then, brethren, stand firm and hold to the traditions which you were taught, whether by word of mouth or by letter from us.

Now may our Lord Jesus **Christ** Himself and God our Father, who has loved us and given us eternal comfort and good hope by grace, comfort and strengthen your hearts in every good work and word.
2 Thessalonians 2:13-17

The Lord is faithful, and He will strengthen and protect you from the evil one. We have confidence in the Lord concerning you, that you are doing and will continue to do what we command.

May the Lord direct your hearts into the love of God and into the steadfastness of **Christ**.

Now we command you, brethren, in the name of our Lord Jesus **Christ**, that you keep away from every brother who leads an unruly life and not according to the tradition which you received from us.
2 Thessalonians 3:3-6

Even when we were with you, we used to give you this order: If anyone is not willing to work, then he is not to eat, either. For we hear that some among you are leading an undisciplined life, doing no work at all, but acting like busybodies. Now such persons we command and exhort in the Lord Jesus **Christ** to work in quiet fashion and eat their own bread.

But as for you, brethren, do not grow weary of doing good.
2 Thessalonians 3:10-13

The grace of our Lord Jesus **Christ** be with you all.   *2 Thessalonians 3:18*

Paul, an apostle of **Christ** Jesus according to the commandment of God our Savior, and of **Christ** Jesus, who is our hope, to Timothy, my true child in the faith: Grace, mercy and peace from God the Father and **Christ** Jesus our Lord.
1 Timothy 1:1-2

I thank **Christ** Jesus our Lord, who has strengthened me, because He considered me faithful, putting me into service, even though I was formerly a blasphemer and a persecutor and a violent aggressor. Yet I was shown mercy because I acted ignorantly in unbelief; and the grace of our Lord was more than abundant, with the faith and love which are found in **Christ** Jesus.

It is a trustworthy statement, deserving full acceptance, that **Christ** Jesus came into the world to save sinners, among whom I am foremost of all.

Yet for this reason I found mercy, so that in me as the foremost, Jesus **Christ** might demonstrate His perfect patience as an example for those who would believe in Him for eternal life.
1 Timothy 1:12-16

First of all, then, I urge that entreaties and prayers, petitions and thanksgivings, be made on behalf of all men, for kings and all who are in authority, so that we may lead a tranquil and quiet life in all godliness and dignity.

This is good and acceptable in the sight of God our Savior, who desires all men to be saved and to come to the knowledge of the truth.

For there is one God, and one mediator also between God and men, the man **Christ** Jesus, who gave Himself as a ransom for all, the testimony given at the proper time.   *1 Timothy 2:1-6*

Deacons must be husbands of only one wife, and good managers of their children and their own households. For those who have served well as deacons obtain for themselves a high standing and great confidence in the faith that is in **Christ** Jesus.   *1 Timothy 3:12-13*

In pointing out these things to the brethren, you will be a good servant of **Christ** Jesus, constantly nourished on the words of the faith and of the sound doctrine which you have been following.
1 Timothy 4:6

A widow is to be put on the list only if she is not less than sixty years old, having been the wife of one man, having a reputation for good works; and if she has brought up children, if she has shown hospitality to strangers, if she has washed the saints' feet, if she has assisted those in distress, and if she has devoted herself to every good work.

But refuse to put younger widows on the list, for when they feel sensual desires in disregard of **Christ**, they want to get married, thus incurring condemnation, because they have set aside their previous pledge. *1 Timothy 5:9-12*

Do not receive an accusation against an elder except on the basis of two or three witnesses. Those who continue in sin, rebuke in the presence of all, so that the rest also will be fearful of sinning.

I solemnly charge you in the presence of God and of **Christ** Jesus and of His chosen angels, to maintain these principles without bias, doing nothing in a spirit of partiality.

Do not lay hands upon anyone too hastily and thereby share responsibility for the sins of others; keep yourself free from sin. *1 Timothy 5:19-22*

If anyone advocates a different doctrine and does not agree with sound words, those of our Lord Jesus **Christ**, and with the doctrine conforming to godliness, he is conceited and understands nothing; but he has a morbid interest in controversial questions and disputes about words, out of which arise envy, strife, abusive language, evil suspicions, and constant friction between men of depraved mind and deprived of the truth, who suppose that godliness is a means of gain. But godliness actually is a means of great gain when accompanied by contentment. *1 Timothy 6:3-6*

I charge you in the presence of God, who gives life to all things, and of **Christ** Jesus, who testified the good confession before Pontius Pilate, that you keep the commandment without stain or reproach until the appearing of our Lord Jesus **Christ**, that you keep the commandment without stain or reproach until the appearing of our Lord Jesus **Christ**, which He

will bring about at the proper time - He who is the blessed and only Sovereign, the King of kings and Lord of lords, who alone possesses immortality and dwells in unapproachable light, whom no man has seen or can see.

To Him be honor and eternal dominion! Amen. *1 Timothy 6:13-16*

Paul, an apostle of **Christ** Jesus by the will of God, according to the promise of life in **Christ** Jesus, to Timothy, my beloved son: Grace, mercy and peace from God the Father and **Christ** Jesus our Lord. *2 Timothy 1:1-2*

God has not given us a spirit of timidity, but of power and love and discipline. Therefore do not be ashamed of the testimony of our Lord or of me His prisoner, but join with me in suffering for the gospel according to the power of God, who has saved us and called us with a holy calling, not according to our works, but according to His own purpose and grace which was granted us in **Christ** Jesus from all eternity, but now has been revealed by the appearing of our Savior **Christ** Jesus, who abolished death and brought life and immortality to light through the gospel, for which I was appointed a preacher and an apostle and a teacher.

For this reason I also suffer these things, but I am not ashamed; for I know whom I have believed and I am convinced that He is able to guard what I have entrusted to Him until that day. Retain the standard of sound words which you have heard from me, in the faith and love which are in **Christ** Jesus. Guard, through the Holy Spirit who dwells in us, the treasure which has been entrusted to you. *2 Timothy 1:7-14*

My son, be strong in the grace that is in **Christ** Jesus. The things which you have heard from me in the presence of many witnesses, entrust these to faithful men who will be able to teach others also. Suffer hardship with me, as a good soldier of **Christ** Jesus.

No soldier in active service entangles

himself in the affairs of everyday life, so that he may please the one who enlisted him as a soldier. Also if anyone competes as an athlete, he does not win the prize unless he competes according to the rules.

The hard-working farmer ought to be the first to receive his share of the crops.

Consider what I say, for the Lord will give you understanding in everything. Remember Jesus **Christ**, risen from the dead, descendant of David, according to my gospel, for which I suffer hardship even to imprisonment as a criminal; but the word of God is not imprisoned.

For this reason I endure all things for the sake of those who are chosen, so that they also may obtain the salvation which is in **Christ** Jesus and with it eternal glory.

It is a trustworthy statement: For if we died with Him, we will also live with Him; if we endure, we will also reign with Him; if we deny Him, He also will deny us; if we are faithless, He remains faithful, for He cannot deny Himself. *2 Timothy 2:1-13*

All who desire to live godly in **Christ** Jesus will be persecuted. But evil men and impostors will proceed from bad to worse, deceiving and being deceived.

You, however, continue in the things you have learned and become convinced of, knowing from whom you have learned them, and that from childhood you have known the sacred writings which are able to give you the wisdom that leads to salvation through faith which is in **Christ** Jesus.

All Scripture is inspired by God and profitable for teaching, for reproof, for correction, for training in righteousness; so that the man of God may be adequate, equipped for every good work.

I solemnly charge you in the presence of God and of **Christ** Jesus, who is to judge the living and the dead, and by His appearing and His kingdom: Preach the word; be ready in season and out of season; reprove, rebuke, exhort, with great patience and instruction.

2 Timothy 3:12 - 4:2

Paul, a bond-servant of God and an apostle of Jesus **Christ**, for the faith of those chosen of God and the knowledge of the truth which is according to godliness, in the hope of eternal life, which God, who cannot lie, promised long ages ago, but at the proper time manifested, even His word, in the proclamation with which I was entrusted according to the commandment of God our Savior, to Titus, my true child in a common faith: Grace and peace from God the Father and **Christ** Jesus our Savior. *Titus 1:1-4*

The grace of God has appeared, bringing salvation to all men, instructing us to deny ungodliness and worldly desires and to live sensibly, righteously and godly in the present age, looking for the blessed hope and the appearing of the glory of our great God and Savior, **Christ** Jesus, who gave Himself for us to redeem us from every lawless deed, and to purify for Himself a people for His own possession, zealous for good deeds. These things speak and exhort and reprove with all authority.

Let no one disregard you. Remind them to be subject to rulers, to authorities, to be obedient, to be ready for every good deed, to malign no one, to be peaceable, gentle, showing every consideration for all men. For we also once were foolish ourselves, disobedient, deceived, enslaved to various lusts and pleasures, spending our life in malice and envy, hateful, hating one another.

But when the kindness of God our Savior and His love for mankind appeared, He saved us, not on the basis of deeds which we have done in righteousness, but according to His mercy, by the washing of regeneration and renewing by the Holy Spirit, whom He poured out upon us richly through Jesus **Christ** our Savior, so that being justified by His grace we would be made heirs according to the hope of eternal life. *Titus 2:11 - 3:7*

Paul, a prisoner of **Christ** Jesus, and Timothy our brother, to Philemon our beloved brother and fellow worker, and to

Apphia our sister, and to Archippus our fellow soldier, and to the church in your house: Grace to you and peace from God our Father and the Lord Jesus **Christ**.

I thank my God always, making mention of you in my prayers, because I hear of your love and of the faith which you have toward the Lord Jesus and toward all the saints; and I pray that the fellowship of your faith may become effective through the knowledge of every good thing which is in you for **Christ's** sake. For I have come to have much joy and comfort in your love, because the hearts of the saints have been refreshed through you, brother.

Therefore, though I have enough confidence in **Christ** to order you to do what is proper, yet for love's sake I rather appeal to you - since I am such a person as Paul, the aged, and now also a prisoner of **Christ** Jesus - I appeal to you for my child Onesimus, whom I have begotten in my imprisonment, who formerly was useless to you, but now is useful both to you and to me. *Philemon 1-11*

Brother, let me benefit from you in the Lord; refresh my heart in **Christ**. Having confidence in your obedience, I write to you, since I know that you will do even more than what I say. At the same time also prepare me a lodging, for I hope that through your prayers I will be given to you.

Epaphras, my fellow prisoner in **Christ** Jesus, greets you, as do Mark, Aristarchus, Demas, Luke, my fellow workers.

The grace of the Lord Jesus **Christ** be with your spirit. *Philemon 1:20-25*

Moses was faithful in all His house as a servant, for a testimony of those things which were to be spoken later; but **Christ** was faithful as a Son over His house - whose house we are, if we hold fast our confidence and the boast of our hope firm until the end. *Hebrews 3:5-6*

Take care, brethren, that there not be in any one of you an evil, unbelieving heart that falls away from the living God. But encourage one another day after day, as long as it is still called "Today," so that none of you will be hardened by the deceitfulness of sin.

For we have become partakers of **Christ**, if we hold fast the beginning of our assurance firm until the end, while it is said, "Today if you hear His voice, do not harden your hearts, as when they provoked Me." *Hebrews 3:12-15*

No one takes the honor to himself, but receives it when he is called by God, even as Aaron was.

So also **Christ** did not glorify Himself so as to become a high priest, but He who said to Him, "You are My Son, today I have begotten You"; just as He says also in another passage, "You are a priest forever according to the order of Melchizedek."

In the days of His flesh, He offered up both prayers and supplications with loud crying and tears to the One able to save Him from death, and He was heard because of His piety.

Although He was a Son, He learned obedience from the things which He suffered. And having been made perfect, He became to all those who obey Him the source of eternal salvation, being designated by God as a high priest according to the order of Melchizedek. *Hebrews 5:4-10*

Leaving the elementary teaching about the **Christ**, let us press on to maturity, not laying again a foundation of repentance from dead works and of faith toward God, of instruction about washings and laying on of hands, and the resurrection of the dead and eternal judgment. And this we will do, if God permits. *Hebrews 6:1-3*

When **Christ** appeared as a high priest of the good things to come, He entered through the greater and more perfect tabernacle, not made with hands, that is to say, not of this creation; and not through the blood of goats and calves, but through His own blood, He entered the holy place once for all, having obtained eternal redemption.

For if the blood of goats and bulls and the ashes of a heifer sprinkling those who have been defiled sanctify for the cleansing of the flesh, how much more will the blood of **Christ**, who through the eternal Spirit offered Himself without blemish to God, cleanse your conscience from dead works to serve the living God?

For this reason He is the mediator of a new covenant, so that, since a death has taken place for the redemption of the transgressions that were committed under the first covenant, those who have been called may receive the promise of the eternal inheritance.   *Hebrews 9:11-15*

According to the Law, one may almost say, all things are cleansed with blood, and without shedding of blood there is no forgiveness.

Therefore it was necessary for the copies of the things in the heavens to be cleansed with these, but the heavenly things themselves with better sacrifices than these.

For **Christ** did not enter a holy place made with hands, a mere copy of the true one, but into heaven itself, now to appear in the presence of God for us; or was it that He would offer Himself often, as the high priest enters the holy place year by year with blood that is not his own. Otherwise, He would have needed to suffer often since the foundation of the world; but now once at the consummation of the ages He has been manifested to put away sin by the sacrifice of Himself.

And inasmuch as it is appointed for men to die once and after this comes judgment, so **Christ** also, having been offered once to bear the sins of many, will appear a second time for salvation without reference to sin, to those who eagerly await Him.

For the Law, since it has only a shadow of the good things to come and not the very form of things, can never, by the same sacrifices which they offer continually year by year, make perfect those who draw near. Otherwise, would they not have ceased to be offered, because the worshipers, having once been cleansed, would no longer have had consciousness of sins?

But in those sacrifices there is a reminder of sins year by year. For it is impossible for the blood of bulls and goats to take away sins.

Therefore, when He comes into the world, He says, "Sacrifice and offering You have not desired, but a body You have prepared for Me; in whole burnt offerings and sacrifices for sin You have taken no pleasure.

Then I said, 'Behold, I have come (in the scroll of the book it is written of Me) to do Your will, O God.' "

After saying above, "Sacrifices and offerings and whole burnt offerings and sacrifices for sin You have not desired, nor have You taken pleasure in them" (which are offered according to the Law), then He said, "Behold, I have come to do Your will." He takes away the first in order to establish the second.

By this will we have been sanctified through the offering of the body of Jesus **Christ** once for all.   *Hebrews 9:23 - 10:10*

By faith Moses, when he was born, was hidden for three months by his parents, because they saw he was a beautiful child; and they were not afraid of the king's edict.

By faith Moses, when he had grown up, refused to be called the son of Pharaoh's daughter, choosing rather to endure ill-treatment with the people of God than to enjoy the passing pleasures of sin, considering the reproach of **Christ** greater riches than the treasures of Egypt; for he was looking to the reward.

By faith he left Egypt, not fearing the wrath of the king; for he endured, as seeing Him who is unseen.   *Hebrews 11:23-27*

Jesus **Christ** is the same yesterday and today and forever.   *Hebrews 13:8*

The God of peace, who brought up from the dead the great Shepherd of the sheep through the blood of the eternal covenant, even Jesus our Lord, equip you in every good thing to do His will, working in us that which is pleasing in His sight, through Jesus **Christ**, to whom be the glory forever and ever. Amen.   *Hebrews 13:20-21*

James, a bond-servant of God and of the Lord Jesus **Christ**, to the twelve tribes who are dispersed abroad: Greetings.

Consider it all joy, my brethren, when you encounter various trials, knowing that the testing of your faith produces endurance.   *James 1:1-3*

My brethren, do not hold your faith in our glorious Lord Jesus **Christ** with an attitude of personal favoritism. For if a man comes into your assembly with a gold ring and dressed in fine clothes, and there also comes in a poor man in dirty clothes, and you pay special attention to the one who is wearing the fine clothes, and say, "You sit here in a good place," and you say to the poor man, "You stand over there, or sit down by my footstool," have you not made distinctions among yourselves, and become judges with evil motives?   *James 2:1-4*

Peter, an apostle of Jesus **Christ**, to those who reside as aliens, scattered throughout Pontus, Galatia, Cappadocia, Asia, and Bithynia, who are chosen according to the foreknowledge of God the Father, by the sanctifying work of the Spirit, to obey Jesus **Christ** and be sprinkled with His blood: May grace and peace be yours in the fullest measure.

Blessed be the God and Father of our Lord Jesus **Christ**, who according to His great mercy has caused us to be born again to a living hope through the resurrection of Jesus **Christ** from the dead, to obtain an inheritance which is imperishable and undefiled and will not fade away, reserved in heaven for you, who are protected by the power of God through faith for a salvation ready to be revealed in the last time.

In this you greatly rejoice, even though now for a little while, if necessary, you have been distressed by various trials, so that the proof of your faith, being more precious than gold which is perishable, even though tested by fire, may be found to result in praise and glory and honor at the revelation of Jesus **Christ**; and though you have not seen Him, you love Him, and though you do not see Him now, but believe in Him, you greatly rejoice with joy inexpressible and full of glory, obtaining as the outcome of your faith the salvation of your souls.

As to this salvation, the prophets who prophesied of the grace that would come to you made careful searches and inquiries, seeking to know what person or time the Spirit of **Christ** within them was indicating as He predicted the sufferings of **Christ** and the glories to follow.

It was revealed to them that they were not serving themselves, but you, in these things which now have been announced to you through those who preached the gospel to you by the Holy Spirit sent from heaven - things into which angels long to look. Therefore, prepare your minds for action, keep sober in spirit, fix your hope completely on the grace to be brought to you at the revelation of Jesus **Christ**.

As obedient children, do not be conformed to the former lusts which were yours in your ignorance, but like the Holy One who called you, be holy yourselves also in all your behavior; because it is written, "You shall be holy, for I am holy."

If you address as Father the One who impartially judges according to each one's work, conduct yourselves in fear during the time of your stay on earth; knowing that you were not redeemed with perishable things like silver or gold from your futile way of life inherited from your forefathers, but with precious blood, as of a lamb unblemished and spotless, the blood of **Christ**.

For He was foreknown before the foundation of the world, but has appeared in these last times for the sake of you who through Him are believers in God, who raised Him from the dead and gave Him glory, so that your faith and hope are in God.   *1 Peter 1:1-21*

Coming to Him as to a living stone which has been rejected by men, but is choice and precious in the sight of God, you also, as living stones, are being built up as a spiritual house for a holy priesthood, to offer up spiritual sacrifices acceptable to God through Jesus **Christ**. For this is contained in Scripture: "Behold, I lay in Zion a choice stone, a precious corner stone, and he who believes in Him will not be disappointed."

This precious value, then, is for you who believe; but for those who disbelieve, "The stone which the builders rejected, this became the very corner stone," and, "A stone of stumbling and a rock of offense"; for they stumble because they are disobedient to the word, and to this doom they were also appointed. *1 Peter 2:4-8*

Honor all people, love the brotherhood, fear God, honor the king. Servants, be submissive to your masters with all respect, not only to those who are good and gentle, but also to those who are unreasonable. For this finds favor, if for the sake of conscience toward God a person bears up under sorrows when suffering unjustly.

For what credit is there if, when you sin and are harshly treated, you endure it with patience? But if when you do what is right and suffer for it you patiently endure it, this finds favor with God.

For you have been called for this purpose, since **Christ** also suffered for you, leaving you an example for you to follow in His steps, who committed no sin, nor was any deceit found in His mouth; and while being reviled, He did not revile in return; while suffering, He uttered no threats, but kept entrusting Himself to Him who judges righteously; and He Himself bore our sins in His body on the cross, so that we might die to sin and live to righteousness; for by His wounds you were healed.

For you were continually straying like sheep, but now you have returned to the Shepherd and Guardian of your souls.

1 Peter 2:17-25

Who is there to harm you if you prove zealous for what is good? But even if you should suffer for the sake of righteousness, you are blessed.

And do not fear their intimidation, and do not be troubled, but sanctify **Christ** as Lord in your hearts, always being ready to make a defense to everyone who asks you to give an account for the hope that is in you, yet with gentleness and reverence; keep a good conscience so that in the thing in which you are slandered, those who revile your good behavior in **Christ** will be put to shame.

For **Christ** also died for sins once for all, the just for the unjust, so that He might bring us to God, having been put to death in the flesh, but made alive in the spirit; in which also He went and made proclamation to the spirits now in prison, who once were disobedient, when the patience of God kept waiting in the days of Noah, during the construction of the ark, in which a few, that is, eight persons, were brought safely through the water.

Corresponding to that, baptism now saves you - not the removal of dirt from the flesh, but an appeal to God for a good conscience - through the resurrection of Jesus **Christ**, who is at the right hand of God, having gone into heaven, after angels and authorities and powers had been subjected to Him.

Therefore, since **Christ** has suffered in the flesh, arm yourselves also with the same purpose, because he who has suffered in the flesh has ceased from sin, so as to live the rest of the time in the flesh no longer for the lusts of men, but for the will of God. *1 Peter 3:13-4:2*

As each one has received a special gift, employ it in serving one another as good stewards of the manifold grace of God. Whoever speaks, is to do so as one who is speaking the utterances of God; whoever serves is to do so as one who is serving by the strength which God supplies; so that in all things God may be glorified through Jesus **Christ**, to whom belongs the glory and dominion forever and ever. Amen.

Beloved, do not be surprised at the fiery ordeal among you, which comes upon you for your testing, as though some strange thing were happening to you; but to the degree that you share the sufferings of **Christ**, keep on rejoicing, so that also at the revelation of His glory you may rejoice with exultation.

If you are reviled for the name of **Christ**, you are blessed, because the Spirit of glory and of God rests on you.

1 Peter 4:10-14

Those also who suffer according to the will of God shall entrust their souls to a faithful Creator in doing what is right.

Therefore, I exhort the elders among you, as your fellow elder and witness of the sufferings of **Christ**, and a partaker also of the glory that is to be revealed, shepherd the flock of God among you, exercising oversight not under compulsion, but voluntarily, according to the will of God; and not for sordid gain, but with eagerness; nor yet as lording it over those allotted to your charge, but proving to be examples to the flock.

And when the Chief Shepherd appears, you will receive the unfading crown of glory. *1 Peter 4:19 - 5:4*

After you have suffered for a little while, the God of all grace, who called you to His eternal glory in **Christ**, will Himself perfect, confirm, strengthen and establish you. To Him be dominion forever and ever. Amen. *1 Peter 5:10-11*

Greet one another with a kiss of love.

Peace be to you all who are in **Christ**.

1 Peter 5:14

Simon Peter, a bond-servant and apostle of Jesus **Christ**, to those who have received a faith of the same kind as ours, by the righteousness of our God and Savior, Jesus **Christ**: Grace and peace be multiplied to you in the knowledge of God and of Jesus our Lord; seeing that His divine power has granted to us everything pertaining to life and godliness, through the true knowledge of Him who called us by His own glory and excellence.

For by these He has granted to us His precious and magnificent promises, so that by them you may become partakers of the divine nature, having escaped the corruption that is in the world by lust.

Now for this very reason also, applying all diligence, in your faith supply moral excellence, and in your moral excellence, knowledge, and in your knowledge, self-control, and in your self-control, perseverance, and in your perseverance, godliness, and in your godliness, brotherly kindness, and in your brotherly kindness, love.

For if these qualities are yours and are increasing, they render you neither useless nor unfruitful in the true knowledge of our Lord Jesus **Christ**. For he who lacks these qualities is blind or short-sighted, having forgotten his purification from his former sins.

Therefore, brethren, be all the more diligent to make certain about His calling and choosing you; for as long as you practice these things, you will never stumble; for in this way the entrance into the eternal kingdom of our Lord and Savior Jesus **Christ** will be abundantly supplied to you.

Therefore, I will always be ready to remind you of these things, even though you already know them, and have been established in the truth which is present with you.

I consider it right, as long as I am in this earthly dwelling, to stir you up by way of reminder, knowing that the laying aside of my earthly dwelling is imminent, as also our Lord Jesus **Christ** has made clear to me. And I will also be diligent that at any time after my departure you will be able to call these things to mind.

For we did not follow cleverly devised tales when we made known to you the power and coming of our Lord Jesus **Christ**, but we were eyewitnesses of His majesty. For when He received honor and glory from God the Father, such an utterance as this was made to Him by the Majestic Glory, "This is My beloved Son with whom I am well-pleased" - and we ourselves heard this utterance made from heaven when we were with Him on the holy mountain.   *2 Peter 1:1-18*

If, after they have escaped the defilements of the world by the knowledge of the Lord and Savior Jesus **Christ**, they are again entangled in them and are overcome, the last state has become worse for them than the first.

For it would be better for them not to have known the way of righteousness, than having known it, to turn away from the holy commandment handed on to them.   *2 Peter 2:20-21*

You therefore, beloved, knowing this beforehand, be on your guard so that you are not carried away by the error of unprincipled men and fall from your own steadfastness, but grow in the grace and knowledge of our Lord and Savior Jesus **Christ**.

To Him be the glory, both now and to the day of eternity. Amen.   *2 Peter 3:17-18*

What was from the beginning, what we have heard, what we have seen with our eyes, what we have looked at and touched with our hands, concerning the Word of Life - and the life was manifested, and we have seen and testify and proclaim to you the eternal life, which was with the Father and was manifested to us - what we have seen and heard we proclaim to you also, so that you too may have fellowship with us; and indeed our fellowship is with the Father, and with His Son Jesus **Christ**.

These things we write, so that our joy may be made complete.   *1 John 1:1-4*

My little children, I am writing these things to you so that you may not sin.

And if anyone sins, we have an Advocate with the Father, Jesus **Christ** the righteous; and He Himself is the propitiation for our sins; and not for ours only, but also for those of the whole world.
                    1 John 2:1-2

Children, it is the last hour; and just as you heard that antichrist is coming, even now many antichrists have appeared; from this we know that it is the last hour.

They went out from us, but they were not really of us; for if they had been of us, they would have remained with us; but they went out, so that it would be shown that they all are not of us.

But you have an anointing from the Holy One, and you all know. I have not written to you because you do not know the truth, but because you do know it, and because no lie is of the truth.

Who is the liar but the one who denies that Jesus is the **Christ**? This is the antichrist, the one who denies the Father and the Son.

Whoever denies the Son does not have the Father; the one who confesses the Son has the Father also. *1 John 2:18-23*

Beloved, if our heart does not condemn us, we have confidence before God; and whatever we ask we receive from Him, because we keep His commandments and do the things that are pleasing in His sight.

This is His commandment, that we believe in the name of His Son Jesus **Christ**, and love one another, just as He commanded us.

The one who keeps His commandments abides in Him, and He in him. We know by this that He abides in us, by the Spirit whom He has given us.

Beloved, do not believe every spirit, but test the spirits to see whether they are from God, because many false prophets have gone out into the world.

By this you know the Spirit of God: Every spirit that confesses that Jesus **Christ** has come in the flesh is from God; and every spirit that does not confess Jesus is not from God; this is the spirit of the antichrist, of which you have heard that it is coming, and now it is already in the world.

You are from God, little children, and have overcome them; because greater is He who is in you than he who is in the world.   *1 John 3:21 - 4:4*

Whoever believes that Jesus is the **Christ** is born of God, and whoever loves the Father loves the child born of Him. By this we know that we love the children of God, when we love God and observe His commandments.

For this is the love of God, that we keep His commandments; and His commandments are not burdensome. For whatever is born of God overcomes the world; and this is the victory that has overcome the world - our faith.

Who is the one who overcomes the world, but he who believes that Jesus is the Son of God?

This is the One who came by water and blood, Jesus **Christ**; not with the water only, but with the water and with the blood.

It is the Spirit who testifies, because the Spirit is the truth. *1 John 5:1-7*

We know that we are of God, and that the whole world lies in the power of the evil one.

And we know that the Son of God has come, and has given us understanding so that we may know Him who is true; and we are in Him who is true, in His Son Jesus **Christ**.

This is the true God and eternal life. *1 John 5:19-20*

Grace, mercy and peace will be with us, from God the Father and from Jesus **Christ**, the Son of the Father, in truth and love.

I was very glad to find some of your children walking in truth, just as we have received commandment to do from the Father.

Now I ask you, lady, not as though I were writing to you a new commandment, but the one which we have had from the beginning, that we love one another.

And this is love, that we walk according to His commandments. This is the commandment, just as you have heard from the beginning, that you should walk in it.

For many deceivers have gone out into the world, those who do not acknowledge Jesus **Christ** as coming in the flesh. This is the deceiver and the antichrist. Watch yourselves, that you do not lose what we have accomplished, but that you may receive a full reward.

Anyone who goes too far and does not abide in the teaching of **Christ**, does not have God; the one who abides in the teaching, he has both the Father and the Son. *2 John 3-9*

Jude, a bond-servant of Jesus **Christ**, and brother of James, to those who are the called, beloved in God the Father, and kept for Jesus **Christ**: May mercy and peace and love be multiplied to you.

Beloved, while I was making every effort to write you about our common salvation, I felt the necessity to write to you appealing that you contend earnestly for the faith which was once for all handed down to the saints.

For certain persons have crept in unnoticed, those who were long beforehand marked out for this condemnation, ungodly persons who turn the grace of our God into licentiousness and deny our only Master and Lord, Jesus **Christ**. *Jude 1-4*

You, beloved, ought to remember the words that were spoken beforehand by the apostles of our Lord Jesus **Christ**, that they were saying to you, "In the last time there will be mockers, following after their own ungodly lusts." These are the ones who cause divisions, worldly-minded, devoid of the Spirit.

But you, beloved, building yourselves up on your most holy faith, praying in the Holy Spirit, keep yourselves in the love of God, waiting anxiously for the mercy of our Lord Jesus **Christ** to eternal life.

And have mercy on some, who are doubting; save others, snatching them out of the fire; and on some have mercy with fear, hating even the garment polluted by the flesh.

Now to Him who is able to keep you from stumbling, and to make you stand in the presence of His glory blameless with great joy, to the only God our Savior, through Jesus Christ our Lord, be glory, majesty, dominion and authority, before all time and now and forever. Amen.

Jude 17-25

The Revelation of Jesus **Christ**, which God gave Him to show to His bond-servants, the things which must soon take place; and He sent and communicated it by His angel to His bond-servant John, who testified to the word of God and to the testimony of Jesus **Christ**, even to all that he saw.

Blessed is he who reads and those who hear the words of the prophecy, and heed the things which are written in it; for the time is near.

John to the seven churches that are in Asia: Grace to you and peace, from Him who is and who was and who is to come, and from the seven Spirits who are before His throne and from Jesus **Christ**, the faithful witness, the firstborn of the dead, and the ruler of the kings of the earth.

To Him who loves us and released us from our sins by His blood - and He has made us to be a kingdom, priests to His God and Father - to Him be the glory and the dominion forever and ever. Amen.

Behold, He is coming with the clouds, and every eye will see Him, even those who pierced Him; and all the tribes of the earth will mourn over Him. So it is to be. Amen.

Revelation 1:1-7

The second woe is past; behold, the third woe is coming quickly.

Then the seventh angel sounded; and there were loud voices in heaven, saying, "The kingdom of the world has become the kingdom of our Lord and of His **Christ**; and He will reign forever and ever."

And the twenty-four elders, who sit on their thrones before God, fell on their faces and worshiped God, saying, "We give You thanks, O Lord God, the Almighty, who are and who were, because You have taken Your great power and have begun to reign."

Revelation 11:14-17

I heard a loud voice in heaven, saying, "Now the salvation, and the power, and the kingdom of our God and the authority of His **Christ** have come, for the accuser of our brethren has been thrown down, he who accuses them before our God day and night.

And they overcame him because of the blood of the Lamb and because of the word of their testimony, and they did not love their life even when faced with death."

Revelation 12:10-11

Then I saw thrones, and they sat on them, and judgment was given to them.

And I saw the souls of those who had been beheaded because of their testimony of Jesus and because of the word of God, and those who had not worshiped the beast or his image, and had not received the mark on their forehead and on their hand; and they came to life and reigned with **Christ** for a thousand years.

The rest of the dead did not come to life until the thousand years were completed. This is the first resurrection.

Blessed and holy is the one who has a part in the first resurrection; over these the second death has no power, but they will be priests of God and of **Christ** and will reign with Him for a thousand years.

Revelation 20:4-6

SON OF GOD^

/ GOD'S SON / SON*

Definitions

Son of God   1. A title in the New Testament that usually denotes Jesus Christ.

2. For most Christians, the second person of the Trinity.

3. A superhuman or divine being; an angel.

4. A term that can denote someone with a special relationship to God.

NEW TESTAMENT

After being baptized, Jesus came up immediately from the water; and behold, the heavens were opened, and he saw the Spirit of God descending as a dove and lighting on Him, and behold, a voice out of the heavens said, "This is My beloved **Son**, in whom I am well-pleased."

Then Jesus was led up by the Spirit into the wilderness to be tempted by the devil. And after He had fasted forty days and forty nights, He then became hungry.

And the tempter came and said to Him, "If You are the **Son of God**, command that these stones become bread."

But He answered and said, "It is written, 'Man shall not live on bread alone, but on every word that proceeds out of the mouth of God.' "

Then the devil took Him into the holy city and had Him stand on the pinnacle of the temple, and said to Him, "If You are the **Son of God**, throw Yourself down; for it is written, 'He will command His angels concerning You'; and 'On their hands they will bear You up, so that You will not strike Your foot against a stone.' "

Jesus said to him, "On the other hand, it is written, 'You shall not put the Lord your God to the test.' "

Matthew 3:16 - 4:7

When He came to the other side into the country of the Gadarenes, two men who were demon-possessed met Him as they were coming out of the tombs. They were so extremely violent that no one could pass by that way.

And they cried out, saying, "What business do we have with each other, **Son of God**? Have You come here to torment us before the time?"

Now there was a herd of many swine feeding at a distance from them. The demons began to entreat Him, saying, "If You are going to cast us out, send us into the herd of swine."

And He said to them, "Go!"

And they came out and went into the swine, and the whole herd rushed down the steep bank into the sea and perished in the waters.   *Matthew 8:28-32*

Immediately He made the disciples get into the boat and go ahead of Him to the other side, while He sent the crowds away.

After He had sent the crowds away, He went up on the mountain by Himself to pray; and when it was evening, He was there alone. But the boat was already a long distance from the land, battered by the waves; for the wind was contrary.

And in the fourth watch of the night He came to them, walking on the sea.

When the disciples saw Him walking on the sea, they were terrified, and said, "It is a ghost!" And they cried out in fear.

But immediately Jesus spoke to them, saying, "Take courage, it is I; do not be afraid."

Peter said to Him, "Lord, if it is You, command me to come to You on the water."

And He said, "Come!"

And Peter got out of the boat, and walked on the water and came toward Jesus.

But seeing the wind, he became frightened, and beginning to sink, he cried out, "Lord, save me!"

Immediately Jesus stretched out His hand and took hold of him, and said to him, "You of little faith, why did you doubt?"

When they got into the boat, the wind stopped. And those who were in the boat worshiped Him, saying, "You are certainly **God's Son**!"   *Matthew 14:22-33*

When Jesus came into the district of Caesarea Philippi, He was asking His disciples, "Who do people say that the Son of Man is?"

And they said, "Some say John the Baptist; and others, Elijah; but still others, Jeremiah, or one of the prophets."

He said to them, "But who do you say that I am?"

Simon Peter answered, "You are the Christ, the **Son of** the living **God**."

And Jesus said to him, "Blessed are you, Simon Barjona, because flesh and blood did not reveal this to you, but My Father who is in heaven.

"I also say to you that you are Peter, and upon this rock I will build My church; and the gates of Hades will not overpower it.

"I will give you the keys of the kingdom of heaven; and whatever you bind on earth shall have been bound in heaven, and whatever you loose on earth shall have been loosed in heaven."

Then He warned the disciples that they should tell no one that He was the Christ.   *Matthew 16:13-20*

Six days later Jesus took with Him Peter and James and John his brother, and led them up on a high mountain by themselves.

And He was transfigured before them; and His face shone like the sun, and His garments became as white as light. And behold, Moses and Elijah ap-

peared to them, talking with Him.

Peter said to Jesus, "Lord, it is good for us to be here; if You wish, I will make three tabernacles here, one for You, and one for Moses, and one for Elijah."

While he was still speaking, a bright cloud overshadowed them, and behold, a voice out of the cloud said, "This is My beloved **Son**, with whom I am well-pleased; listen to Him!"

When the disciples heard this, they fell face down to the ground and were terrified.

And Jesus came to them and touched them and said, "Get up, and do not be afraid." And lifting up their eyes, they saw no one except Jesus Himself alone.

As they were coming down from the mountain, Jesus commanded them, saying, "Tell the vision to no one until the Son of Man has risen from the dead."

Matthew 17:1-9

The high priest stood up and said to Him, "Do You not answer? What is it that these men are testifying against You?" But Jesus kept silent.

And the high priest said to Him, "I adjure You by the living God, that You tell us whether You are the Christ, the **Son of God**."

Jesus said to him, "You have said it yourself; nevertheless I tell you, hereafter you will see the Son of Man sitting at the right hand of Power, and coming on the clouds of heaven."   *Matthew 26:62-68*

Two robbers were crucified with Him, one on the right and one on the left.

And those passing by were hurling abuse at Him, wagging their heads and saying, "You who are going to destroy the temple and rebuild it in three days, save Yourself! If You are the **Son of God**, come down from the cross."

In the same way the chief priests also, along with the scribes and elders, were mocking Him and saying, "He saved others; He cannot save Himself. He is the King of Israel; let Him now come down from the cross, and we will believe in Him. He trusts in God; let God rescue

Him now, if He delights in Him; for He said, 'I am the **Son of God**.' "

The robbers who had been crucified with Him were also insulting Him with the same words. *Matthew 27:38-44*

Jesus cried out again with a loud voice, and yielded up His spirit.

And behold, the veil of the temple was torn in two from top to bottom; and the earth shook and the rocks were split.

The tombs were opened, and many bodies of the saints who had fallen asleep were raised; and coming out of the tombs after His resurrection they entered the holy city and appeared to many.

Now the centurion, and those who were with him keeping guard over Jesus, when they saw the earthquake and the things that were happening, became very frightened and said, "Truly this was the **Son of God**!" *Matthew 27:50-54*

The beginning of the gospel of Jesus Christ, the **Son of God**. As it is written in Isaiah the prophet: "Behold, I send My messenger ahead of You, who will prepare Your way; the voice of one crying in the wilderness, 'Make ready the way of the Lord, make His paths straight.' " *Mark 1:1-3*

In those days Jesus came from Nazareth in Galilee and was baptized by John in the Jordan.

Immediately coming up out of the water, He saw the heavens opening, and the Spirit like a dove descending upon Him; and a voice came out of the heavens: "You are My beloved **Son**, in You I am well-pleased." *Mark 1:9-11*

Whenever the unclean spirits saw Him, they would fall down before Him and shout, "You are the **Son of God**!"

And He earnestly warned them not to tell who He was. *Mark 3:11-12*

They came to the other side of the sea, into the country of the Gerasenes.

When He got out of the boat, immediately a man from the tombs with an un-clean spirit met Him, and he had his dwelling among the tombs.

And no one was able to bind him anymore, even with a chain; because he had often been bound with shackles and chains, and the chains had been torn apart by him and the shackles broken in pieces, and no one was strong enough to subdue him. Constantly, night and day, he was screaming among the tombs and in the mountains, and gashing himself with stones.

Seeing Jesus from a distance, he ran up and bowed down before Him; and shouting with a loud voice, he said, "What business do we have with each other, Jesus, **Son of** the Most High **God**? I implore You by God, do not torment me!" For He had been saying to him, "Come out of the man, you unclean spirit!" *Mark 5:1-8*

Six days later, Jesus took with Him Peter and James and John, and brought them up on a high mountain by themselves. And He was transfigured before them; and His garments became radiant and exceedingly white, as no launderer on earth can whiten them.

Elijah appeared to them along with Moses; and they were talking with Jesus.

Peter said to Jesus, "Rabbi, it is good for us to be here; let us make three taber-nacles, one for You, and one for Moses, and one for Elijah." For he did not know what to answer; for they became terrified.

Then a cloud formed, overshadowing them, and a voice came out of the cloud, "This is My beloved **Son**, listen to Him!"

All at once they looked around and saw no one with them anymore, except Jesus alone.

As they were coming down from the mountain, He gave them orders not to relate to anyone what they had seen, until the Son of Man rose from the dead. *Mark 9:2-9*

At the ninth hour Jesus cried out with a loud voice, "Eloi, eloi, lama sabachthani?" which is translated, "My God, My God, why have You forsaken Me?"

When some of the bystanders heard it, they began saying, "Behold, He is calling for Elijah."

Someone ran and filled a sponge with sour wine, put it on a reed, and gave Him a drink, saying, "Let us see whether Elijah will come to take Him down."

And Jesus uttered a loud cry, and breathed His last.

And the veil of the temple was torn in two from top to bottom.

When the centurion, who was standing right in front of Him, saw the way He breathed His last, he said, "Truly this man was the **Son of God!**" *Mark 15:34-39*

In the sixth month the angel Gabriel was sent from God to a city in Galilee called Nazareth, to a virgin engaged to a man whose name was Joseph, of the descendants of David; and the virgin's name was Mary.

And coming in, he said to her, "Greetings, favored one! The Lord is with you." But she was very perplexed at this statement, and kept pondering what kind of salutation this was.

The angel said to her, "Do not be afraid, Mary; for you have found favor with God.

"And behold, you will conceive in your womb and bear a son, and you shall name Him Jesus. He will be great and will be called the **Son** of the Most High; and the Lord God will give Him the throne of His father David; and He will reign over the house of Jacob forever, and His kingdom will have no end."

Mary said to the angel, "How can this be, since I am a virgin?"

The angel answered and said to her, "The Holy Spirit will come upon you, and the power of the Most High will overshadow you; and for that reason the holy Child shall be called the **Son of God.**"
Luke 1:26-35

When all the people were baptized, Jesus was also baptized, and while He was praying, heaven was opened, and the Holy Spirit descended upon Him in bodily form like a dove, and a voice came out of heaven, "You are My beloved **Son**, in You I am well-pleased."

When He began His ministry, Jesus Himself was about thirty years of age, being, as was supposed, the son of Joseph, the son of Eli, ..*<list>*.. the son of Cainan, the son of Arphaxad, the son of Shem, the son of Noah, the son of Lamech, the son of Methuselah, the son of Enoch, the son of Jared, the son of Mahalaleel, the son of Cainan, the son of Enosh, the son of Seth, the son of Adam, the **son of God**. *Luke 3:21-23 > 3:36-38*

Jesus, full of the Holy Spirit, returned from the Jordan and was led around by the Spirit in the wilderness for forty days, being tempted by the devil. And He ate nothing during those days, and when they had ended, He became hungry.

And the devil said to Him, "If You are the **Son of God**, tell this stone to become bread."

And Jesus answered him, "It is written, 'Man shall not live on bread alone.' "
Luke 4:1-4

He led Him to Jerusalem and had Him stand on the pinnacle of the temple, and said to Him, "If You are the **Son of God**, throw Yourself down from here; for it is written, 'He will command His angels concerning You to guard You,' and, 'On their hands they will bear You up, so that You will not strike Your foot against a stone.' "

And Jesus answered and said to him, "It is said, 'You shall not put the Lord your God to the test.' "

When the devil had finished every temptation, he left Him until an opportune time. *Luke 4:9-13*

While the sun was setting, all those who had any who were sick with various diseases brought them to Him; and laying His hands on each one of them, He was healing them. Demons also were coming out of many, shouting, "You are the **Son of God!**"

But rebuking them, He would not allow them to speak, because they knew Him to be the Christ. *Luke 4:40-41*

When it was day, the Council of elders of the people assembled, both chief priests and scribes, and they led Him away to their council chamber, saying, "If You are the Christ, tell us."

But He said to them, "If I tell you, you will not believe; and if I ask a question, you will not answer.

"But from now on the Son of Man will be seated at the right hand of the power of God."

And they all said, "Are You the **Son of God**, then?"

And He said to them, "Yes, I am."

Then they said, "What further need do we have of testimony? For we have heard it ourselves from His own mouth."

Then the whole body of them got up and brought Him before Pilate.

Luke 22:66 - 23:1

The next day he saw Jesus coming to him and said, "Behold, the Lamb of God who takes away the sin of the world!

"This is He on behalf of whom I said, 'After me comes a Man who has a higher rank than I, for He existed before me.' I did not recognize Him, but so that He might be manifested to Israel, I came baptizing in water."

John testified saying, "I have seen the Spirit descending as a dove out of heaven, and He remained upon Him.

"I did not recognize Him, but He who sent me to baptize in water said to me, 'He upon whom you see the Spirit descending and remaining upon Him, this is the One who baptizes in the Holy Spirit.'

I myself have seen, and have testified that this is the **Son of God**."   *John 1:29-34*

Jesus saw Nathanael coming to Him, and said of him, "Behold, an Israelite indeed, in whom there is no deceit!"

Nathanael said to Him, "How do You know me?"

Jesus answered and said to him, "Before Philip called you, when you were under the fig tree, I saw you."

Nathanael answered Him, "Rabbi, You are the **Son of God**; You are the King of Israel."

Jesus answered and said to him, "Because I said to you that I saw you under the fig tree, do you believe? You will see greater things than these."

And He said to him, "Truly, truly, I say to you, you will see the heavens opened and the angels of God ascending and descending on the Son of Man."

John 1:47-51

As Moses lifted up the serpent in the wilderness, even so must the Son of Man be lifted up; so that whoever believes will in Him have eternal life.

For God so loved the world, that He gave His only begotten **Son**, that whoever believes in Him shall not perish, but have eternal life.

For God did not send the **Son** into the world to judge the world, but that the world might be saved through Him.

He who believes in Him is not judged; he who does not believe has been judged already, because he has not believed in the name of the only begotten **Son of God**.

This is the judgment, that the Light has come into the world, and men loved the darkness rather than the Light, for their deeds were evil. For everyone who does evil hates the Light, and does not come to the Light for fear that his deeds will be exposed.   *John 3:14-20*

The man went away, and told the Jews that it was Jesus who had made him well. For this reason the Jews were persecuting Jesus, because He was doing these things on the Sabbath.

But He answered them, "My Father is working until now, and I Myself am working."

For this reason therefore the Jews were seeking all the more to kill Him, because He not only was breaking the Sabbath, but also was calling God His own Father, making Himself equal with God.

Therefore Jesus answered and was saying to them, "Truly, truly, I say to you, the **Son** can do nothing of Himself, unless it is something He sees the Father doing;

for whatever the Father does, these things the **Son** also does in like manner.

"For the Father loves the **Son**, and shows Him all things that He Himself is doing; and the Father will show Him greater works than these, so that you will marvel. For just as the Father raises the dead and gives them life, even so the **Son** also gives life to whom He wishes.

"For not even the Father judges anyone, but He has given all judgment to the **Son**, so that all will honor the **Son** even as they honor the Father.

"He who does not honor the **Son** does not honor the Father who sent Him.

"Truly, truly, I say to you, he who hears My word, and believes Him who sent Me, has eternal life, and does not come into judgment, but has passed out of death into life.

"Truly, truly, I say to you, an hour is coming and now is, when the dead will hear the voice of the **Son of God**, and those who hear will live.

"For just as the Father has life in Himself, even so He gave to the **Son** also to have life in Himself; and He gave Him authority to execute judgment, because He is the Son of Man."   *John 5:15-27*

At that time the Feast of the Dedication took place at Jerusalem; it was winter, and Jesus was walking in the temple in the portico of Solomon.

The Jews then gathered around Him, and were saying to Him, "How long will You keep us in suspense? If You are the Christ, tell us plainly."

Jesus answered them, "I told you, and you do not believe; the works that I do in My Father's name, these testify of Me. But you do not believe because you are not of My sheep.

"My sheep hear My voice, and I know them, and they follow Me; and I give eternal life to them, and they will never perish; and no one will snatch them out of My hand.

"My Father, who has given them to Me, is greater than all; and no one is able to snatch them out of the Father's hand. I and the Father are one."

The Jews picked up stones again to stone Him.

Jesus answered them, "I showed you many good works from the Father; for which of them are you stoning Me?"

The Jews answered Him, "For a good work we do not stone You, but for blasphemy; and because You, being a man, make Yourself out to be God."

Jesus answered them, "Has it not been written in your Law, 'I said, you are gods'? If he called them gods, to whom the word of God came (and the Scripture cannot be broken), do you say of Him, whom the Father sanctified and sent into the world, 'You are blaspheming,' because I said, 'I am the **Son of God**'?

"If I do not do the works of My Father, do not believe Me; but if I do them, though you do not believe Me, believe the works, so that you may know and understand that the Father is in Me, and I in Father."

Therefore they were seeking again to seize Him, and He eluded their grasp.
          John 10:22-39

A certain man was sick, Lazarus of Bethany, the village of Mary and her sister Martha. It was the Mary who anointed the Lord with ointment, and wiped His feet with her hair, whose brother Lazarus was sick.

So the sisters sent word to Him, saying, "Lord, behold, he whom You love is sick."

But when Jesus heard this, He said, "This sickness is not to end in death, but for the glory of God, so that the **Son of God** may be glorified by it."   *John 11:1-4*

Martha said to Jesus, "Lord, if You had been here, my brother would not have died. Even now I know that whatever You ask of God, God will give You."

Jesus said to her, "Your brother will rise again."

Martha said to Him, "I know that he will rise again in the resurrection on the last day."

Jesus said to her, "I am the resurrection and the life; he who believes in Me will live even if he dies, and everyone who lives and believes in Me will never die. Do you believe this?"

She said to Him, "Yes, Lord; I have believed that You are the Christ, the **Son of God**, even He who comes into the world."   *John 11:21-27*

Jesus then came out, wearing the crown of thorns and the purple robe.

Pilate said to them, "Behold, the Man!"

So when the chief priests and the officers saw Him, they cried out saying, "Crucify, crucify!"

Pilate said to them, "Take Him yourselves and crucify Him, for I find no guilt in Him."

The Jews answered him, "We have a law, and by that law He ought to die because He made Himself out to be the **Son of God**."

Therefore when Pilate heard this statement, he was even more afraid; and he entered into the Praetorium again and said to Jesus, "Where are You from?"

But Jesus gave him no answer.
                                    John 19:5-9

Many other signs Jesus also performed in the presence of the disciples, which are not written in this book; but these have been written so that you may believe that Jesus is the Christ, the **Son of God**; and that believing you may have life in His name.   *John 20:30-31*

Philip opened his mouth, and beginning from this Scripture he preached Jesus to him.

As they went along the road they came to some water; and the eunuch said, "Look! Water! What prevents me from being baptized?"

[And Philip said, "If you believe with all your heart, you may."

And he answered and said, "I believe that Jesus Christ is the **Son of God**."]

And he ordered the chariot to stop; and they both went down into the water, Philip as well as the eunuch, and he baptized him.   *Acts 8:35-38*

Ananias departed and entered the house, and after laying his hands on him said, "Brother Saul, the Lord Jesus, who appeared to you on the road by which you were coming, has sent me so that you may regain your sight and be filled with the Holy Spirit."

And immediately there fell from his eyes something like scales, and he regained his sight, and he got up and was baptized; and he took food and was strengthened.

Now for several days he was with the disciples who were at Damascus, and immediately he began to proclaim Jesus in the synagogues, saying, "He is the **Son of God**."

All those hearing him continued to be amazed, and were saying, "Is this not he who in Jerusalem destroyed those who called on this name, and who had come here for the purpose of bringing them bound before the chief priests?"
                                    Acts 9:17-21

Paul, a bond-servant of Christ Jesus, called as an apostle, set apart for the gospel of God, which He promised beforehand through His prophets in the holy Scriptures, concerning His **Son**, who was born of a descendant of David according to the flesh, who was declared the **Son of God** with power by the resurrection from the dead, according to the Spirit of holiness, Jesus Christ our Lord, through whom we have received grace and apostleship to bring about the obedience of faith among all the Gentiles for His name's sake, among whom you also are the called of Jesus Christ; to all who are beloved of God in Rome, called as saints: Grace to you and peace from God our Father and the Lord Jesus Christ.

First, I thank my God through Jesus Christ for you all, because your faith is being proclaimed throughout the whole world. For God, whom I serve in my spirit in the preaching of the gospel of His **Son**, is my witness as to how unceasingly I make mention of you, always in my prayers making request, if perhaps now at last by the will of God I may succeed in coming to you.   *Romans 1:1-10*

As God is faithful, our word to you is not yes and no.

For the **Son of God**, Christ Jesus, who was preached among you by us - by me and Silvanus and Timothy - was not yes and no, but is yes in Him.

For as many as are the promises of God, in Him they are yes; therefore also through Him is our Amen to the glory of God through us.   *2 Corinthians 1:18-20*

Through the Law I died to the Law, so that I might live to God.

I have been crucified with Christ; and it is no longer I who live, but Christ lives in me; and the life which I now live in the flesh I live by faith in the **Son of God**, who loved me and gave Himself up for me.   *Galatians 2:19-20*

He gave some as apostles, and some as prophets, and some as evangelists, and some as pastors and teachers, for the equipping of the saints for the work of service, to the building up of the body of Christ; until we all attain to the unity of the faith, and of the knowledge of the **Son of God**, to a mature man, to the measure of the stature which belongs to the fullness of Christ.

As a result, we are no longer to be children, tossed here and there by waves and carried about by every wind of doctrine, by the trickery of men, by craftiness in deceitful scheming; but speaking the truth in love, we are to grow up in all aspects into Him who is the head, even Christ, from whom the whole body, being fitted and held together by what every joint supplies, according to the proper working of each individual part, causes the growth of the body for the building up of itself in love.   *Ephesians 4:11-16*

Since the day we heard of it, we have not ceased to pray for you and to ask that you may be filled with the knowledge of His will in all spiritual wisdom and understanding, so that you will walk in a manner worthy of the Lord, to please Him in all respects, bearing fruit in every good work and increasing in the knowledge of God; strengthened with all power, according to His glorious might, for the attaining of all steadfastness and patience; joyously giving thanks to the Father, who has qualified us to share in the inheritance of the saints in Light.

For He rescued us from the domain of darkness, and transferred us to the kingdom of His beloved **Son**, in whom we have redemption, the forgiveness of sins.

He is the image of the invisible God, the firstborn of all creation. For by Him all things were created, both in the heavens and on earth, visible and invisible, whether thrones or dominions or rulers or authorities - all things have been created through Him and for Him.

He is before all things, and in Him all things hold together.

He is also head of the body, the church; and He is the beginning, the firstborn from the dead, so that He Himself will come to have first place in everything.

For it was the Father's good pleasure for all the fullness to dwell in Him, and through Him to reconcile all things to Himself, having made peace through the blood of His cross; through Him, I say, whether things on earth or things in heaven.   *Colossians 1:9-20*

Since we have a great high priest who has passed through the heavens, Jesus the **Son of God**, let us hold fast our confession. For we do not have a high priest who cannot sympathize with our weaknesses, but One who has been tempted in all things as we are, yet without sin.
                    Hebrews 4:14-15

Leaving the elementary teaching about the Christ, let us press on to maturity, not laying again a foundation of repentance from dead works and of faith toward God, of instruction about washings and laying on of hands, and the resurrection of the dead and eternal judgment. And this we will do, if God permits.

For in the case of those who have once been enlightened and have tasted of the heavenly gift and have been made partakers of the Holy Spirit, and have tasted the good word of God and the powers of the age to come, and then have fallen away, it is impossible to renew them again to repentance, since they again crucify to themselves the **Son of God** and put Him to open shame.

Hebrews 6:1-6

This Melchizedek, king of Salem, priest of the Most High God, who met Abraham as he was returning from the slaughter of the kings and blessed him, to whom also Abraham apportioned a tenth part of all the spoils, was first of all, by the translation of his name, king of righteousness, and then also king of Salem, which is king of peace.

Without father, without mother, without genealogy, having neither beginning of days nor end of life, but made like the **Son of God**, he remains a priest perpetually.

Hebrews 7:1-3

If we go on sinning willfully after receiving the knowledge of the truth, there no longer remains a sacrifice for sins, but a terrifying expectation of judgment and the fury of a fire which will consume the adversaries.

Anyone who has set aside the Law of Moses dies without mercy on the testimony of two or three witnesses. How much severer punishment do you think he will deserve who has trampled under foot the **Son of God**, and has regarded as unclean the blood of the covenant by which he was sanctified, and has insulted the Spirit of grace?

Hebrews 10:26-29

We did not follow cleverly devised tales when we made known to you the power and coming of our Lord Jesus Christ, but we were eyewitnesses of His majesty.

For when He received honor and glory from God the Father, such an utterance as this was made to Him by the Majestic Glory, "This is My beloved **Son** with whom I am well-pleased" - and we ourselves heard this utterance made from heaven when we were with Him on the holy mountain.

2 Peter 1:16-18

Everyone who practices sin also practices lawlessness; and sin is lawlessness. You know that He appeared in order to take away sins; and in Him there is no sin.

No one who abides in Him sins; no one who sins has seen Him or knows Him.

Little children, make sure no one deceives you; the one who practices righteousness is righteous, just as He is righteous; the one who practices sin is of the devil; for the devil has sinned from the beginning.

The **Son of God** appeared for this purpose, to destroy the works of the devil. No one who is born of God practices sin, because His seed abides in him; and he cannot sin, because he is born of God.

By this the children of God and the children of the devil are obvious: anyone who does not practice righteousness is not of God, nor the one who does not love his brother.

1 John 3:4-10

Beloved, let us love one another, for love is from God; and everyone who loves is born of God and knows God. The one who does not love does not know God, for God is love.

By this the love of God was manifested in us, that God has sent His only begotten **Son** into the world so that we might live through Him.

In this is love, not that we loved God, but that He loved us and sent His **Son** to be the propitiation for our sins.

Beloved, if God so loved us, we also ought to love one another.

No one has seen God at any time; if we love one another, God abides in us, and His love is perfected in us.

By this we know that we abide in Him and He in us, because He has given us of His Spirit.

We have seen and testify that the Father has sent the **Son** to be the Savior of the world.

Whoever confesses that Jesus is the **Son of God**, God abides in him, and he in God. *1 John 4:7-15*

Whoever believes that Jesus is the Christ is born of God, and whoever loves the Father loves the child born of Him.

By this we know that we love the children of God, when we love God and observe His commandments.

For this is the love of God, that we keep His commandments; and His commandments are not burdensome.

For whatever is born of God overcomes the world; and this is the victory that has overcome the world - our faith.

Who is the one who overcomes the world, but he who believes that Jesus is the **Son of God**? This is the One who came by water and blood, Jesus Christ; not with the water only, but with the water and with the blood.

It is the Spirit who testifies, because the Spirit is the truth. For there are three that testify: the Spirit and the water and the blood; and the three are in agreement.

If we receive the testimony of men, the testimony of God is greater; for the testimony of God is this, that He has testified concerning His **Son**.

The one who believes in the **Son of God** has the testimony in himself; the one who does not believe God has made Him a liar, because he has not believed in the testimony that God has given concerning His **Son**.

And the testimony is this, that God has given us eternal life, and this life is in His **Son**.

He who has the **Son** has the life; he who does not have the **Son of God** does not have the life.

These things I have written to you who believe in the name of the **Son of God**, so that you may know that you have eternal life. *1 John 5:1-13*

We know that no one who is born of God sins; but He who was born of God keeps him, and the evil one does not touch him.

We know that we are of God, and that the whole world lies in the power of the evil one.

And we know that the **Son of God** has come, and has given us understanding so that we may know Him who is true; and we are in Him who is true, in His **Son** Jesus Christ.

This is the true God and eternal life. *1 John 5:18-20*

To the angel of the church in Thyatira write: The **Son of God**, who has eyes like a flame of fire, and His feet are like burnished bronze, says this: "I know your deeds, and your love and faith and service and perseverance, and that your deeds of late are greater than at first.

"But I have this against you, that you tolerate the woman Jezebel, who calls herself a prophetess, and she teaches and leads My bond-servants astray so that they commit acts of immorality and eat things sacrificed to idols." *Revelation 2:18 -20*

SON OF MAN*

*Not including the term "**son of man**" which God uses to address Ezekiel & Daniel.*

Definitions

Son of Man   1. A term in the Old Testament that refers to a mortal human being.

          2. A title in the New Testament that often denotes Jesus Christ as God's representative destined to preside over the final judgment of the world.

OLD TESTAMENT

God is not a man, that He should lie, nor a **son of man**, that He should repent; has He said, and will He not do it? Or has He spoken, and will He not make it good?
Numbers 23:19

Bildad the Shuhite answered, "Dominion and awe belong to Him who establishes peace in His heights. Is there any number to His troops? And upon whom does His light not rise?

"How then can a man be just with God? Or how can he be clean who is born of woman?

"If even the moon has no brightness and the stars are not pure in His sight, how much less man, that maggot, and the **son of man**, that worm!"
Job 25:1-6

If you have sinned, what do you accomplish against Him? And if your transgressions are many, what do you do to Him?

If you are righteous, what do you give to Him, or what does He receive from your hand?

Your wickedness is for a man like yourself, and your righteousness is for a **son of man**.
Job 35:6-8

When I consider Your heavens, the work of Your fingers, the moon and the stars, which You have ordained; what is man that You take thought of him, and the **son of man** that You care for him?

Yet You have made him a little lower than God, and You crown him with glory and majesty!

You make him to rule over the works of Your hands; You have put all things under his feet, all sheep and oxen, and also the beasts of the field, the birds of the heavens and the fish of the sea, whatever passes through the paths of the seas.
Psalm 8:3-8

O Lord, what is man, that You take knowledge of him? Or the **son of man**, that You think of him?

Man is like a mere breath; his days are like a passing shadow.
Psalm 144:3-4

I, even I, am He who comforts you. Who are you that you are afraid of man who dies and of the **son of man** who is made like grass, that you have forgotten the Lord your maker, who stretched out the heavens and laid the foundations of the earth, that you fear continually all day long because of the fury of the oppressor, as he makes ready to destroy? But where is the fury of the oppressor?
Isaiah 51:12-13

Thus says the Lord, "Preserve justice and do righteousness, for My salvation is about to come and My righteousness to be revealed.

"How blessed is the man who does this, and the **son of man** who takes hold of it; who keeps from profaning the sabbath, and keeps his hand from doing any evil."
Isaiah 56:1-2

"Edom will become an object of horror; everyone who passes by it will be horrified and will hiss at all its wounds.

"Like the overthrow of Sodom and Gomorrah with its neighbors," says the Lord, "no one will live there, nor will a **son of man** reside in it." *Jeremiah 49:17-18*

Hazor will become a haunt of jackals, a desolation forever; no one will live there, nor will a **son of man** reside in it.
Jeremiah 49:33

"A sword against the Chaldeans," declares the Lord, "and against the inhabitants of Babylon and against her officials and her wise men! A sword against the oracle priests, and they will become fools! A sword against her mighty men, and they will be shattered!

"A sword against their horses and against their chariots and against all the foreigners who are in the midst of her, and they will become women!

"A sword against her treasures, and they will be plundered! A drought on her waters, and they will be dried up! For it is a land of idols, and they are mad over fearsome idols.

"Therefore the desert creatures will live there along with the jackals; the ostriches also will live in it, and it will never again be inhabited or dwelt in from generation to generation.

"As when God overthrew Sodom and Gomorrah with its neighbors," declares the Lord, "No man will live there, nor will any **son of man** reside in it."
Jeremiah 50:35-40

How Sheshak has been captured, and the praise of the whole earth been seized! How Babylon has become an object of horror among the nations!

The sea has come up over Babylon; she has been engulfed with its tumultuous waves. Her cities have become an object of horror, a parched land and a desert, a land in which no man lives and through which no **son of man** passes.

I will punish Bel in Babylon, and I will make what he has swallowed come out of his mouth; and the nations will no longer stream to him. Even the wall of Babylon has fallen down!

Come forth from her midst, My people, and each of you save yourselves from the fierce anger of the Lord.
Jeremiah 51:41-45

I kept looking in the night visions, and behold, with the clouds of heaven one like a **Son of Man** was coming, and He came up to the Ancient of Days and was presented before Him.

And to Him was given dominion, glory and a kingdom, that all the peoples, nations and men of every language might serve Him.

His dominion is an everlasting dominion which will not pass away; and His kingdom is one which will not be destroyed.

As for me, Daniel, my spirit was distressed within me, and the visions in my mind kept alarming me. *Daniel 7:13-15*

NEW TESTAMENT

When Jesus saw a crowd around Him, He gave orders to depart to the other side of the sea.

Then a scribe came and said to Him, "Teacher, I will follow You wherever You go."

Jesus said to him, "The foxes have holes and the birds of the air have nests, but the **Son of Man** has nowhere to lay His head." *Matthew 8:18-20*

Getting into a boat, Jesus crossed over the sea and came to His own city. And they brought to Him a paralytic lying on a bed.

Seeing their faith, Jesus said to the paralytic, "Take courage, son; your sins are forgiven."

And some of the scribes said to themselves, "This fellow blasphemes."

And Jesus knowing their thoughts said, "Why are you thinking evil in your hearts? Which is easier, to say, 'Your sins are forgiven,' or to say, 'Get up, and walk'?

"But so that you may know that the **Son of Man** has authority on earth to forgive sins" - then He said to the paralytic, "Get up, pick up your bed and go home." And he got up and went home.

But when the crowds saw this, they were awestruck, and glorified God, who had given such authority to men.
Matthew 9:1-8

Brother will betray brother to death, and a father his child; and children will rise up against parents and cause them to be put to death.

You will be hated by all because of My name, but it is the one who has endured to the end who will be saved.

But whenever they persecute you in one city, flee to the next; for truly I say to you, you will not finish going through the cities of Israel until the **Son of Man** comes. *Matthew 10:21-23*

To what shall I compare this generation? It is like children sitting in the market places, who call out to the other children, and say, "We played the flute for you, and you did not dance; we sang a dirge, and you did not mourn." For John came neither eating nor drinking, and they say, "He has a demon!"

The **Son of Man** came eating and drinking, and they say, "Behold, a gluttonous man and a drunkard, a friend of tax collectors and sinners!"

Yet wisdom is vindicated by her deeds. *Matthew 11:16-19*

At that time Jesus went through the grainfields on the Sabbath, and His disciples became hungry and began to pick the heads of grain and eat.

But when the Pharisees saw this, they said to Him, "Look, Your disciples do what is not lawful to do on a Sabbath."

But He said to them, "Have you not read what David did when he became hungry, he and his companions, how he entered the house of God, and they ate the consecrated bread, which was not lawful for him to eat nor for those with him, but for the priests alone?

"Or have you not read in the Law, that on the Sabbath the priests in the temple break the Sabbath and are innocent? But I say to you that something greater than the temple is here.

"But if you had known what this means, 'I desire compassion, and not a sacrifice,' you would not have condemned the innocent. For the **Son of Man** is Lord of the Sabbath." *Matthew 12:1-8*

He who is not with Me is against Me; and he who does not gather with Me scatters.

Therefore I say to you, any sin and blasphemy shall be forgiven people, but blasphemy against the Spirit shall not be forgiven.

Whoever speaks a word against the **Son of Man**, it shall be forgiven him; but whoever speaks against the Holy Spirit, it shall not be forgiven him, either in this age or in the age to come. *Matthew 12:30-32*

Some of the scribes and Pharisees said to Him, "Teacher, we want to see a sign from You."

But He answered and said to them, "An evil and adulterous generation craves for a sign; and yet no sign will be given to it but the sign of Jonah the prophet; for just as Jonah was three days and three nights in the belly of the sea monster, so will the **Son of Man** be three days and three nights in the heart of the earth."

Matthew 12:38-40

He left the crowds and went into the house. And His disciples came to Him and said, "Explain to us the parable of the tares of the field."

And He said, "The one who sows the good seed is the **Son of Man**, and the field is the world; and as for the good seed, these are the sons of the kingdom; and the tares are the sons of the evil one; and the enemy who sowed them is the devil, and the harvest is the end of the age; and the reapers are angels.

"So just as the tares are gathered up and burned with fire, so shall it be at the end of the age.

"The **Son of Man** will send forth His angels, and they will gather out of His kingdom all stumbling blocks, and those who commit lawlessness, and will throw them into the furnace of fire; in that place there will be weeping and gnashing of teeth.

"Then the righteous will shine forth as the sun in the kingdom of their Father. He who has ears, let him hear."

Matthew 13:36-43

When Jesus came into the district of Caesarea Philippi, He was asking His disciples, "Who do people say that the **Son of Man** is?"

And they said, "Some say John the Baptist; and others, Elijah; but still others, Jeremiah, or one of the prophets."

He said to them, "But who do you say that I am?"

Simon Peter answered, "You are the Christ, the Son of the living God."

And Jesus said to him, "Blessed are you, Simon Barjona, because flesh and blood did not reveal this to you, but My Father who is in heaven." *Matthew 16:13-17*

Jesus said to His disciples, "If anyone wishes to come after Me, he must deny himself, and take up his cross and follow Me. For whoever wishes to save his life will lose it; but whoever loses his life for My sake will find it.

"For what will it profit a man if he gains the whole world and forfeits his soul? Or what will a man give in exchange for his soul?

"For the **Son of Man** is going to come in the glory of His Father with His angels, and will then repay every man according to his deeds.

"Truly I say to you, there are some of those who are standing here who will not taste death until they see the **Son of Man** coming in His kingdom."

Six days later Jesus took with Him Peter and James and John his brother, and led them up on a high mountain by themselves.

And He was transfigured before them; and His face shone like the sun, and His garments became as white as light.

And behold, Moses and Elijah appeared to them, talking with Him.

Peter said to Jesus, "Lord, it is good for us to be here; if You wish, I will make three tabernacles here, one for You, and one for Moses, and one for Elijah."

While he was still speaking, a bright cloud overshadowed them, and behold, a voice out of the cloud said, "This is My beloved Son, with whom I am well-pleased; listen to Him!"

When the disciples heard this, they fell face down to the ground and were terrified.

And Jesus came to them and touched them and said, "Get up, and do not be afraid."

And lifting up their eyes, they saw no one except Jesus Himself alone.

As they were coming down from the mountain, Jesus commanded them, saying, "Tell the vision to no one until the **Son of Man** has risen from the dead."

And His disciples asked Him, "Why then do the scribes say that Elijah must come first?"

And He answered and said, "Elijah is coming and will restore all things; but I say to you that Elijah already came, and they did not recognize him, but did to him whatever they wished.

"So also the **Son of Man** is going to suffer at their hands."

Then the disciples understood that He had spoken to them about John the Baptist. *Matthew 16:24 - 7:13*

While they were gathering together in Galilee, Jesus said to them, "The **Son of Man** is going to be delivered into the hands of men; and they will kill Him, and He will be raised on the third day."

And they were deeply grieved. *Matthew 17:22-23*

See that you do not despise one of these little ones, for I say to you that their angels in heaven continually see the face of My Father who is in heaven. [For the **Son of Man** has come to save that which was lost.]

What do you think? If any man has a hundred sheep, and one of them has gone astray, does he not leave the ninety-nine on the mountains and go and search for the one that is straying? If it turns out that he finds it, truly I say to you, he rejoices over it more than over the ninety-nine which have not gone astray.

So it is not the will of your Father who is in heaven that one of these little ones perish. *Matthew 18:10-14*

Peter said to Him, "Behold, we have left everything and followed You; what then will there be for us?"

And Jesus said to them, "Truly I say to you, that you who have followed Me, in the regeneration when the **Son of Man** will sit on His glorious throne, you also shall sit upon twelve thrones, judging the twelve tribes of Israel.

"And everyone who has left houses or brothers or sisters or father or mother or children or farms for My name's sake, will receive many times as much, and will inherit eternal life." *Matthew 19:27-29*

As Jesus was about to go up to Jerusalem, He took the twelve disciples aside by themselves, and on the way He said to them, "Behold, we are going up to Jerusalem; and the **Son of Man** will be delivered to the chief priests and scribes, and they will condemn Him to death, and will hand Him over to the Gentiles to mock and scourge and crucify Him, and on the third day He will be raised up."

Then the mother of the sons of Zebedee came to Jesus with her sons, bowing down and making a request of Him.

And He said to her, "What do you wish?"

She said to Him, "Command that in Your kingdom these two sons of mine may sit one on Your right and one on Your left."

But Jesus answered, "You do not know what you are asking. Are you able to drink the cup that I am about to drink?"

They said to Him, "We are able."

He said to them, "My cup you shall drink; but to sit on My right and on My left, this is not Mine to give, but it is for those for whom it has been prepared by My Father."

And hearing this, the ten became indignant with the two brothers.

But Jesus called them to Himself and said, "You know that the rulers of the Gentiles lord it over them, and their great men exercise authority over them. It is not this way among you, but whoever wishes to become great among you shall be your servant, and whoever wishes to be first among you shall be your slave; just as the **Son of Man** did not come to be served, but to serve, and to give His life a ransom for many." *Matthew 20:17-28*

Pray that your flight will not be in the winter, or on a Sabbath. For then there will be a great tribulation, such as has not occurred since the beginning of the world until now, nor ever will.

Unless those days had been cut short, no life would have been saved; but for the sake of the elect those days will be cut short.

Then if anyone says to you, "Behold, here is the Christ," or "There He is," do not believe him. For false Christs and false prophets will arise and will show great signs and wonders, so as to mislead, if possible, even the elect. Behold, I have told you in advance.

So if they say to you, "Behold, He is in the wilderness," do not go out, or, "Behold, He is in the inner rooms," do not believe them. For just as the lightning comes from the east and flashes even to the west, so will the coming of the **Son of Man** be.

Wherever the corpse is, there the vultures will gather. But immediately after the tribulation of those days the sun will be darkened, and the moon will not give its light, and the stars will fall from the sky, and the powers of the heavens will be shaken.

And then the sign of the **Son of Man** will appear in the sky, and then all the tribes of the earth will mourn, and they will see the **Son of Man** coming on the clouds of the sky with power and great glory.

And He will send forth His angels with a great trumpet and they will gather together His elect from the four winds, from one end of the sky to the other.

Now learn the parable from the fig tree: when its branch has already become tender and puts forth its leaves, you know that summer is near; so, you too, when you see all these things, recognize that He is near, right at the door.

Truly I say to you, this generation will not pass away until all these things take place. Heaven and earth will pass away, but My words will not pass away.

But of that day and hour no one knows, not even the angels of heaven, nor the Son, but the Father alone. For the coming of the **Son of Man** will be just like the days of Noah.

For as in those days before the flood they were eating and drinking, marrying and giving in marriage, until the day that Noah entered the ark, and they did not understand until the flood came and took them all away; so will the coming of the **Son of Man** be.

Then there will be two men in the field; one will be taken and one will be left. Two women will be grinding at the mill; one will be taken and one will be left.

Therefore be on the alert, for you do not know which day your Lord is coming.

But be sure of this, that if the head of the house had known at what time of the night the thief was coming, he would have been on the alert and would not have allowed his house to be broken into.

For this reason you also must be ready; for the **Son of Man** is coming at an hour when you do not think He will.

Matthew 24:20-44

When the **Son of Man** comes in His glory, and all the angels with Him, then He will sit on His glorious throne. All the nations will be gathered before Him; and He will separate them from one another, as the shepherd separates the sheep from the goats; and He will put the sheep on His right, and the goats on the left.

Then the King will say to those on His right, "Come, you who are blessed of My Father, inherit the kingdom prepared for you from the foundation of the world."

Then the King will say to those on His right, "Come, you who are blessed of My Father, inherit the kingdom prepared for you from the foundation of the world.

"For I was hungry, and you gave Me something to eat; I was thirsty, and you gave Me something to drink; I was a stranger, and you invited Me in; naked, and you clothed Me; I was sick, and you visited Me; I was in prison, and you came to Me."

Then the righteous will answer Him, "Lord, when did we see You hungry, and feed You, or thirsty, and give You something to drink? And when did we see You a stranger, and invite You in, or naked, and clothe You? When did we see You sick, or in prison, and come to You?"

The King will answer and say to them, "Truly I say to you, to the extent that you did it to one of these brothers of

Mine, even the least of them, you did it to Me."

Then He will also say to those on His left, "Depart from Me, accursed ones, into the eternal fire which has been prepared for the devil and his angels; for I was hungry, and you gave Me nothing to eat; I was thirsty, and you gave Me nothing to drink; I was a stranger, and you did not invite Me in; naked, and you did not clothe Me; sick, and in prison, and you did not visit Me."

Then they themselves also will answer, "Lord, when did we see You hungry, or thirsty, or a stranger, or naked, or sick, or in prison, and did not take care of You?"

Then He will answer them, "Truly I say to you, to the extent that you did not do it to one of the least of these, you did not do it to Me."

These will go away into eternal punishment, but the righteous into eternal life.
Matthew 25:31-46

When Jesus had finished all these words, He said to His disciples, "You know that after two days the Passover is coming, and the **Son of Man** is to be handed over for crucifixion."

Then the chief priests and the elders of the people were gathered together in the court of the high priest, named Caiaphas; and they plotted together to seize Jesus by stealth and kill Him. But they were saying, "Not during the festival, otherwise a riot might occur among the people."
Matthew 26:1-5

When evening came, Jesus was reclining at the table with the twelve disciples.

As they were eating, He said, "Truly I say to you that one of you will betray Me."

Being deeply grieved, they each one began to say to Him, "Surely not I, Lord?"

And He answered, "He who dipped his hand with Me in the bowl is the one who will betray Me.

"The **Son of Man** is to go, just as it is written of Him; but woe to that man by whom the **Son of Man** is betrayed! It would have been good for that man if he had not been born."

And Judas, who was betraying Him, said, "Surely it is not I, Rabbi?"

Jesus said to him, "You have said it yourself."
Matthew 26:20-25

He came to the disciples and said to them, "Are you still sleeping and resting? Behold, the hour is at hand and the **Son of Man** is being betrayed into the hands of sinners. Get up, let us be going; behold, the one who betrays Me is at hand!"

While He was still speaking, behold, Judas, one of the twelve, came up accompanied by a large crowd with swords and clubs, who came from the chief priests and elders of the people.

Now he who was betraying Him gave them a sign, saying, "Whomever I kiss, He is the one; seize Him."

Immediately Judas went to Jesus and said, "Hail, rabbi!" and kissed Him.

And Jesus said to him, "Friend, do what you have come for."

Then they came and laid hands on Jesus and seized Him. *Matthew 26:45-50*

The high priest stood up and said to Him, "Do You not answer? What is it that these men are testifying against You?" But Jesus kept silent.

And the high priest said to Him, "I adjure You by the living God, that You tell us whether You are the Christ, the Son of God."

Jesus said to him, "You have said it yourself; nevertheless I tell you, hereafter you will see the **Son of Man** sitting at the right hand of Power, and coming on the clouds of heaven."

Then the high priest tore his robes and said, "He has blasphemed! What further need do we have of witnesses? Behold, you have now heard the blasphemy; what do you think?"

They answered, "He deserves death!"
Matthew 26:62-66

When He had come back to Capernaum several days afterward, it was heard that He was at home. And many were gathered together, so that there was no longer room, not even near the door; and He was speaking the word to them.

And they came, bringing to Him a paralytic, carried by four men. Being unable to get to Him because of the crowd, they removed the roof above Him; and when they had dug an opening, they let down the pallet on which the paralytic was lying.

And Jesus seeing their faith said to the paralytic, "Son, your sins are forgiven."

But some of the scribes were sitting there and reasoning in their hearts, "Why does this man speak that way? He is blaspheming; who can forgive sins but God alone?"

Immediately Jesus, aware in His spirit that they were reasoning that way within themselves, said to them, "Why are you reasoning about these things in your hearts? Which is easier, to say to the paralytic, 'Your sins are forgiven'; or to say, 'Get up, and pick up your pallet and walk'?

"But so that you may know that the **Son of Man** has authority on earth to forgive sins" - He said to the paralytic, "I say to you, get up, pick up your pallet and go home."

And he got up and immediately picked up the pallet and went out in the sight of everyone, so that they were all amazed and were glorifying God, saying, "We have never seen anything like this."

Mark 2:1-12

It happened that He was passing through the grainfields on the Sabbath, and His disciples began to make their way along while picking the heads of grain.

The Pharisees were saying to Him, "Look, why are they doing what is not lawful on the Sabbath?"

And He said to them, "Have you never read what David did when he was in need and he and his companions became hungry; how he entered the house of God in the time of Abiathar the high priest, and ate the consecrated bread, which is not lawful for anyone to eat except the priests, and he also gave it to those who

were with him?"

Jesus said to them, "The Sabbath was made for man, and not man for the Sabbath. So the **Son of Man** is Lord even of the Sabbath." *Mark 2:23-28*

He began to teach them that the **Son of Man** must suffer many things and be rejected by the elders and the chief priests and the scribes, and be killed, and after three days rise again. And He was stating the matter plainly.

And Peter took Him aside and began to rebuke Him.

But turning around and seeing His disciples, He rebuked Peter and said, "Get behind Me, Satan; for you are not setting your mind on God's interests, but man's."

And He summoned the crowd with His disciples, and said to them, "If anyone wishes to come after Me, he must deny himself, and take up his cross and follow Me. For whoever wishes to save his life will lose it, but whoever loses his life for My sake and the gospel's will save it.

"For what does it profit a man to gain the whole world, and forfeit his soul? For what will a man give in exchange for his soul?

"For whoever is ashamed of Me and My words in this adulterous and sinful generation, the **Son of Man** will also be ashamed of him when He comes in the glory of His Father with the holy angels."

Mark 8:31-38

Six days later, Jesus took with Him Peter and James and John, and brought them up on a high mountain by themselves.

And He was transfigured before them; and His garments became radiant and exceedingly white, as no launderer on earth can whiten them.

Elijah appeared to them along with Moses; and they were talking with Jesus.

Peter said to Jesus, "Rabbi, it is good for us to be here; let us make three tabernacles, one for You, and one for Moses, and one for Elijah." For he did not know what to answer; for they became terrified.

Then a cloud formed, overshadowing them, and a voice came out of the cloud, "This is My beloved Son, listen to Him!"

All at once they looked around and saw no one with them anymore, except Jesus alone.

As they were coming down from the mountain, He gave them orders not to relate to anyone what they had seen, until the **Son of Man** rose from the dead. They seized upon that statement, discussing with one another what rising from the dead meant.

They asked Him, saying, "Why is it that the scribes say that Elijah must come first?"

And He said to them, "Elijah does first come and restore all things. And yet how is it written of the **Son of Man** that He will suffer many things and be treated with contempt?

"But I say to you that Elijah has indeed come, and they did to him whatever they wished, just as it is written of him."
Mark 9:2-13

They went out and began to go through Galilee, and He did not want anyone to know about it. For He was teaching His disciples and telling them, "The **Son of Man** is to be delivered into the hands of men, and they will kill Him; and when He has been killed, He will rise three days later."

But they did not understand this statement, and they were afraid to ask Him. *Mark 9:30-32*

They were on the road going up to Jerusalem, and Jesus was walking on ahead of them; and they were amazed, and those who followed were fearful.

And again He took the twelve aside and began to tell them what was going to happen to Him, saying, "Behold, we are going up to Jerusalem, and the **Son of Man** will be delivered to the chief priests and the scribes; and they will condemn Him to death and will hand Him over to the Gentiles.

They will mock Him and spit on Him, and scourge Him and kill Him, and three days later He will rise again." *Mark 10:32-34*

Calling them to Himself, Jesus said to them, "You know that those who are recognized as rulers of the Gentiles lord it over them; and their great men exercise authority over them.

But it is not this way among you, but whoever wishes to become great among you shall be your servant; and whoever wishes to be first among you shall be slave of all.

"For even the **Son of Man** did not come to be served, but to serve, and to give His life a ransom for many."
Mark 10:42-45

In those days, after that tribulation, the sun will be darkened and the moon will not give its light, and the stars will be falling from heaven, and the powers that are in the heavens will be shaken.

Then they will see the **Son of Man** coming in clouds with great power and glory.

And then He will send forth the angels, and will gather together His elect from the four winds, from the farthest end of the earth to the farthest end of heaven.
Mark 13:24-27

When it was evening He came with the twelve.

As they were reclining at the table and eating, Jesus said, "Truly I say to you that one of you will betray Me - one who is eating with Me."

They began to be grieved and to say to Him one by one, "Surely not I?"

And He said to them, "It is one of the twelve, one who dips with Me in the bowl.

"For the **Son of Man** is to go just as it is written of Him; but woe to that man by whom the **Son of Man** is betrayed! It would have been good for that man if he had not been born." *Mark 14:17-21*

He came the third time, and said to them, "Are you still sleeping and resting? It is enough; the hour has come; behold, the **Son of Man** is being betrayed into the hands of sinners.

"Get up, let us be going; behold, the one who betrays Me is at hand!"

Immediately while He was still speaking, Judas, one of the twelve, came up accompanied by a crowd with swords and clubs, who were from the chief priests and the scribes and the elders.

Now he who was betraying Him had given them a signal, saying, "Whomever I kiss, He is the one; seize Him and lead Him away under guard."

After coming, Judas immediately went to Him, saying, "Rabbi!" and kissed Him.

They laid hands on Him and seized Him. *Mark 14:41-46*

The high priest stood up and came forward and questioned Jesus, saying, "Do You not answer? What is it that these men are testifying against You?" But He kept silent and did not answer.

Again the high priest was questioning Him, and saying to Him, "Are You the Christ, the Son of the Blessed One?"

And Jesus said, "I am; and you shall see the **Son of Man** sitting at the right hand of Power, and coming with the clouds of heaven."

Tearing his clothes, the high priest said, "What further need do we have of witnesses? You have heard the blasphemy; how does it seem to you?"

And they all condemned Him to be deserving of death. *Mark 14:60-64*

Some men were carrying on a bed a man who was paralyzed; and they were trying to bring him in and to set him down in front of Him. But not finding any way to bring him in because of the crowd, they went up on the roof and let him down through the tiles with his stretcher, into the middle of the crowd, in front of Jesus.

Seeing their faith, He said, "Friend, your sins are forgiven you."

The scribes and the Pharisees began to reason, saying, "Who is this man who speaks blasphemies? Who can forgive sins, but God alone?"

But Jesus, aware of their reasonings, answered and said to them, "Why are you reasoning in your hearts? Which is easier, to say, 'Your sins have been forgiven you,' or to say, 'Get up and walk'?

"But, so that you may know that the **Son of Man** has authority on earth to forgive sins," - He said to the paralytic - "I say to you, get up, and pick up your stretcher and go home."

Immediately he got up before them, and picked up what he had been lying on, and went home glorifying God.

They were all struck with astonishment and began glorifying God; and they were filled with fear, saying, "We have seen remarkable things today." *Luke 5:18-26*

It happened that He was passing through some grainfields on a Sabbath; and His disciples were picking the heads of grain, rubbing them in their hands, and eating the grain.

But some of the Pharisees said, "Why do you do what is not lawful on the Sabbath?"

And Jesus answering them said, "Have you not even read what David did when he was hungry, he and those who were with him, how he entered the house of God, and took and ate the consecrated bread which is not lawful for any to eat except the priests alone, and gave it to his companions?"

And He was saying to them, "The **Son of Man** is Lord of the Sabbath." *Luke 6:1-5*

Turning His gaze toward His disciples, He began to say, "Blessed are you who are poor, for yours is the kingdom of God.

"Blessed are you who hunger now, for you shall be satisfied.

"Blessed are you who weep now, for you shall laugh.

"Blessed are you when men hate you, and ostracize you, and insult you, and scorn your name as evil, for the sake of the **Son of Man**.

"Be glad in that day and leap for joy, for behold, your reward is great in heaven. For in the same way their fathers used to treat the prophets." *Luke 6:20-23*

To what then shall I compare the men of this generation, and what are they like?

They are like children who sit in the market place and call to one another, and they say, "We played the flute for you, and you did not dance; we sang a dirge, and you did not weep."

For John the Baptist has come eating no bread and drinking no wine, and you say, "He has a demon!"

The **Son of Man** has come eating and drinking, and you say, "Behold, a gluttonous man and a drunkard, a friend of tax collectors and sinners!"

Yet wisdom is vindicated by all her children. *Luke 7:31-35*

It happened that while He was praying alone, the disciples were with Him, and He questioned them, saying, "Who do the people say that I am?"

They answered and said, "John the Baptist, and others say Elijah; but others, that one of the prophets of old has risen again."

And He said to them, "But who do you say that I am?"

And Peter answered and said, "The Christ of God."

But He warned them and instructed them not to tell this to anyone, saying, "The **Son of Man** must suffer many things and be rejected by the elders and chief priests and scribes, and be killed and be raised up on the third day."

And He was saying to them all, "If anyone wishes to come after Me, he must deny himself, and take up his cross daily and follow Me. For whoever wishes to save his life will lose it, but whoever loses his life for My sake, he is the one who will save it.

"For what is a man profited if he gains the whole world, and loses or forfeits himself?

"For whoever is ashamed of Me and My words, the **Son of Man** will be ashamed of him when He comes in His glory, and the glory of the Father and of the holy angels." *Luke 9:18-26*

They were all amazed at the greatness of God. But while everyone was marveling at all that He was doing, He said to His disciples, "Let these words sink into your ears; for the **Son of Man** is going to be delivered into the hands of men."

But they did not understand this statement, and it was concealed from them so that they would not perceive it; and they were afraid to ask Him about this statement. *Luke 9:43-45*

When the days were approaching for His ascension, He was determined to go to Jerusalem; and He sent messengers on ahead of Him, and they went and entered a village of the Samaritans to make arrangements for Him. But they did not receive Him, because He was traveling toward Jerusalem.

When His disciples James and John saw this, they said, "Lord, do You want us to command fire to come down from heaven and consume them?"

But He turned and rebuked them, [and said, "You do not know what kind of spirit you are of; for the **Son of Man** did not come to destroy men's lives, but to save them."]

And they went on to another village. As they were going along the road, someone said to Him, "I will follow You wherever You go."

And Jesus said to him, "The foxes have holes and the birds of the air have nests, but the **Son of Man** has nowhere to lay His head." *Luke 9:51-58*

As the crowds were increasing, He began to say, "This generation is a wicked generation; it seeks for a sign, and yet no sign will be given to it but the sign of Jonah.

"For just as Jonah became a sign to the Ninevites, so will the **Son of Man** be to this generation." *Luke 11:29-30*

I say to you, everyone who confesses Me before men, the **Son of Man** will confess him also before the angels of God; but he who denies Me before men will be denied before the angels of God.

And everyone who speaks a word against the **Son of Man**, it will be forgiven him; but he who blasphemes against the Holy Spirit, it will not be forgiven him.

Luke 12:8-10

"Be dressed in readiness, and keep your lamps lit. Be like men who are waiting for their master when he returns from the wedding feast, so that they may immediately open the door to him when he comes and knocks.

"Blessed are those slaves whom the master will find on the alert when he comes; truly I say to you, that he will gird himself to serve, and have them recline at the table, and will come up and wait on them.

"Whether he comes in the second watch, or even in the third, and finds them so, blessed are those slaves.

"But be sure of this, that if the head of the house had known at what hour the thief was coming, he would not have allowed his house to be broken into.

"You too, be ready; for the **Son of Man** is coming at an hour that you do not expect."

Peter said, "Lord, are You addressing this parable to us, or to everyone else as well?"

And the Lord said, "Who then is the faithful and sensible steward, whom his master will put in charge of his servants, to give them their rations at the proper time?

"Blessed is that slave whom his master finds so doing when he comes. Truly I say to you that he will put him in charge of all his possessions." *Luke 12:35-44*

Having been questioned by the Pharisees as to when the kingdom of God was coming, He answered them and said, "The kingdom of God is not coming with signs to be observed; nor will they say, 'Look, here it is!' or, 'There it is!' for behold, the kingdom of God is in your midst."

And He said to the disciples, "The days will come when you will long to see one of the days of the **Son of Man**, and you will not see it.

"They will say to you, 'Look there! Look here!' Do not go away, and do not run after them. For just like the lightning, when it flashes out of one part of the sky, shines to the other part of the sky, so will the **Son of Man** be in His day.

"But first He must suffer many things and be rejected by this generation.

"And just as it happened in the days of Noah, so it will be also in the days of the **Son of Man**: they were eating, they were drinking, they were marrying, they were being given in marriage, until the day that Noah entered the ark, and the flood came and destroyed them all.

"It was the same as happened in the days of Lot: they were eating, they were drinking, they were buying, they were selling, they were planting, they were building; but on the day that Lot went out from Sodom it rained fire and brimstone from heaven and destroyed them all.

"It will be just the same on the day that the **Son of Man** is revealed."

Luke 17:20-30

The Lord said, "Hear what the unrighteous judge said; now, will not God bring about justice for His elect who cry to Him day and night, and will He delay long over them? I tell you that He will bring about justice for them quickly.

"However, when the **Son of Man** comes, will He find faith on the earth?"

Luke 18:6-8

He took the twelve aside and said to them, "Behold, we are going up to Jerusalem, and all things which are written through the prophets about the **Son of Man** will be accomplished.

"For He will be handed over to the Gentiles, and will be mocked and mistreated and spit upon, and after they have scourged Him, they will kill Him; and the third day He will rise again."

But the disciples understood none of these things, and the meaning of this statement was hidden from them, and they did not comprehend the things that were said. *Luke 18:31-34*

He entered Jericho and was passing through. And there was a man called by the name of Zaccheus; he was a chief tax collector and he was rich. Zaccheus was trying to see who Jesus was, and was unable because of the crowd, for he was small in stature.

So he ran on ahead and climbed up into a sycamore tree in order to see Him, for He was about to pass through that way.

When Jesus came to the place, He looked up and said to him, "Zaccheus, hurry and come down, for today I must stay at your house."

And he hurried and came down and received Him gladly.

When they saw it, they all began to grumble, saying, "He has gone to be the guest of a man who is a sinner."

Zaccheus stopped and said to the Lord, "Behold, Lord, half of my possessions I will give to the poor, and if I have defrauded anyone of anything, I will give back four times as much."

And Jesus said to him, "Today salvation has come to this house, because he, too, is a son of Abraham. For the **Son of Man** has come to seek and to save that which was lost." *Luke 19:1-10*

By your endurance you will gain your lives.

But when you see Jerusalem surrounded by armies, then recognize that her desolation is near.

Then those who are in Judea must flee to the mountains, and those who are in the midst of the city must leave, and those who are in the country must not enter the city; because these are days of vengeance, so that all things which are written will be fulfilled.

Woe to those who are pregnant and to those who are nursing babies in those days; for there will be great distress upon the land and wrath to this people; and they will fall by the edge of the sword, and will be led captive into all the nations; and Jerusalem will be trampled under foot by the Gentiles until the times of the Gentiles are fulfilled.

There will be signs in sun and moon and stars, and on the earth dismay among nations, in perplexity at the roaring of the sea and the waves, men fainting from fear and the expectation of the things which are coming upon the world; for the powers of the heavens will be shaken.

Then they will see the **Son of Man** coming in a cloud with power and great glory.

But when these things begin to take place, straighten up and lift up your heads, because your redemption is drawing near. *Luke 21:19-28*

Be on guard, so that your hearts will not be weighted down with dissipation and drunkenness and the worries of life, and that day will not come on you suddenly like a trap; for it will come upon all those who dwell on the face of all the earth.

But keep on the alert at all times, praying that you may have strength to escape all these things that are about to take place, and to stand before the **Son of Man**. *Luke 21:34-36*

When the hour had come, He reclined at the table, and the apostles with Him.

And He said to them, "I have earnestly desired to eat this Passover with you before I suffer; for I say to you, I shall never again eat it until it is fulfilled in the kingdom of God."

And when He had taken a cup and given thanks, He said, "Take this and share it among yourselves; for I say to you, I will not drink of the fruit of the vine from now on until the kingdom of God comes."

And when He had taken some bread and given thanks, He broke it and gave it to them, saying, "This is My body which is given for you; do this in remembrance of Me."

And in the same way He took the cup after they had eaten, saying, "This cup which is poured out for you is the new covenant in My blood.

"But behold, the hand of the one betraying Me is with Mine on the table. For indeed, the **Son of Man** is going as it has been determined; but woe to that man by whom He is betrayed!"

And they began to discuss among themselves which one of them it might be who was going to do this thing.

Luke 22:14-23

When He rose from prayer, He came to the disciples and found them sleeping from sorrow, and said to them, "Why are you sleeping? Get up and pray that you may not enter into temptation."

While He was still speaking, behold, a crowd came, and the one called Judas, one of the twelve, was preceding them; and he approached Jesus to kiss Him.

But Jesus said to him, "Judas, are you betraying the **Son of Man** with a kiss?"

Luke 22:45-48

When it was day, the Council of elders of the people assembled, both chief priests and scribes, and they led Him away to their council chamber, saying, "If You are the Christ, tell us."

But He said to them, "If I tell you, you will not believe; and if I ask a question, you will not answer. But from now on the **Son of Man** will be seated at the right hand of the power of God."

And they all said, "Are You the Son of God, then?"

And He said to them, "Yes, I am."

Then they said, "What further need do we have of testimony? For we have heard it ourselves from His own mouth."

Then the whole body of them got up and brought Him before Pilate.

Luke 22:66 - 23:1

On the first day of the week, at early dawn, they came to the tomb bringing the spices which they had prepared.

And they found the stone rolled away from the tomb, but when they entered, they did not find the body of the Lord Jesus.

While they were perplexed about this, behold, two men suddenly stood near them in dazzling clothing; and as the women were terrified and bowed their faces to the ground, the men said to them, "Why do you seek the living One among the dead? He is not here, but He has risen.

"Remember how He spoke to you while He was still in Galilee, saying that the **Son of Man** must be delivered into the hands of sinful men, and be crucified, and the third day rise again."

And they remembered His words, and returned from the tomb and reported all these things to the eleven and to all the rest.

Luke 24:1-9

Jesus saw Nathanael coming to Him, and said of him, "Behold, an Israelite indeed, in whom there is no deceit!"

Nathanael said to Him, "How do You know me?"

Jesus answered and said to him, "Before Philip called you, when you were under the fig tree, I saw you."

Nathanael answered Him, "Rabbi, You are the Son of God; You are the King of Israel."

Jesus answered and said to him, "Because I said to you that I saw you under the fig tree, do you believe? You will see greater things than these."

And He said to him, "Truly, truly, I say to you, you will see the heavens opened and the angels of God ascending and descending on the **Son of Man**."

John 1:47-51

Truly, truly, I say to you, we speak of what we know and testify of what we have seen, and you do not accept our testimony.

If I told you earthly things and you do not believe, how will you believe if I tell you heavenly things?

No one has ascended into heaven, but He who descended from heaven: The **Son of Man**.

As Moses lifted up the serpent in the wilderness, even so must the **Son of Man** be lifted up; so that whoever believes will in Him have eternal life.

John 3:11-15

Truly, truly, I say to you, he who hears My word, and believes Him who sent Me, has eternal life, and does not come into judgment, but has passed out of death into life.

Truly, truly, I say to you, an hour is coming and now is, when the dead will hear the voice of the Son of God, and those who hear will live.

For just as the Father has life in Himself, even so He gave to the Son also to have life in Himself; and He gave Him authority to execute judgment, because He is the **Son of Man**.

Do not marvel at this; for an hour is coming, in which all who are in the tombs will hear His voice, and will come forth; those who did the good deeds to a resurrection of life, those who committed the evil deeds to a resurrection of judgment.

John 5:24-29

When the crowd saw that Jesus was not there, nor His disciples, they themselves got into the small boats, and came to Capernaum seeking Jesus.

When they found Him on the other side of the sea, they said to Him, "Rabbi, when did You get here?"

Jesus answered them and said, "Truly, truly, I say to you, you seek Me, not because you saw signs, but because you ate of the loaves and were filled.

"Do not work for the food which perishes, but for the food which endures to eternal life, which the **Son of Man** will give to you, for on Him the Father, God, has set His seal."

Therefore they said to Him, "What shall we do, so that we may work the works of God?"

Jesus answered and said to them, "This is the work of God, that you believe in Him whom He has sent." *John 6:24-27*

"Truly, truly, I say to you, he who believes has eternal life. I am the bread of life. Your fathers ate the manna in the wilderness, and they died.

"This is the bread which comes down out of heaven, so that one may eat of it and not die.

"I am the living bread that came down out of heaven; if anyone eats of this bread, he will live forever; and the bread also which I will give for the life of the world is My flesh."

Then the Jews began to argue with one another, saying, "How can this man give us His flesh to eat?"

So Jesus said to them, "Truly, truly, I say to you, unless you eat the flesh of the **Son of Man** and drink His blood, you have no life in yourselves.

"He who eats My flesh and drinks My blood has eternal life, and I will raise him up on the last day.

"For My flesh is true food, and My blood is true drink. He who eats My flesh and drinks My blood abides in Me, and I in him.

"As the living Father sent Me, and I live because of the Father, so he who eats Me, he also will live because of Me.

"This is the bread which came down out of heaven; not as the fathers ate and died; he who eats this bread will live forever."

These things He said in the synagogue as He taught in Capernaum. Therefore many of His disciples, when they heard this said, "This is a difficult statement; who can listen to it?"

But Jesus, conscious that His disciples grumbled at this, said to them, "Does this cause you to stumble? What then if you see the **Son of Man** ascending to where He was before?

"It is the Spirit who gives life; the flesh profits nothing; the words that I have spoken to you are spirit and are life. But there are some of you who do not believe."

For Jesus knew from the beginning who they were who did not believe, and who it was that would betray Him.

John 6:47-64

He was saying to them, "You are from below, I am from above; you are of this world, I am not of this world.

"Therefore I said to you that you will die in your sins; for unless you believe that I am He, you will die in your sins."

So they were saying to Him, "Who are You?"

Jesus said to them, "What have I been saying to you from the beginning? I have many things to speak and to judge concerning you, but He who sent Me is true; and the things which I heard from Him, these I speak to the world."

They did not realize that He had been speaking to them about the Father.

So Jesus said, "When you lift up the **Son of Man**, then you will know that I am He, and I do nothing on My own initiative, but I speak these things as the Father taught Me.

"And He who sent Me is with Me; He has not left Me alone, for I always do the things that are pleasing to Him."

As He spoke these things, many came to believe in Him. *John 8:23-30*

"We know that God does not hear sinners; but if anyone is God-fearing and does His will, He hears him.

"Since the beginning of time it has never been heard that anyone opened the eyes of a person born blind. If this man were not from God, He could do nothing."

They answered him, "You were born entirely in sins, and are you teaching us?" So they put him out.

Jesus heard that they had put him out, and finding him, He said, "Do you believe in the **Son of Man**?"

He answered, "Who is He, Lord, that I may believe in Him?"

Jesus said to him, "You have both seen Him, and He is the one who is talking with you."

And he said, "Lord, I believe." And he worshiped Him. *John 9:31-38*

There were some Greeks among those who were going up to worship at the feast; these then came to Philip, who was from Bethsaida of Galilee, and began to ask him, saying, "Sir, we wish to see Jesus."

Philip came and told Andrew; Andrew and Philip came and told Jesus.

And Jesus answered them, saying, "The hour has come for the **Son of Man** to be glorified. Truly, truly, I say to you, unless a grain of wheat falls into the earth and dies, it remains alone; but if it dies, it bears much fruit.

"He who loves his life loses it, and he who hates his life in this world will keep it to life eternal.

"If anyone serves Me, he must follow Me; and where I am, there My servant will be also; if anyone serves Me, the Father will honor him.

"Now My soul has become troubled; and what shall I say, 'Father, save Me from this hour'? But for this purpose I came to this hour. Father, glorify Your name."

Then a voice came out of heaven: "I have both glorified it, and will glorify it again."

So the crowd of people who stood by and heard it were saying that it had thundered; others were saying, "An angel has spoken to Him."

Jesus answered and said, "This voice has not come for My sake, but for your sakes.

"Now judgment is upon this world; now the ruler of this world will be cast out. And I, if I am lifted up from the earth, will draw all men to Myself."

But He was saying this to indicate the kind of death by which He was to die.

The crowd then answered Him, "We have heard out of the Law that the Christ is to remain forever; and how can You say, 'The **Son of Man** must be lifted up'? Who is this **Son of Man**?"

So Jesus said to them, "For a little while longer the Light is among you. Walk while you have the Light, so that darkness will not overtake you; he who walks in the darkness does not know where he goes.

"While you have the Light, believe in the Light, so that you may become sons of Light."

These things Jesus spoke, and He went away and hid Himself from them.
John 12:20-36

"I do not speak of all of you. I know the ones I have chosen; but it is that the Scripture may be fulfilled, 'He who eats My bread has lifted up his heel against

Me.' From now on I am telling you before it comes to pass, so that when it does occur, you may believe that I am He.

"Truly, truly, I say to you, he who receives whomever I send receives Me; and he who receives Me receives Him who sent Me."

When Jesus had said this, He became troubled in spirit, and testified and said, "Truly, truly, I say to you, that one of you will betray Me."

The disciples began looking at one another, at a loss to know of which one He was speaking.

There was reclining on Jesus' bosom one of His disciples, whom Jesus loved. So Simon Peter gestured to him, and said to him, "Tell us who it is of whom He is speaking."

He, leaning back thus on Jesus' bosom, said to Him, "Lord, who is it?"

Jesus then answered, "That is the one for whom I shall dip the morsel and give it to him."

So when He had dipped the morsel, He took and gave it to Judas, the son of Simon Iscariot.

After the morsel, Satan then entered into him. Therefore Jesus said to him, "What you do, do quickly."

Now no one of those reclining at the table knew for what purpose He had said this to him. For some were supposing, because Judas had the money box, that Jesus was saying to him, "Buy the things we have need of for the feast"; or else, that he should give something to the poor.

So after receiving the morsel he went out immediately; and it was night. Therefore when he had gone out, Jesus said, "Now is the **Son of Man** glorified, and God is glorified in Him; if God is glorified in Him, God will also glorify Him in Himself, and will glorify Him immediately."

John 13:18-32

"You men who are stiff-necked and uncircumcised in heart and ears are always resisting the Holy Spirit; you are doing just as your fathers did. Which one of the prophets did your fathers not persecute? They killed those who had previously announced the coming of the Righteous One, whose betrayers and murderers you have now become; you who received the law as ordained by angels, and yet did not keep it."

Now when they heard this, they were cut to the quick, and they began gnashing their teeth at him.

But being full of the Holy Spirit, he gazed intently into heaven and saw the glory of God, and Jesus standing at the right hand of God; and he said, "Behold, I see the heavens opened up and the **Son of Man** standing at the right hand of God."

But they cried out with a loud voice, and covered their ears and rushed at him with one impulse.

When they had driven him out of the city, they began stoning him; and the witnesses laid aside their robes at the feet of a young man named Saul.

They went on stoning Stephen as he called on the Lord and said, "Lord Jesus, receive my spirit!"

Then falling on his knees, he cried out with a loud voice, "Lord, do not hold this sin against them!"

Having said this, he fell asleep.

Acts 7:51-60

One has testified somewhere, saying, "What is man, that You remember him? Or the **son of man**, that You are concerned about him?

"You have made him for a little while lower than the angels; You have crowned him with glory and honor, and have appointed him over the works of Your hands; You have put all things in subjection under his feet."

For in subjecting all things to him, He left nothing that is not subject to him. But now we do not yet see all things subjected to him. But we do see Him who was made for a little while lower than the angels, namely, Jesus, because of the suffering of death crowned with glory and honor, so that by the grace of God He might taste death for everyone.

For it was fitting for Him, for whom are all things, and through whom are all things, in bringing many sons to glory, to perfect the author of their salvation through sufferings. *Hebrews 2:6-10*

I, John, your brother and fellow partaker in the tribulation and kingdom and perseverance which are in Jesus, was on the island called Patmos because of the word of God and the testimony of Jesus.

I was in the Spirit on the Lord's day, and I heard behind me a loud voice like the sound of a trumpet, saying, "Write in a book what you see, and send it to the seven churches: to Ephesus and to Smyrna and to Pergamum and to Thyatira and to Sardis and to Philadelphia and to Laodicea."

Then I turned to see the voice that was speaking with me.

And having turned I saw seven golden lampstands; and in the middle of the lampstands I saw one like a **son of man**, clothed in a robe reaching to the feet, and girded across His chest with a golden sash. His head and His hair were white like white wool, like snow; and His eyes were like a flame of fire.

His feet were like burnished bronze, when it has been made to glow in a furnace, and His voice was like the sound of many waters.

In His right hand He held seven stars, and out of His mouth came a sharp two-edged sword; and His face was like the sun shining in its strength.

When I saw Him, I fell at His feet like a dead man.

And He placed His right hand on me, saying, "Do not be afraid; I am the first and the last, and the living One; and I was dead, and behold, I am alive forevermore, and I have the keys of death and of Hades.

"Therefore write the things which you have seen, and the things which are, and the things which will take place after these things." *Revelation 1:9-19*

I looked, and behold, a white cloud, and sitting on the cloud was one like a **son of man**, having a golden crown on His head and a sharp sickle in His hand.

And another angel came out of the temple, crying out with a loud voice to Him who sat on the cloud, "Put in your sickle and reap, for the hour to reap has come, because the harvest of the earth is ripe."

Then He who sat on the cloud swung His sickle over the earth, and the earth was reaped. *Revelation 14:14-16*

HOLY SPIRIT
/ SPIRIT OF GOD^ / SPIRIT OF THE LORD^ / SPIRIT*

Definitions

Holy Spirit   1. The Spirit of God.

2. God as present and active in the universe.

3. For most Christians, the third member of the Trinity; the "Holy Ghost".

OLD TESTAMENT

In the beginning God created the heavens and the earth.

The earth was formless and void, and darkness was over the surface of the deep, and the **Spirit of God** was moving over the surface of the waters.

Then God said, "Let there be light"; and there was light. God saw that the light was good; and God separated the light from the darkness.

God called the light day, and the darkness He called night. And there was evening and there was morning, one day.

Genesis 1:1-5

It came about, when men began to multiply on the face of the land, and daughters were born to them, that the sons of God saw that the daughters of men were beautiful; and they took wives for themselves, whomever they chose.

Then the Lord said, "My **Spirit** shall not strive with man forever, because he also is flesh; nevertheless his days shall be one hundred and twenty years."

Genesis 6:1-3

The Lord spoke to Moses, saying, "See, I have called by name Bezalel, the son of Uri, the son of Hur, of the tribe of Judah.

"I have filled him with the **Spirit of God** in wisdom, in understanding, in knowledge, and in all kinds of craftsmanship, to make artistic designs for work in gold, in silver, and in bronze, and in the cutting of stones for settings, and in the

carving of wood, that he may work in all kinds of craftsmanship.

"And behold, I Myself have appointed with him Oholiab, the son of Ahisamach, of the tribe of Dan; and in the hearts of all who are skillful I have put skill, that they may make all that I have commanded you: the tent of meeting, and the ark of testimony, and the mercy seat upon it, and all the furniture of the tent," ~

Exodus 31:1-7

Moses said to the sons of Israel, "See, the Lord has called by name Bezalel the son of Uri, the son of Hur, of the tribe of Judah.

"And He has filled him with the **Spirit of God**, in wisdom, in understanding and in knowledge and in all craftsmanship; to make designs for working in gold and in silver and in bronze, and in the cutting of stones for settings and in the carving of wood, so as to perform in every inventive work.

"He also has put in his heart to teach, both he and Oholiab, the son of Ahisamach, of the tribe of Daniel. He has filled them with skill to perform every work of an engraver and of a designer and of an embroiderer, in blue and in purple and in scarlet material, and in fine linen, and of a weaver, as performers of every work and makers of designs.

"Now Bezalel and Oholiab, and every skillful person in whom the Lord has put skill and understanding to know how to perform all the work in the construction of the sanctuary, shall perform in accordance with all that the Lord has commanded."

Then Moses called Bezalel and Oholiab and every skillful person in whom the Lord had put skill, everyone whose heart stirred him, to come to the work to perform it.   *Exodus 35:30 - 36:2*

The Lord said to Moses, "Gather for Me seventy men from the elders of Israel, whom you know to be the elders of the people and their officers and bring them to the tent of meeting, and let them take their stand there with you.

"Then I will come down and speak with you there, and I will take of the **Spirit** who is upon you, and will put Him upon them; and they shall bear the burden of the people with you, so that you will not bear it all alone."   *Numbers 11:16-17*

Moses went out and told the people the words of the Lord. Also, he gathered seventy men of the elders of the people, and stationed them around the tent.

Then the Lord came down in the cloud and spoke to him; and He took of the **Spirit** who was upon him and placed Him upon the seventy elders.

And when the **Spirit** rested upon them, they prophesied. But they did not do it again.

But two men had remained in the camp; the name of one was Eldad and the name of the other Medad. And the **Spirit** rested upon them (now they were among those who had been registered, but had not gone out to the tent), and they prophesied in the camp.

So a young man ran and told Moses and said, "Eldad and Medad are prophesying in the camp."

Then Joshua the son of Nun, the attendant of Moses from his youth, said, "Moses, my lord, restrain them."

But Moses said to him, "Are you jealous for my sake? Would that all the Lord's people were prophets, that the Lord would put His **Spirit** upon them!"

Then Moses returned to the camp, both he and the elders of Israel.
          Numbers 11:24-30

When Balaam saw that it pleased the Lord to bless Israel, he did not go as at other times to seek omens but he set his face toward the wilderness.

And Balaam lifted up his eyes and saw Israel camping tribe by tribe; and the **Spirit of God** came upon him.

He took up his discourse and said, "The oracle of Balaam the son of Beor, and the oracle of the man whose eye is opened; the oracle of him who hears the words of God, who sees the vision of the Almighty, falling down, yet having his eyes uncovered, how fair are your tents, O Jacob, your dwellings, O Israel!"
          Numbers 24:1-5

Moses spoke to the Lord, saying, "May the Lord, the God of the spirits of all flesh, appoint a man over the congregation, who will go out and come in before them, and who will lead them out and bring them in, so that the congregation of the Lord will not be like sheep which have no shepherd."

So the Lord said to Moses, "Take Joshua the son of Nun, a man in whom is the **Spirit**, and lay your hand on him; and have him stand before Eleazar the priest and before all the congregation, and commission him in their sight. You shall put some of your authority on him, in order that all the congregation of the sons of Israel may obey him.

"Moreover, he shall stand before Eleazar the priest, who shall inquire for him by the judgment of the Urim before the Lord. At his command they shall go out and at his command they shall come in, both he and the sons of Israel with him, even all the congregation."

Moses did just as the Lord commanded him; and he took Joshua and set him before Eleazar the priest and before all the congregation.

Then he laid his hands on him and commissioned him, just as the Lord had spoken through Moses.   *Numbers 27:15-23*

The sons of Israel lived among the Canaanites, the Hittites, the Amorites, the Perizzites, the Hivites, and the Jebusites;

and they took their daughters for themselves as wives, and gave their own daughters to their sons, and served their gods.

The sons of Israel did what was evil in the sight of the Lord, and forgot the Lord their God and served the Baals and the Asheroth.

Then the anger of the Lord was kindled against Israel, so that He sold them into the hands of Cushan-rishathaim king of Mesopotamia; and the sons of Israel served Cushan-rishathaim eight years.

When the sons of Israel cried to the Lord, the Lord raised up a deliverer for the sons of Israel to deliver them, Othniel the son of Kenaz, Caleb's younger brother. The **Spirit of the Lord** came upon him, and he judged Israel.

When he went out to war, the Lord gave Cushan-rishathaim king of Mesopotamia into his hand, so that he prevailed over Cushan-rishathaim.

Then the land had rest forty years. And Othniel the son of Kenaz died.
Judges 3:5-11

All the Midianites and the Amalekites and the sons of the east assembled themselves; and they crossed over and camped in the valley of Jezreel.

So the **Spirit of the Lord** came upon Gideon; and he blew a trumpet, and the Abiezrites were called together to follow him.

He sent messengers throughout Manasseh, and they also were called together to follow him; and he sent messengers to Asher, Zebulun, and Naphtali, and they came up to meet them.   *Judges 6:33-35*

The **Spirit of the Lord** came upon Jephthah, so that he passed through Gilead and Manasseh; then he passed through Mizpah of Gilead, and from Mizpah of Gilead he went on to the sons of Ammon.

Jephthah made a vow to the Lord and said, "If You will indeed give the sons of Ammon into my hand, then it shall be that whatever comes out of the doors of my house to meet me when I return in peace from the sons of Ammon, it shall

be the Lord's, and I will offer it up as a burnt offering."

So Jephthah crossed over to the sons of Ammon to fight against them; and the Lord gave them into his hand. He struck them with a very great slaughter from Aroer to the entrance of Minnith, twenty cities, and as far as Abel-keramim.

So the sons of Ammon were subdued before the sons of Israel.   *Judges 11:29-33*

The woman gave birth to a son and named him Samson; and the child grew up and the Lord blessed him.

And the **Spirit of the Lord** began to stir him in Mahaneh-dan, between Zorah and Eshtaol.   *Judges 13:24-25*

Samson went down to Timnah with his father and mother, and came as far as the vineyards of Timnah; and behold, a young lion came roaring toward him.

The **Spirit of the Lord** came upon him mightily, so that he tore him as one tears a young goat though he had nothing in his hand; but he did not tell his father or mother what he had done.   *Judges 14:5-6*

The men of the city said to him on the seventh day before the sun went down, "What is sweeter than honey? And what is stronger than a lion?"

And he said to them, "If you had not plowed with my heifer, you would not have found out my riddle."

Then the **Spirit of the Lord** came upon him mightily, and he went down to Ashkelon and killed thirty of them and took their spoil and gave the changes of clothes to those who told the riddle.

And his anger burned, and he went up to his father's house.   *Judges 14:18-19*

The Philistines went up and camped in Judah, and spread out in Lehi.

The men of Judah said, "Why have you come up against us?"

And they said, "We have come up to bind Samson in order to do to him as he did to us."

Then 3,000 men of Judah went down to the cleft of the rock of Etam and said to

Samson, "Do you not know that the Philistines are rulers over us? What then is this that you have done to us?"

And he said to them, "As they did to me, so I have done to them."

They said to him, "We have come down to bind you so that we may give you into the hands of the Philistines."

And Samson said to them, "Swear to me that you will not kill me."

So they said to him, "No, but we will bind you fast and give you into their hands; yet surely we will not kill you."

Then they bound him with two new ropes and brought him up from the rock.

When he came to Lehi, the Philistines shouted as they met him. And the **Spirit of the Lord** came upon him mightily so that the ropes that were on his arms were as flax that is burned with fire, and his bonds dropped from his hands.

He found a fresh jawbone of a donkey, so he reached out and took it and killed a thousand men with it.

Then Samson said, "With the jawbone of a donkey, heaps upon heaps, with the jawbone of a donkey I have killed a thousand men."   *Judges 15:9-16*

"Afterward you will come to the hill of God where the Philistine garrison is; and it shall be as soon as you have come there to the city, that you will meet a group of prophets coming down from the high place with harp, tambourine, flute, and a lyre before them, and they will be prophesying.

"Then the **Spirit of the Lord** will come upon you mightily, and you shall prophesy with them and be changed into another man. It shall be when these signs come to you, do for yourself what the occasion requires, for God is with you.

"And you shall go down before me to Gilgal; and behold, I will come down to you to offer burnt offerings and sacrifice peace offerings. You shall wait seven days until I come to you and show you what you should do."

Then it happened when he turned his back to leave Samuel, God changed his heart; and all those signs came about on that day.

When they came to the hill there, behold, a group of prophets met him; and the **Spirit of God** came upon him mightily, so that he prophesied among them.

It came about, when all who knew him previously saw that he prophesied now with the prophets, that the people said to one another, "What has happened to the son of Kish? Is Saul also among the prophets?"

A man there said, "Now, who is their father?" Therefore it became a proverb: "Is Saul also among the prophets?"

When he had finished prophesying, he came to the high place. *1 Samuel 10:5-13*

Behold, Saul was coming from the field behind the oxen, and he said, "What is the matter with the people that they weep?" So they related to him the words of the men of Jabesh.

Then the **Spirit of God** came upon Saul mightily when he heard these words, and he became very angry.

He took a yoke of oxen and cut them in pieces, and sent them throughout the territory of Israel by the hand of messengers, saying, "Whoever does not come out after Saul and after Samuel, so shall it be done to his oxen."

Then the dread of the Lord fell on the people, and they came out as one man.
1 Samuel 11:5-7

Jesse made seven of his sons pass before Samuel. But Samuel said to Jesse, "The Lord has not chosen these."

And Samuel said to Jesse, "Are these all the children?"

And he said, "There remains yet the youngest, and behold, he is tending the sheep."

Then Samuel said to Jesse, "Send and bring him; for we will not sit down until he comes here." So he sent and brought him in.

Now he was ruddy, with beautiful eyes and a handsome appearance.

And the Lord said, "Arise, anoint him; for this is he."

Then Samuel took the horn of oil and

anointed him in the midst of his brothers; and the **Spirit of the Lord** came mightily upon David from that day forward. And Samuel arose and went to Ramah.

Now the **Spirit of the Lord** departed from Saul, and an evil spirit from the Lord terrorized him. Saul's servants then said to him, "Behold now, an evil spirit from God is terrorizing you. Let our lord now command your servants who are before you.

"Let them seek a man who is a skillful player on the harp; and it shall come about when the evil spirit from God is on you, that he shall play the harp with his hand, and you will be well."

So Saul said to his servants, "Provide for me now a man who can play well and bring him to me."

Then one of the young men said, "Behold, I have seen a son of Jesse the Bethlehemite who is a skillful musician, a mighty man of valor, a warrior, one prudent in speech, and a handsome man; and the Lord is with him."

So Saul sent messengers to Jesse and said, "Send me your son David who is with the flock."

Jesse took a donkey loaded with bread and a jug of wine and a young goat, and sent them to Saul by David his son.   *1 Samuel 16:10-20*

David fled and escaped and came to Samuel at Ramah, and told him all that Saul had done to him. And he and Samuel went and stayed in Naioth.

It was told Saul, saying, "Behold, David is at Naioth in Ramah."

Then Saul sent messengers to take David, but when they saw the company of the prophets prophesying, with Samuel standing and presiding over them, the **Spirit of God** came upon the messengers of Saul; and they also prophesied.

When it was told Saul, he sent other messengers, and they also prophesied. So Saul sent messengers again the third time, and they also prophesied. Then he himself went to Ramah and came as far as the large well that is in Secu; and he asked and said, "Where are Samuel and David?"

And someone said, "Behold, they are at Naioth in Ramah."

He proceeded there to Naioth in Ramah; and the **Spirit of God** came upon him also, so that he went along prophesying continually until he came to Naioth in Ramah. He also stripped off his clothes, and he too prophesied before Samuel and lay down naked all that day and all that night.

Therefore they say, "Is Saul also among the prophets?"   *1 Samuel 19:18-24*

These are the last words of David.

David the son of Jesse declares, the man who was raised on high declares, the anointed of the God of Jacob, and the sweet psalmist of Israel, "The **Spirit of the Lord** spoke by me, and His word was on my tongue.

The God of Israel said, the Rock of Israel spoke to me, 'He who rules over men righteously, who rules in the fear of God, is as the light of the morning when the sun rises, a morning without clouds, when the tender grass springs out of the earth, through sunshine after rain.'

"Truly is not my house so with God? For He has made an everlasting covenant with me, ordered in all things, and secured; for all my salvation and all my desire, will He not indeed make it grow?"   *2 Samuel 23:1-5*

As Obadiah was on the way, behold, Elijah met him, and he recognized him and fell on his face and said, "Is this you, Elijah my master?"

He said to him, "It is I. Go, say to your master, 'Behold, Elijah is here.' "

He said, "What sin have I committed, that you are giving your servant into the hand of Ahab to put me to death?

"As the Lord your God lives, there is no nation or kingdom where my master has not sent to search for you; and when they said, 'He is not here,' he made the kingdom or nation swear that they could not find you. And now you are saying, 'Go, say to your master, "Behold, Elijah is here." '

"It will come about when I leave you that the **Spirit of the Lord** will carry you where I do not know; so when I come and tell Ahab and he cannot find you, he will kill me, although I your servant have feared the Lord from my youth."

1 Kings 18:7-12

Micaiah said, "Therefore, hear the word of the Lord.

"I saw the Lord sitting on His throne, and all the host of heaven standing by Him on His right and on His left.

The Lord said, 'Who will entice Ahab to go up and fall at Ramoth-gilead?' And one said this while another said that.

"Then a spirit came forward and stood before the Lord and said, 'I will entice him.'

"The Lord said to him, 'How?'

"And he said, 'I will go out and be a deceiving spirit in the mouth of all his prophets.' Then He said, 'You are to entice him and also prevail. Go and do so.'

"Now therefore, behold, the Lord has put a deceiving spirit in the mouth of all these your prophets; and the Lord has proclaimed disaster against you."

Then Zedekiah the son of Chenaanah came near and struck Micaiah on the cheek and said, "How did the **Spirit of the Lord** pass from me to speak to you?"

Micaiah said, "Behold, you shall see on that day when you enter an inner room to hide yourself."   *1 Kings 22:19-25*

When the sons of the prophets who were at Jericho opposite him saw him, they said, "The spirit of Elijah rests on Elisha."

And they came to meet him and bowed themselves to the ground before him.

They said to him, "Behold now, there are with your servants fifty strong men, please let them go and search for your master; perhaps the **Spirit of the Lord** has taken him up and cast him on some mountain or into some valley."

And he said, "You shall not send." But when they urged him until he was ashamed, he said, "Send."

They sent therefore fifty men; and they searched three days but did not find him.

They returned to him while he was staying at Jericho; and he said to them, "Did I not say to you, 'Do not go'?"

2 Kings 2:15-18

The **Spirit** came upon Amasai, who was the chief of the thirty, and he said, "We are yours, O David, and with you, O son of Jesse! Peace, peace to you, and peace to him who helps you; indeed, your God helps you!"

Then David received them and made them captains of the band.

1 Chronicles 12:18

The **Spirit of God** came on Azariah the son of Oded, and he went out to meet Asa and said to him, "Listen to me, Asa, and all Judah and Benjamin: The Lord is with you when you are with Him.

"And if you seek Him, He will let you find Him; but if you forsake Him, He will forsake you."

For many days Israel was without the true God and without a teaching priest and without law. But in their distress they turned to the Lord God of Israel, and they sought Him, and He let them find Him.

2 Chronicles 15:1-4

The king of Israel said to Jehoshaphat, Micaiah said, "Therefore, hear the word of the Lord. I saw the Lord sitting on His throne, and all the host of heaven standing on His right and on His left.

The Lord said, 'Who will entice Ahab king of Israel to go up and fall at Ramoth-gilead?' And one said this while another said that.

"Then a spirit came forward and stood before the Lord and said, 'I will entice him.'

And the Lord said to him, 'How?'

He said, 'I will go and be a deceiving spirit in the mouth of all his prophets.'

Then He said, 'You are to entice him and prevail also. Go and do so.'

"Now therefore, behold, the Lord has put a deceiving spirit in the mouth of these your prophets, for the Lord has proclaimed disaster against you."

Then Zedekiah the son of Chenaanah came near and struck Micaiah on the cheek and said, "How did the **Spirit of the Lord** pass from me to speak to you?"

Micaiah said, "Behold, you will see on that day when you enter an inner room to hide yourself." *2 Chronicles 18:18-24*

All Judah was standing before the Lord, with their infants, their wives and their children.

Then in the midst of the assembly the **Spirit of the Lord** came upon Jahaziel the son of Zechariah, the son of Benaiah, the son of Jeiel, the son of Mattaniah, the Levite of the sons of Asaph; and he said, "Listen, all Judah and the inhabitants of Jerusalem and King Jehoshaphat: Thus says the Lord to you, 'Do not fear or be dismayed because of this great multitude, for the battle is not yours but God's.

"Tomorrow go down against them. Behold, they will come up by the ascent of Ziz, and you will find them at the end of the valley in front of the wilderness of Jeruel.

'You need not fight in this battle; station yourselves, stand and see the salvation of the Lord on your behalf, O Judah and Jerusalem. Do not fear or be dismayed; tomorrow go out to face them, for the Lord is with you.' "

Jehoshaphat bowed his head with his face to the ground, and all Judah and the inhabitants of Jerusalem fell down before the Lord, worshiping the Lord.
2 Chronicles 20:13-18

When Jehoiada reached a ripe old age he died; he was one hundred and thirty years old at his death. They buried him in the city of David among the kings, because he had done well in Israel and to God and His house.

But after the death of Jehoiada the officials of Judah came and bowed down to the king, and the king listened to them.

They abandoned the house of the Lord, the God of their fathers, and served the Asherim and the idols; so wrath came upon Judah and Jerusalem for this their guilt.

Yet He sent prophets to them to bring them back to the Lord; though they testified against them, they would not listen.

Then the **Spirit of God** came on Zechariah the son of Jehoiada the priest; and he stood above the people and said to them, "Thus God has said, 'Why do you transgress the commandments of the Lord and do not prosper? Because you have forsaken the Lord, He has also forsaken you.' "

So they conspired against him and at the command of the king they stoned him to death in the court of the house of the Lord. *2 Chronicles 24:15-21*

When they made for themselves a calf of molten metal and said, "This is your God who brought you up from Egypt," and committed great blasphemies, You, in Your great compassion, did not forsake them in the wilderness; the pillar of cloud did not leave them by day, to guide them on their way, nor the pillar of fire by night, to light for them the way in which they were to go.

You gave Your good **Spirit** to instruct them, Your manna You did not withhold from their mouth, and You gave them water for their thirst.

Indeed, forty years You provided for them in the wilderness and they were not in want; their clothes did not wear out, nor did their feet swell. *Nehemiah 9:18-21*

They became disobedient and rebelled against You, and cast Your law behind their backs and killed Your prophets who had admonished them so that they might return to You, and they committed great blasphemies.

Therefore You delivered them into the hand of their oppressors who oppressed them, but when they cried to You in the time of their distress, You heard from heaven, and according to Your great compassion You gave them deliverers who delivered them from the hand of their oppressors.

But as soon as they had rest, they did evil again before You; therefore You abandoned them to the hand of their enemies, so that they ruled over them.

When they cried again to You, You heard from heaven, and many times You rescued them according to Your compassion, and admonished them in order to turn them back to Your law.

Yet they acted arrogantly and did not listen to Your commandments but sinned against Your ordinances, by which if a man observes them he shall live. And they turned a stubborn shoulder and stiffened their neck, and would not listen.

However, You bore with them for many years, and admonished them by Your **Spirit** through Your prophets, yet they would not give ear. Therefore You gave them into the hand of the peoples of the lands.

Nevertheless, in Your great compassion You did not make an end of them or forsake them, for You are a gracious and compassionate God. *Nehemiah 9:26-31*

The **Spirit of God** has made me, and the breath of the Almighty gives me life.
Job 33:4

Hide Your face from my sins and blot out all my iniquities. Create in me a clean heart, O God, and renew a steadfast spirit within me.

Do not cast me away from Your presence and do not take Your **Holy Spirit** from me.

Restore to me the joy of Your salvation and sustain me with a willing spirit. Then I will teach transgressors Your ways, and sinners will be converted to You. *Psalm 51:9-13*

They all wait for You to give them their food in due season. You give to them, they gather it up; You open Your hand, they are satisfied with good.

You hide Your face, they are dismayed; You take away their spirit, they expire and return to their dust.

You send forth Your **Spirit**, they are created; and You renew the face of the ground. *Psalm 104:27-30*

They also provoked Him to wrath at the waters of Meribah, so that it went hard with Moses on their account; because they were rebellious against His **Spirit**, he spoke rashly with his lips. *Psalm 106:32-33*

Where can I go from Your **Spirit**? Or where can I flee from Your presence?

If I ascend to heaven, You are there; if I make my bed in Sheol, behold, You are there. If I take the wings of the dawn, if I dwell in the remotest part of the sea, even there Your hand will lead me, and Your right hand will lay hold of me.
Psalm 139:7-10

Teach me to do Your will, for You are my God; let Your good **Spirit** lead me on level ground.

For the sake of Your name, O Lord, revive me. In Your righteousness bring my soul out of trouble. *Psalm 143:10-11*

Behold, the Lord, the God of hosts, will lop off the boughs with a terrible crash; those also who are tall in stature will be cut down and those who are lofty will be abased. He will cut down the thickets of the forest with an iron axe, and Lebanon will fall by the Mighty One.

Then a shoot will spring from the stem of Jesse, and a branch from his roots will bear fruit.

The **Spirit of the Lord** will rest on Him, the spirit of wisdom and understanding, the spirit of counsel and strength, the spirit of knowledge and the fear of the Lord.

And He will delight in the fear of the Lord, and He will not judge by what His eyes see, nor make a decision by what His ears hear; but with righteousness He will judge the poor, and decide with fairness for the afflicted of the earth; and He will strike the earth with the rod of His mouth, and with the breath of His lips He will slay the wicked. *Isaiah 10:33 - 11:4*

"Woe to the rebellious children," declares the Lord, "who execute a plan, but not Mine, and make an alliance, but not of My **Spirit**, in order to add sin to sin; who proceed down to Egypt without consulting Me, to take refuge in the safety of Pharaoh and to seek shelter in the shadow of Egypt!

"Therefore the safety of Pharaoh will be your shame and the shelter in the shadow of Egypt, your humiliation."

Isaiah 30:1-3

Tremble, you women who are at ease; be troubled, you complacent daughters; strip, undress and put sackcloth on your waist, beat your breasts for the pleasant fields, for the fruitful vine, for the land of my people in which thorns and briars shall come up; yea, for all the joyful houses and for the jubilant city. Because the palace has been abandoned, the populated city forsaken.

Hill and watch-tower have become caves forever, a delight for wild donkeys, a pasture for flocks; until the **Spirit** is poured out upon us from on high, and the wilderness becomes a fertile field, and the fertile field is considered as a forest.

Then justice will dwell in the wilderness and righteousness will abide in the fertile field. And the work of righteousness will be peace, and the service of righteousness, quietness and confidence forever.

Then my people will live in a peaceful habitation, and in secure dwellings and in undisturbed resting places; ~

Isaiah 32:11-18

Seek from the book of the Lord, and read: Not one of these will be missing; none will lack its mate. For His mouth has commanded, and His **Spirit** has gathered them.

He has cast the lot for them, and His hand has divided it to them by line. They shall possess it forever; from generation to generation they will dwell in it.

Isaiah 34:16-17

Who has directed the **Spirit of the Lord**, or as His counselor has informed Him? With whom did He consult and who gave Him understanding?

And who taught Him in the path of justice and taught Him knowledge and

informed Him of the way of understanding?

Behold, the nations are like a drop from a bucket, and are regarded as a speck of dust on the scales; behold, He lifts up the islands like fine dust. Even Lebanon is not enough to burn, nor its beasts enough for a burnt offering.

All the nations are as nothing before Him, they are regarded by Him as less than nothing and meaningless.

To whom then will you liken God? Or what likeness will you compare with Him?

Isaiah 40:13-18

Behold, My Servant, whom I uphold; My chosen one in whom My soul delights. I have put My **Spirit** upon Him; He will bring forth justice to the nations.

He will not cry out or raise His voice, nor make His voice heard in the street. A bruised reed He will not break and a dimly burning wick He will not extinguish; He will faithfully bring forth justice.

He will not be disheartened or crushed until He has established justice in the earth; and the coastlands will wait expectantly for His law. *Isaiah 42:1-4*

Listen, O Jacob, My servant, and Israel, whom I have chosen: thus says the Lord who made you and formed you from the womb, who will help you, "Do not fear, O Jacob My servant; and you Jeshurun whom I have chosen.

"For I will pour out water on the thirsty land and streams on the dry ground; I will pour out My **Spirit** on your offspring and My blessing on your descendants; and they will spring up among the grass like poplars by streams of water.

"This one will say, 'I am the Lord's'; and that one will call on the name of Jacob; and another will write on his hand, 'Belonging to the Lord,' and will name Israel's name with honor." *Isaiah 44:1-5*

Come near to Me, listen to this: from the first I have not spoken in secret, from the time it took place, I was there. And now the Lord God has sent Me, and His **Spirit**.

Thus says the Lord, your Redeemer,

the Holy One of Israel, "I am the Lord your God, who teaches you to profit, who leads you in the way you should go."

Isaiah 48:16-17

"A Redeemer will come to Zion, and to those who turn from transgression in Jacob," declares the Lord.

"As for Me, this is My covenant with them," says the Lord: "My **Spirit** which is upon you, and My words which I have put in your mouth shall not depart from your mouth, nor from the mouth of your off-spring, nor from the mouth of your off-spring's offspring," says the Lord, "from now and forever.

"Arise, shine; for your light has come, and the glory of the Lord has risen upon you. For behold, darkness will cover the earth and deep darkness the peoples; but the Lord will rise upon you and His glory will appear upon you.

Nations will come to your light, and kings to the brightness of your rising."

Isaiah 59:20 - 60:3

The **Spirit of the Lord God** is upon me, because the Lord has anointed me to bring good news to the afflicted; He has sent me to bind up the brokenhearted, to proclaim liberty to captives and freedom to prisoners; to proclaim the favorable year of the Lord and the day of venge-ance of our God; to comfort all who mourn, to grant those who mourn in Zion, giving them a garland instead of ashes, the oil of gladness instead of mourning, the mantle of praise instead of a spirit of fainting.

So they will be called oaks of right-eousness, the planting of the Lord, that He may be glorified. *Isaiah 61:1-3*

I shall make mention of the lovingkind-nesses of the Lord, the praises of the Lord, according to all that the Lord has granted us, and the great goodness to-ward the house of Israel, which He has granted them according to His compas-sion and according to the abundance of His lovingkindnesses.

For He said, "Surely, they are My people, sons who will not deal falsely."

So He became their Savior. In all their affliction He was afflicted, and the angel of His presence saved them; in His love and in His mercy He redeemed them, and He lifted them and carried them all the days of old.

But they rebelled and grieved His **Holy Spirit**; therefore He turned Himself to become their enemy, He fought against them.

Then His people remembered the days of old, of Moses. Where is He who brought them up out of the sea with the shepherds of His flock?

Where is He who put His **Holy Spirit** in the midst of them, who caused His glorious arm to go at the right hand of Moses, who divided the waters before them to make for Himself an everlasting name, who led them through the depths?

Like the horse in the wilderness, they did not stumble; as the cattle which go down into the valley, the **Spirit of the Lord** gave them rest. So You led Your people, to make for Yourself a glorious name. *Isaiah 63:7-14*

He said to me, "Son of man, stand on your feet that I may speak with you!"

As He spoke to me the **Spirit** entered me and set me on my feet; and I heard Him speaking to me.

Then He said to me, "Son of man, I am sending you to the sons of Israel, to a rebellious people who have rebelled against Me; they and their fathers have transgressed against Me to this very day. I am sending you to them who are stub-born and obstinate children, and you shall say to them, 'Thus says the Lord God.'

"As for them, whether they listen or not - for they are a rebellious house - they will know that a prophet has been among them." *Ezekiel 2:1-5*

He said to me, "Son of man, take into your heart all My words which I will speak to you and listen closely. Go to the ex-iles, to the sons of your people, and speak to them and tell them, whether they listen or not, 'Thus says the Lord God.' "

Then the **Spirit** lifted me up, and I

heard a great rumbling sound behind me, "Blessed be the glory of the Lord in His place."

And I heard the sound of the wings of the living beings touching one another and the sound of the wheels beside them, even a great rumbling sound.

So the **Spirit** lifted me up and took me away; and I went embittered in the rage of my spirit, and the hand of the Lord was strong on me.

Then I came to the exiles who lived beside the river Chebar at Tel-abib, and I sat there seven days where they were living, causing consternation among them.

At the end of seven days the word of the Lord came to me, saying, "Son of man, I have appointed you a watchman to the house of Israel; whenever you hear a word from My mouth, warn them from Me." *Ezekiel 3:10-17*

The hand of the Lord was on me there, and He said to me, "Get up, go out to the plain, and there I will speak to you."

So I got up and went out to the plain; and behold, the glory of the Lord was standing there, like the glory which I saw by the river Chebar, and I fell on my face.

The **Spirit** then entered me and made me stand on my feet, and He spoke with me and said to me, "Go, shut yourself up in your house.

"As for you, son of man, they will put ropes on you and bind you with them so that you cannot go out among them.

"Moreover, I will make your tongue stick to the roof of your mouth so that you will be mute and cannot be a man who rebukes them, for they are a rebellious house.

"But when I speak to you, I will open your mouth and you will say to them, 'Thus says the Lord God.'

"He who hears, let him hear; and he who refuses, let him refuse; for they are a rebellious house." *Ezekiel 3:22-27*

It came about in the sixth year, on the fifth day of the sixth month, as I was sitting in my house with the elders of Judah sitting

before me, that the hand of the Lord God fell on me there.

Then I looked, and behold, a likeness as the appearance of a man; from His loins and downward there was the appearance of fire, and from His loins and upward the appearance of brightness, like the appearance of glowing metal.

He stretched out the form of a hand and caught me by a lock of my head; and the **Spirit** lifted me up between earth and heaven and brought me in the visions of God to Jerusalem, to the entrance of the north gate of the inner court, where the seat of the idol of jealousy, which provokes to jealousy, was located.

And behold, the glory of the God of Israel was there, like the appearance which I saw in the plain. *Ezekiel 8:1-4*

The **Spirit** lifted me up and brought me to the east gate of the Lord's house which faced eastward.

And behold, there were twenty-five men at the entrance of the gate, and among them I saw Jaazaniah son of Azzur and Pelatiah son of Benaiah, leaders of the people.

He said to me, "Son of man, these are the men who devise iniquity and give evil advice in this city, who say, 'The time is not near to build houses. This city is the pot and we are the flesh.' Therefore, prophesy against them, son of man, prophesy!"

Then the **Spirit of the Lord** fell upon me, and He said to me, "Say, 'Thus says the Lord, "So you think, house of Israel, for I know your thoughts. You have multiplied your slain in this city, filling its streets with them."

Therefore, thus says the Lord God, "Your slain whom you have laid in the midst of the city are the flesh and this city is the pot; but I will bring you out of it.

"You have feared a sword; so I will bring a sword upon you,"'" the Lord God declares. *Ezekiel 11:1-8*

The **Spirit** lifted me up and brought me in a vision by the **Spirit of God** to the exiles in Chaldea. So the vision that I had seen left me.

Then I told the exiles all the things that the Lord had shown me.

Ezekiel 11:24-25

Say to the house of Israel, "Thus says the Lord God, 'It is not for your sake, O house of Israel, that I am about to act, but for My holy name, which you have profaned among the nations where you went.

'I will vindicate the holiness of My great name which has been profaned among the nations, which you have profaned in their midst.

'Then the nations will know that I am the Lord,' declares the Lord God, 'when I prove Myself holy among you in their sight. For I will take you from the nations, gather you from all the lands and bring you into your own land.

'Then I will sprinkle clean water on you, and you will be clean; I will cleanse you from all your filthiness and from all your idols.

'Moreover, I will give you a new heart and put a new spirit within you; and I will remove the heart of stone from your flesh and give you a heart of flesh.

'I will put My **Spirit** within you and cause you to walk in My statutes, and you will be careful to observe My ordinances. You will live in the land that I gave to your forefathers; so you will be My people, and I will be your God.' " *Ezekiel 36:22-28*

The hand of the Lord was upon me, and He brought me out by the **Spirit of the Lord** and set me down in the middle of the valley; and it was full of bones. He caused me to pass among them round about, and behold, there were very many on the surface of the valley; and lo, they were very dry.

He said to me, "Son of man, can these bones live?"

And I answered, "O Lord God, You know."

Again He said to me, "Prophesy over these bones and say to them, 'O dry bones, hear the word of the Lord.'

Thus says the Lord God to these bones, 'Behold, I will cause breath to enter you that you may come to life.

"I will put sinews on you, make flesh grow back on you, cover you with skin and put breath in you that you may come alive; and you will know that I am the Lord.' "

So I prophesied as I was commanded; and as I prophesied, there was a noise, and behold, a rattling; and the bones came together, bone to its bone.

And I looked, and behold, sinews were on them, and flesh grew and skin covered them; but there was no breath in them.

Then He said to me, "Prophesy to the breath, prophesy, son of man, and say to the breath, 'Thus says the Lord God, "Come from the four winds, O breath, and breathe on these slain, that they come to life." ' "

So I prophesied as He commanded me, and the breath came into them, and they came to life and stood on their feet, an exceedingly great army.

Then He said to me, "Son of man, these bones are the whole house of Israel; behold, they say, 'Our bones are dried up and our hope has perished. We are completely cut off.'

"Therefore prophesy and say to them, 'Thus says the Lord God, "Behold, I will open your graves and cause you to come up out of your graves, My people; and I will bring you into the land of Israel.

"Then you will know that I am the Lord, when I have opened your graves and caused you to come up out of your graves, My people.

"I will put My **Spirit** within you and you will come to life, and I will place you on your own land.

"Then you will know that I, the Lord, have spoken and done it," ' " declares the Lord. *Ezekiel 37:1-14*

Thus says the Lord God, "Now I will restore the fortunes of Jacob and have mercy on the whole house of Israel; and I will be jealous for My holy name.

"They will forget their disgrace and all their treachery which they perpetrated against Me, when they live securely on their own land with no one to make them afraid.

"When I bring them back from the peoples and gather them from the lands of their enemies, then I shall be sanctified through them in the sight of the many nations.

"Then they will know that I am the Lord their God because I made them go into exile among the nations, and then gathered them again to their own land; and I will leave none of them there any longer.

"I will not hide My face from them any longer, for I will have poured out My **Spirit** on the house of Israel," declares the Lord God.   *Ezekiel 39:25-29*

He led me to the gate, the gate facing toward the east; and behold, the glory of the God of Israel was coming from the way of the east. And His voice was like the sound of many waters; and the earth shone with His glory.

And it was like the appearance of the vision which I saw, like the vision which I saw when He came to destroy the city. And the visions were like the vision which I saw by the river Chebar; and I fell on my face.

And the glory of the Lord came into the house by the way of the gate facing toward the east.

And the **Spirit** lifted me up and brought me into the inner court; and behold, the glory of the Lord filled the house.   *Ezekiel 43:1-5*

It will come about after this that I will pour out My **Spirit** on all mankind; and your sons and daughters will prophesy, your old men will dream dreams, your young men will see visions.

Even on the male and female servants I will pour out My **Spirit** in those days.

I will display wonders in the sky and on the earth, blood, fire and columns of smoke. The sun will be turned into darkness and the moon into blood before the great and awesome day of the Lord comes.   *Joel 2:28-31*

Is it being said, O house of Jacob: "Is the **Spirit of the Lord** impatient? Are these His doings?" Do not My words do good to the one walking uprightly?

Recently My people have arisen as an enemy - you strip the robe off the garment from unsuspecting passersby, from those returned from war.   *Micah 2:7-8*

The seers will be ashamed and the diviners will be embarrassed. Indeed, they will all cover their mouths because there is no answer from God.

On the other hand I am filled with power - with the **Spirit of the Lord** - and with justice and courage to make known to Jacob his rebellious act, even to Israel his sin.   *Micah 3:7-8*

"Take courage, Zerubbabel," declares the Lord, "take courage also, Joshua son of Jehozadak, the high priest, and all you people of the land take courage," declares the Lord, "and work; for I am with you," declares the Lord of hosts.

"As for the promise which I made you when you came out of Egypt, My **Spirit** is abiding in your midst; do not fear!"
                              Haggai 2:4-5

The angel who was speaking with me returned and roused me, as a man who is awakened from his sleep. He said to me, "What do you see?"

And I said, "I see, and behold, a lampstand all of gold with its bowl on the top of it, and its seven lamps on it with seven spouts belonging to each of the lamps which are on the top of it; also two olive trees by it, one on the right side of the bowl and the other on its left side."

Then I said to the angel who was speaking with me saying, "What are these, my lord?"

So the angel who was speaking with me answered and said to me, "Do you not know what these are?"

And I said, "No, my lord."

Then he said to me, "This is the word of the Lord to Zerubbabel saying, 'Not by might nor by power, but by My **Spirit**,' says the Lord of hosts."   *Zechariah 4:1-6*

The word of the Lord came to Zechariah saying, "Thus has the Lord of hosts said, 'Dispense true justice and practice kindness and compassion each to his brother; and do not oppress the widow or the orphan, the stranger or the poor; and do not devise evil in your hearts against one another.'

"But they refused to pay attention and turned a stubborn shoulder and stopped their ears from hearing. They made their hearts like flint so that they could not hear the law and the words which the Lord of hosts had sent by His **Spirit** through the former prophets; therefore great wrath came from the Lord of hosts.

"And just as He called and they would not listen, so they called and I would not listen," says the Lord of hosts; "but I scattered them with a storm wind among all the nations whom they have not known.

"Thus the land is desolated behind them so that no one went back and forth, for they made the pleasant land desolate."   *Zechariah 7:8-14*

In that day I will set about to destroy all the nations that come against Jerusalem.

I will pour out on the house of David and on the inhabitants of Jerusalem, the **Spirit** of grace and of supplication, so that they will look on Me whom they have pierced; and they will mourn for Him, as one mourns for an only son, and they will weep bitterly over Him like the bitter weeping over a firstborn.

In that day there will be great mourning in Jerusalem, like the mourning of Hadadrimmon in the plain of Megiddo.
                    Zechariah 12:9-11

"This is another thing you do: you cover the altar of the Lord with tears, with weeping and with groaning, because He no longer regards the offering or accepts it with favor from your hand.

"Yet you say, 'For what reason?' Because the Lord has been a witness between you and the wife of your youth, against whom you have dealt treacherously, though she is your companion and your wife by covenant.

"But not one has done so who has a remnant of the **Spirit**. And what did that one do while he was seeking a godly offspring?

"Take heed then to your spirit, and let no one deal treacherously against the wife of your youth. For I hate divorce," says the Lord, the God of Israel, "and him who covers his garment with wrong," says the Lord of hosts.

"So take heed to your spirit, that you do not deal treacherously." *Malachi 2:13-16*

NEW TESTAMENT

The birth of Jesus Christ was as follows: When His mother Mary had been betrothed to Joseph, before they came together she was found to be with child by the **Holy Spirit**.

And Joseph her husband, being a righteous man and not wanting to disgrace her, planned to send her away secretly.

But when he had considered this, behold, an angel of the Lord appeared to him in a dream, saying, "Joseph, son of David, do not be afraid to take Mary as your wife; for the Child who has been conceived in her is of the **Holy Spirit**.

"She will bear a Son; and you shall call His name Jesus, for He will save His people from their sins."

Now all this took place to fulfill what was spoken by the Lord through the prophet: "Behold, the virgin shall be with child and shall bear a Son, and they shall call His name Immanuel," which translated means, "God with us."   *Matthew 1:18-23*

As for me, I baptize you with water for repentance, but He who is coming after me is mightier than I, and I am not fit to remove His sandals; He will baptize you with the **Holy Spirit** and fire.

His winnowing fork is in His hand, and He will thoroughly clear His threshing floor; and He will gather His wheat into the barn, but He will burn up the chaff with unquenchable fire.

Then Jesus arrived from Galilee at the Jordan coming to John, to be baptized by him. But John tried to prevent Him, saying, "I have need to be baptized by You, and do You come to me?"

But Jesus answering said to him, "Permit it at this time; for in this way it is fitting for us to fulfill all righteousness." Then he permitted Him.

After being baptized, Jesus came up immediately from the water; and behold, the heavens were opened, and he saw the **Spirit of God** descending as a dove and lighting on Him, and behold, a voice out of the heavens said, "This is My beloved Son, in whom I am well-pleased."

Then Jesus was led up by the **Spirit** into the wilderness to be tempted by the devil.   *Matthew 3:11 - 4:1*

Behold, I send you out as sheep in the midst of wolves; so be shrewd as serpents and innocent as doves.

But beware of men, for they will hand you over to the courts and scourge you in their synagogues; and you will even be brought before governors and kings for My sake, as a testimony to them and to the Gentiles.

But when they hand you over, do not worry about how or what you are to say; for it will be given you in that hour what you are to say. For it is not you who speak, but it is the **Spirit** of your Father who speaks in you.   *Matthew 10:16-20*

This was to fulfill what was spoken through Isaiah the prophet: "Behold, My Servant whom I have chosen; My Beloved in whom My soul is well-pleased; I will put My **Spirit** upon Him, and He shall proclaim justice to the Gentiles.

"He will not quarrel, nor cry out; nor will anyone hear His voice in the streets. A battered reed He will not break off, and a smoldering wick He will not put out, until He leads justice to victory.

"And in His name the Gentiles will hope."

Then a demon-possessed man who was blind and mute was brought to Jesus, and He healed him, so that the mute man spoke and saw.

All the crowds were amazed, and were saying, "This man cannot be the Son of David, can he?"

But when the Pharisees heard this, they said, "This man casts out demons only by Beelzebul the ruler of the demons."

And knowing their thoughts Jesus said to them, "Any kingdom divided against itself is laid waste; and any city or house divided against itself will not stand. If Satan casts out Satan, he is divided against himself; how then will his kingdom stand?

"If I by Beelzebul cast out demons, by whom do your sons cast them out? For this reason they will be your judges.

"But if I cast out demons by the **Spirit of God**, then the kingdom of God has come upon you. Or how can anyone enter the strong man's house and carry off his property, unless he first binds the strong man? And then he will plunder his house.

"He who is not with Me is against Me; and he who does not gather with Me scatters.

"Therefore I say to you, any sin and blasphemy shall be forgiven people, but blasphemy against the **Spirit** shall not be forgiven.

"Whoever speaks a word against the Son of Man, it shall be forgiven him; but whoever speaks against the **Holy Spirit**, it shall not be forgiven him, either in this age or in the age to come."

Matthew 12:17-32

While the Pharisees were gathered together, Jesus asked them a question: "What do you think about the Christ, whose son is He?"

They said to Him, "The son of David."

He said to them, "Then how does David in the **Spirit** call Him 'Lord,' saying, 'The Lord said to my Lord, "Sit at My right hand, until I put Your enemies beneath Your feet" '? If David then calls Him 'Lord,' how is He his son?"

No one was able to answer Him a word, nor did anyone dare from that day on to ask Him another question.

Matthew 22:41-46

The eleven disciples proceeded to Galilee, to the mountain which Jesus had designated. When they saw Him, they worshiped Him; but some were doubtful.

And Jesus came up and spoke to them, saying, "All authority has been given to Me in heaven and on earth.

"Go therefore and make disciples of all the nations, baptizing them in the name of the Father and the Son and the **Holy Spirit**, teaching them to observe all

that I commanded you; and lo, I am with you always, even to the end of the age."

Matthew 28:16-20

John the Baptist appeared in the wilderness preaching a baptism of repentance for the forgiveness of sins. And all the country of Judea was going out to him, and all the people of Jerusalem; and they were being baptized by him in the Jordan River, confessing their sins.

John was clothed with camel's hair and wore a leather belt around his waist, and his diet was locusts and wild honey.

And he was preaching, and saying, "After me One is coming who is mightier than I, and I am not fit to stoop down and untie the thong of His sandals. I baptized you with water; but He will baptize you with the **Holy Spirit**."

In those days Jesus came from Nazareth in Galilee and was baptized by John in the Jordan.

Immediately coming up out of the water, He saw the heavens opening, and the **Spirit** like a dove descending upon Him; and a voice came out of the heavens: "You are My beloved Son, in You I am well-pleased."

Immediately the **Spirit** impelled Him to go out into the wilderness. And He was in the wilderness forty days being tempted by Satan; and He was with the wild beasts, and the angels were ministering to Him.

Mark 1:4-13

Truly I say to you, all sins shall be forgiven the sons of men, and whatever blasphemies they utter; but whoever blasphemes against the **Holy Spirit** never has forgiveness, but is guilty of an eternal sin because they were saying, "He has an unclean spirit."

Mark 3:28-30

Jesus began to say, as He taught in the temple, "How is it that the scribes say that the Christ is the son of David? David himself said in the **Holy Spirit**, 'The Lord said to my Lord, "Sit at My right hand, until I put Your enemies beneath Your feet." '

"David himself calls Him 'Lord'; so in what sense is He his son?"

And the large crowd enjoyed listening to Him.   *Mark 12:35-37*

Be on your guard; for they will deliver you to the courts, and you will be flogged in the synagogues, and you will stand before governors and kings for My sake, as a testimony to them. The gospel must first be preached to all the nations.

When they arrest you and hand you over, do not worry beforehand about what you are to say, but say whatever is given you in that hour; for it is not you who speak, but it is the **Holy Spirit**.
                                      Mark 13:9-11

An angel of the Lord appeared to him, standing to the right of the altar of incense. Zacharias was troubled when he saw the angel, and fear gripped him.

But the angel said to him, "Do not be afraid, Zacharias, for your petition has been heard, and your wife Elizabeth will bear you a son, and you will give him the name John.

"You will have joy and gladness, and many will rejoice at his birth. For he will be great in the sight of the Lord; and he will drink no wine or liquor, and he will be filled with the **Holy Spirit** while yet in his mother's womb.

"And he will turn many of the sons of Israel back to the Lord their God.

"It is he who will go as a forerunner before Him in the **Spirit** and power of Elijah, to turn the hearts of the fathers back to the children, and the disobedient to the attitude of the righteous, so as to make ready a people prepared for the Lord."

Zacharias said to the angel, "How will I know this for certain? For I am an old man and my wife is advanced in years."

The angel answered and said to him, "I am Gabriel, who stands in the presence of God, and I have been sent to speak to you and to bring you this good news."
                                      Luke 1:11-19

In the sixth month the angel Gabriel was sent from God to a city in Galilee called Nazareth, to a virgin engaged to a man whose name was Joseph, of the descendants of David; and the virgin's name was Mary.

And coming in, he said to her, "Greetings, favored one! The Lord is with you."

But she was very perplexed at this statement, and kept pondering what kind of salutation this was.

The angel said to her, "Do not be afraid, Mary; for you have found favor with God.

"And behold, you will conceive in your womb and bear a son, and you shall name Him Jesus. He will be great and will be called the Son of the Most High; and the Lord God will give Him the throne of His father David; and He will reign over the house of Jacob forever, and His kingdom will have no end."

Mary said to the angel, "How can this be, since I am a virgin?"

The angel answered and said to her, "The **Holy Spirit** will come upon you, and the power of the Most High will overshadow you; and for that reason the Holy Child shall be called the Son of God.

"And behold, even your relative Elizabeth has also conceived a son in her old age; and she who was called barren is now in her sixth month. For nothing will be impossible with God."

And Mary said, "Behold, the bondslave of the Lord; may it be done to me according to your word." And the angel departed from her.

Now at this time Mary arose and went in a hurry to the hill country, to a city of Judah, and entered the house of Zacharias and greeted Elizabeth.

When Elizabeth heard Mary's greeting, the baby leaped in her womb; and Elizabeth was filled with the **Holy Spirit**.

And she cried out with a loud voice and said, "Blessed are you among women, and blessed is the fruit of your womb!

"And how has it happened to me, that the mother of my Lord would come to me? For behold, when the sound of your greeting reached my ears, the baby leaped in my womb for joy.

"And blessed is she who believed that there would be a fulfillment of what had been spoken to her by the Lord."

And Mary said: "My soul exalts the Lord, and my spirit has rejoiced in God my Savior. For He has had regard for the humble state of His bondslave; for behold, from this time on all generations will count me blessed.

"For the Mighty One has done great things for me; and holy is His name."

Luke 1:26-49

His father Zacharias was filled with the **Holy Spirit**, and prophesied, saying: "Blessed be the Lord God of Israel, for He has visited us and accomplished redemption for His people, and has raised up a horn of salvation for us In the house of David His servant - as He spoke by the mouth of His Holy prophets from of old - salvation from our enemies, and from the hand of all who hate us; to show mercy toward our fathers, and to remember His Holy covenant, the oath which He swore to Abraham our father, to grant us that we, being rescued from the hand of our enemies, might serve Him without fear, in holiness and righteousness before Him all our days.

"And you, child, will be called the prophet of the Most High; for you will go on before the Lord to prepare His ways; to give to His people the knowledge of salvation by the forgiveness of their sins, because of the tender mercy of our God, with which the Sunrise from on high will visit us, to shine upon those who sit in darkness and the shadow of death, to guide our feet into the way of peace."

And the child continued to grow and to become strong in **Spirit**, and he lived in the deserts until the day of his public appearance to Israel. *Luke 1:67-80*

There was a man in Jerusalem whose name was Simeon; and this man was righteous and devout, looking for the consolation of Israel; and the **Holy Spirit** was upon him. And it had been revealed to him by the **Holy Spirit** that he would not see death before he had seen the Lord's Christ.

And he came in the **Spirit** into the temple; and when the parents brought in the child Jesus, to carry out for Him the custom of the Law, then he took Him into his arms, and blessed God, and said, "Now Lord, You are releasing Your bondservant to depart in peace, according to Your word; for my eyes have seen Your salvation, which You have prepared in the presence of all peoples, a Light of revelation to the Gentiles, and the glory of Your people Israel."

And His father and mother were amazed at the things which were being said about Him. *Luke 2:25-33*

While the people were in a state of expectation and all were wondering in their hearts about John, as to whether he was the Christ, John answered and said to them all, "As for me, I baptize you with water; but One is coming who is mightier than I, and I am not fit to untie the thong of His sandals; He will baptize you with the **Holy Spirit** and fire.

"His winnowing fork is in His hand to thoroughly clear His threshing floor, and to gather the wheat into His barn; but He will burn up the chaff with unquenchable fire."

So with many other exhortations he preached the gospel to the people.

Luke 3:15-18

When all the people were baptized, Jesus was also baptized, and while He was praying, heaven was opened, and the **Holy Spirit** descended upon Him in bodily form like a dove, and a voice came out of heaven, "You are My beloved Son, in You I am well-pleased." *Luke 3:21-22*

Jesus, full of the **Holy Spirit**, returned from the Jordan and was led around by the **Spirit** in the wilderness for forty days, being tempted by the devil. And He ate nothing during those days, and when they had ended, He became hungry.

And the devil said to Him, "If You are the Son of God, tell this stone to become bread."

And Jesus answered him, "It is written, 'Man shall not live on bread alone.' "

Luke 4:1-4

When the devil had finished every temptation, he left Him until an opportune time.

And Jesus returned to Galilee in the power of the **Spirit**, and news about Him spread through all the surrounding district. And He began teaching in their synagogues and was praised by all.

And He came to Nazareth, where He had been brought up; and as was His custom, He entered the synagogue on the Sabbath, and stood up to read.

And the book of the prophet Isaiah was handed to Him. And He opened the book and found the place where it was written, "The **Spirit of the Lord** is upon Me, because He anointed Me to preach the gospel to the poor.

"He has sent Me to proclaim release to the captives, and recovery of sight to the blind, to set free those who are oppressed, to proclaim the favorable year of the Lord."

And He closed the book, gave it back to the attendant and sat down; and the eyes of all in the synagogue were fixed on Him.

And He began to say to them, "Today this Scripture has been fulfilled in your hearing."

And all were speaking well of Him, and wondering at the gracious words which were falling from His lips; and they were saying, "Is this not Joseph's son?"

Luke 4:13-22

The seventy returned with joy, saying, "Lord, even the demons are subject to us in Your name."

And He said to them, "I was watching Satan fall from heaven like lightning.

"Behold, I have given you authority to tread on serpents and scorpions, and over all the power of the enemy, and nothing will injure you.

"Nevertheless do not rejoice in this, that the spirits are subject to you, but rejoice that your names are recorded in heaven."

At that very time He rejoiced greatly in the **Holy Spirit**, and said, "I praise You, O Father, Lord of heaven and earth, that You have hidden these things from the wise and intelligent and have revealed them to infants. Yes, Father, for this way was well-pleasing in Your sight."

Luke 10:17-21

He said to them, "Suppose one of you has a friend, and goes to him at midnight and says to him, 'Friend, lend me three loaves; for a friend of mine has come to me from a journey, and I have nothing to set before him'; and from inside he answers and says, 'Do not bother me; the door has already been shut and my children and I are in bed; I cannot get up and give you anything.'

"I tell you, even though he will not get up and give him anything because he is his friend, yet because of his persistence he will get up and give him as much as he needs.

"So I say to you, ask, and it will be given to you; seek, and you will find; knock, and it will be opened to you.

"For everyone who asks, receives; and he who seeks, finds; and to him who knocks, it will be opened.

"Now suppose one of you fathers is asked by his son for a fish; he will not give him a snake instead of a fish, will he? Or if he is asked for an egg, he will not give him a scorpion, will he?

"If you then, being evil, know how to give good gifts to your children, how much more will your heavenly Father give the **Holy Spirit** to those who ask Him?"

Luke 11:5-13

I say to you, everyone who confesses Me before men, the Son of Man will confess him also before the angels of God; but he who denies Me before men will be denied before the angels of God.

And everyone who speaks a word against the Son of Man, it will be forgiven him; but he who blasphemes against the **Holy Spirit**, it will not be forgiven him.

When they bring you before the synagogues and the rulers and the authorities, do not worry about how or what you are to speak in your defense, or what you are to say; for the **Holy Spirit** will teach you in that very hour what you ought to say.

Luke 12:8-12

"You are witnesses of these things. And behold, I am sending forth the promise of My Father upon you; but you are to stay in the city until you are clothed with power from on high."

And He led them out as far as Bethany, and He lifted up His hands and blessed them.
While He was blessing them, He parted from them and was carried up into heaven.

And they, after worshiping Him, returned to Jerusalem with great joy, and were continually in the temple praising God. *Luke 12:48-53*

The next day he saw Jesus coming to him and said, "Behold, the Lamb of God who takes away the sin of the world!

"This is He on behalf of whom I said, 'After me comes a Man who has a higher rank than I, for He existed before me.' I did not recognize Him, but so that He might be manifested to Israel, I came baptizing in water."

John testified saying, "I have seen the **Spirit** descending as a dove out of heaven, and He remained upon Him. I did not recognize Him, but He who sent me to baptize in water said to me, 'He upon whom you see the **Spirit** descending and remaining upon Him, this is the One who baptizes in the **Holy Spirit**.'

"I myself have seen, and have testified that this is the Son of God."

John 1:29-34

There was a man of the Pharisees, named Nicodemus, a ruler of the Jews; this man came to Jesus by night and said to Him, "Rabbi, we know that You have come from God as a teacher; for no one can do these signs that You do unless God is with him."

Jesus answered and said to him, "Truly, truly, I say to you, unless one is born again he cannot see the kingdom of God."

Nicodemus said to Him, "How can a man be born when he is old? He cannot enter a second time into his mother's womb and be born, can he?"

Jesus answered, "Truly, truly, I say to you, unless one is born of water and the **Spirit** he cannot enter into the kingdom of God. That which is born of the flesh is flesh, and that which is born of the **Spirit** is spirit.

"Do not be amazed that I said to you, 'You must be born again.' The wind blows where it wishes and you hear the sound of it, but do not know where it comes from and where it is going; so is everyone who is born of the **Spirit**."

Nicodemus said to Him, "How can these things be?"

Jesus answered and said to him, "Are you the teacher of Israel and do not understand these things?

"Truly, truly, I say to you, we speak of what we know and testify of what we have seen, and you do not accept our testimony.

"If I told you earthly things and you do not believe, how will you believe if I tell you heavenly things?" *John 3:1-12*

He who comes from above is above all, he who is of the earth is from the earth and speaks of the earth. He who comes from heaven is above all.

What He has seen and heard, of that He testifies; and no one receives His testimony.

He who has received His testimony has set his seal to this, that God is true. For He whom God has sent speaks the words of God; for He gives the **Spirit** without measure.

The Father loves the Son and has given all things into His hand. He who believes in the Son has eternal life; but he who does not obey the Son will not see life, but the wrath of God abides on him.

John 3:31-36

The woman said to Him, "Sir, I perceive that You are a prophet. Our fathers worshiped in this mountain, and you people say that in Jerusalem is the place where men ought to worship."

Jesus said to her, "Woman, believe Me, an hour is coming when neither in this mountain nor in Jerusalem will you worship the Father.

"You worship what you do not know; we worship what we know, for salvation is from the Jews.

"But an hour is coming, and now is, when the true worshipers will worship the Father in spirit and truth; for such people the Father seeks to be His worshipers. God is **spirit**, and those who worship Him must worship in spirit and truth."

The woman said to Him, "I know that Messiah is coming (He who is called Christ); when that One comes, He will declare all things to us."

Jesus said to her, "I who speak to you am He." *John 4:19-26*

"It is the **Spirit** who gives life; the flesh profits nothing; the words that I have spoken to you are spirit and are life. But there are some of you who do not believe."

For Jesus knew from the beginning who they were who did not believe, and who it was that would betray Him.
John 6:63-64

On the last day, the great day of the feast, Jesus stood and cried out, saying, "If anyone is thirsty, let him come to Me and drink. He who believes in Me, as the Scripture said, 'From his innermost being will flow rivers of living water.' "

But this He spoke of the **Spirit**, whom those who believed in Him were to receive; for the **Spirit** was not yet given, because Jesus was not yet glorified.

Some of the people therefore, when they heard these words, were saying, "This certainly is the Prophet." Others were saying, "This is the Christ."

Still others were saying, "Surely the Christ is not going to come from Galilee, is He?" *John 7:37-41*

Philip said to Him, "Lord, show us the Father, and it is enough for us."

Jesus said to him, "Have I been so long with you, and yet you have not come to know Me, Philip?

"He who has seen Me has seen the Father; how can you say, 'Show us the Father'? Do you not believe that I am in the Father, and the Father is in Me?

"The words that I say to you I do not speak on My own initiative, but the Father abiding in Me does His works.

"Believe Me that I am in the Father and the Father is in Me; otherwise believe because of the works themselves.

"Truly, truly, I say to you, he who believes in Me, the works that I do, he will do also; and greater works than these he will do; because I go to the Father.

"Whatever you ask in My name, that will I do, so that the Father may be glorified in the Son. If you ask Me anything in My name, I will do it.

"If you love Me, you will keep My commandments. I will ask the Father, and He will give you another Helper, that He may be with you forever; that is the **Spirit** of truth, whom the world cannot receive, because it does not see Him or know Him, but you know Him because He abides with you and will be in you.

"I will not leave you as orphans; I will come to you. After a little while the world will no longer see Me, but you will see Me; because I live, you will live also. In that day you will know that I am in My Father, and you in Me, and I in you.

"He who has My commandments and keeps them is the one who loves Me; and he who loves Me will be loved by My Father, and I will love him and will disclose Myself to him."

Judas (not Iscariot) said to Him, "Lord, what then has happened that You are going to disclose Yourself to us and not to the world?"

Jesus answered and said to him, "If anyone loves Me, he will keep My word; and My Father will love him, and We will come to him and make Our abode with him.

"He who does not love Me does not keep My words; and the word which you hear is not Mine, but the Father's who sent Me.

"These things I have spoken to you while abiding with you. But the Helper, the **Holy Spirit**, whom the Father will send in My name, He will teach you all things, and bring to your remembrance all that I said to you.

"Peace I leave with you; My peace I give to you; not as the world gives do I give to you.

"Do not let your heart be troubled, nor let it be fearful."   *John 14:8-27*

When the Helper comes, whom I will send to you from the Father, that is the **Spirit** of truth who proceeds from the Father, He will testify about Me, and you will testify also, because you have been with Me from the beginning.

These things I have spoken to you so that you may be kept from stumbling.

They will make you outcasts from the synagogue, but an hour is coming for everyone who kills you to think that he is offering service to God.

These things they will do because they have not known the Father or Me. But these things I have spoken to you, so that when their hour comes, you may remember that I told you of them.

These things I did not say to you at the beginning, because I was with you. But now I am going to Him who sent Me; and none of you asks Me, "Where are You going?"

But because I have said these things to you, sorrow has filled your heart.

But I tell you the truth, it is to your advantage that I go away; for if I do not go away, the Helper will not come to you; but if I go, I will send Him to you.

And He, when He comes, will convict the world concerning sin and righteousness and judgment; concerning sin, because they do not believe in Me; and concerning righteousness, because I go to the Father and you no longer see Me; and concerning judgment, because the ruler of this world has been judged.

I have many more things to say to you, but you cannot bear them now. But when He, the **Spirit** of truth, comes, He will guide you into all the truth; for He will not speak on His own initiative, but whatever He hears, He will speak; and He will disclose to you what is to come.

He will glorify Me, for He will take of Mine and will disclose it to you. All things that the Father has are Mine; therefore I said that He takes of Mine and will disclose it to you.

A little while, and you will no longer see Me; and again a little while, and you will see Me.   *John 15:26 - 16:16*

Mary Magdalene came, announcing to the disciples, "I have seen the Lord," and that He had said these things to her.

So when it was evening on that day, the first day of the week, and when the doors were shut where the disciples were, for fear of the Jews, Jesus came and stood in their midst and said to them, "Peace be with you."

And when He had said this, He showed them both His hands and His side.

The disciples then rejoiced when they saw the Lord.

So Jesus said to them again, "Peace be with you; as the Father has sent Me, I also send you."

And when He had said this, He breathed on them and said to them, "Receive the **Holy Spirit**.

"If you forgive the sins of any, their sins have been forgiven them; if you retain the sins of any, they have been retained."   *John 20:18-23*

The first account I composed, Theophilus, about all that Jesus began to do and teach, until the day when He was taken up to heaven, after He had by the **Holy Spirit** given orders to the apostles whom He had chosen.

To these He also presented Himself alive after His suffering, by many convincing proofs, appearing to them over a period of forty days and speaking of the things concerning the kingdom of God.

Gathering them together, He commanded them not to leave Jerusalem, but to wait for what the Father had promised, "Which," He said, "you heard of from Me; for John baptized with water, but you will be baptized with the **Holy Spirit** not many days from now."

So when they had come together, they were asking Him, saying, "Lord, is it at this time You are restoring the kingdom to Israel?"

He said to them, "It is not for you to know times or epochs which the Father has fixed by His own authority; but you will receive power when the **Holy Spirit** has come upon you; and you shall be My witnesses both in Jerusalem, and in all Judea and Samaria, and even to the remotest part of the earth."

And after He had said these things, He was lifted up while they were looking on, and a cloud received Him out of their sight.   *Acts 1:1-9*

At this time Peter stood up in the midst of the brethren (a gathering of about one hundred and twenty persons was there together), and said, "Brethren, the Scripture had to be fulfilled, which the **Holy Spirit** foretold by the mouth of David concerning Judas, who became a guide to those who arrested Jesus. For he was counted among us and received his share in this ministry."   *Acts 1:15-17*

When the day of Pentecost had come, they were all together in one place.

And suddenly there came from heaven a noise like a violent rushing wind, and it filled the whole house where they were sitting.

And there appeared to them tongues as of fire distributing themselves, and they rested on each one of them.

And they were all filled with the **Holy Spirit** and began to speak with other tongues, as the **Spirit** was giving them utterance.

Now there were Jews living in Jerusalem, devout men from every nation under heaven. And when this sound occurred, the crowd came together, and were bewil-

dered because each one of them was hearing them speak in his own language.

They were amazed and astonished, saying, "Why, are not all these who are speaking Galileans?

"And how is it that we each hear them in our own language to which we were born? Parthians and Medes and Elamites, and residents of Mesopotamia, Judea and Cappadocia, Pontus and Asia, Phrygia and Pamphylia, Egypt and the districts of Libya around Cyrene, and visitors from Rome, both Jews and proselytes, Cretans and Arabs - we hear them in our own tongues speaking of the mighty deeds of God."

And they all continued in amazement and great perplexity, saying to one another, "What does this mean?"

But others were mocking and saying, "They are full of sweet wine."

But Peter, taking his stand with the eleven, raised his voice and declared to them: "Men of Judea and all you who live in Jerusalem, let this be known to you and give heed to my words. For these men are not drunk, as you suppose, for it is only the third hour of the day; but this is what was spoken of through the prophet Joel: 'And it shall be in the last days,' God says, 'that I will pour forth of My **Spirit** on all mankind; and your sons and your daughters shall prophesy, and your young men shall see visions, and your old men shall dream dreams; even on My bond-slaves, both men and women, I will in those days pour forth of My **Spirit** and they shall prophesy.

'And I will grant wonders in the sky above and signs on the earth below, blood, and fire, and vapor of smoke. The sun will be turned into darkness and the moon into blood, before the great and glorious day of the Lord shall come.

"And it shall be that everyone who calls on the name of the Lord will be saved.' "   *Acts 2:1-21*

"This Jesus God raised up again, to which we are all witnesses. Therefore having been exalted to the right hand of God, and having received from the Father the promise of the **Holy Spirit**, He has poured forth this which you both see and hear.

"For it was not David who ascended into heaven, but he himself says: 'The Lord said to my Lord, "Sit at My right hand, until I make Your enemies a footstool for Your feet." '

"Therefore let all the house of Israel know for certain that God has made Him both Lord and Christ - this Jesus whom you crucified."

Now when they heard this, they were pierced to the heart, and said to Peter and the rest of the apostles, "Brethren, what shall we do?"

Peter said to them, "Repent, and each of you be baptized in the name of Jesus Christ for the forgiveness of your sins; and you will receive the gift of the **Holy Spirit**. For the promise is for you and your children and for all who are far off, as many as the Lord our God will call to Himself."

And with many other words he solemnly testified and kept on exhorting them, saying, "Be saved from this perverse generation!"   *Acts 2:32-40*

When they had placed them in the center, they began to inquire, "By what power, or in what name, have you done this?"

Then Peter, filled with the **Holy Spirit**, said to them, "Rulers and elders of the people, if we are on trial today for a benefit done to a sick man, as to how this man has been made well, it be known to all of you and to all the people of Israel, that by the name of Jesus Christ the Nazarene, whom you crucified, whom God raised from the dead - by this name this man stands here before you in good health.

"He is the stone which was rejected by you, the builders, but which became the chief corner stone.

"And there is salvation in no one else; for there is no other name under heaven that has been given among men by which we must be saved."   *Acts 4:7-12*

When they had been released, they went to their own companions and reported all that the chief priests and the elders had said to them.

And when they heard this, they lifted their voices to God with one accord and said, "O Lord, it is You who made the heaven and the earth and the sea, and all that is in them, who by the **Holy Spirit**, through the mouth of our father David Your servant, said, 'Why did the Gentiles rage, and the peoples devise futile things? The kings of the earth took their stand, and the rulers were gathered together against the Lord and against His Christ.'

"For truly in this city there were gathered together against Your Holy servant Jesus, whom You anointed, both Herod and Pontius Pilate, along with the Gentiles and the peoples of Israel, to do whatever Your hand and Your purpose predestined to occur.

"And now, Lord, take note of their threats, and grant that Your bondservants may speak Your word with all confidence, while You extend Your hand to heal, and signs and wonders take place through the name of Your Holy servant Jesus."

And when they had prayed, the place where they had gathered together was shaken, and they were all filled with the **Holy Spirit** and began to speak the word of God with boldness.   *Acts 4:23-31*

Joseph, a Levite of Cyprian birth, who was also called Barnabas by the apostles (which translated means Son of Encouragement), and who owned a tract of land, sold it and brought the money and laid it at the apostles' feet.

But a man named Ananias, with his wife Sapphira, sold a piece of property, and kept back some of the price for himself, with his wife's full knowledge, and bringing a portion of it, he laid it at the apostles' feet.

But Peter said, "Ananias, why has Satan filled your heart to lie to the **Holy Spirit** and to keep back some of the price of the land? While it remained unsold, did it not remain your own? And after it was sold, was it not under your control? Why is it that you have conceived this deed in your heart? You have not lied to men but to God."

And as he heard these words, Ananias fell down and breathed his last; and great fear came over all who heard of it.

The young men got up and covered him up, and after carrying him out, they buried him.

Now there elapsed an interval of about three hours, and his wife came in, not knowing what had happened.

And Peter responded to her, "Tell me whether you sold the land for such and such a price?"

And she said, "Yes, that was the price."

Then Peter said to her, "Why is it that you have agreed together to put the **Spirit of the Lord** to the test?

"Behold, the feet of those who have buried your husband are at the door, and they will carry you out as well."

And immediately she fell at his feet and breathed her last, and the young men came in and found her dead, and they carried her out and buried her beside her husband.

And great fear came over the whole church, and over all who heard of these things.

At the hands of the apostles many signs and wonders were taking place among the people; and they were all with one accord in Solomon's portico.

Acts 4:36 - 5:12

When they had brought them, they stood them before the Council.

The high priest questioned them, saying, "We gave you strict orders not to continue teaching in this name, and yet, you have filled Jerusalem with your teaching and intend to bring this man's blood upon us."

But Peter and the apostles answered, "We must obey God rather than men.

"The God of our fathers raised up Jesus, whom you had put to death by hanging Him on a cross.

"He is the one whom God exalted to His right hand as a Prince and a Savior,

to grant repentance to Israel, and forgiveness of sins.

"And we are witnesses of these things; and so is the **Holy Spirit**, whom God has given to those who obey Him."

But when they heard this, they were cut to the quick and intended to kill them.

Acts 5:27-33

While the disciples were increasing in number, a complaint arose on the part of the Hellenistic Jews against the native Hebrews, because their widows were being overlooked in the daily serving of food.

So the twelve summoned the congregation of the disciples and said, "It is not desirable for us to neglect the word of God in order to serve tables.

"Therefore, brethren, select from among you seven men of good reputation, full of the **Spirit** and of wisdom, whom we may put in charge of this task.

"But we will devote ourselves to prayer and to the ministry of the word."

The statement found approval with the whole congregation; and they chose Stephen, a man full of faith and of the **Holy Spirit**, and Philip, Prochorus, Nicanor, Timon, Parmenas and Nicolas, a proselyte from Antioch. And these they brought before the apostles; and after praying, they laid their hands on them.

The word of God kept on spreading; and the number of the disciples continued to increase greatly in Jerusalem, and a great many of the priests were becoming obedient to the faith.

And Stephen, full of grace and power, was performing great wonders and signs among the people.

But some men from what was called the Synagogue of the Freedmen, including both Cyrenians and Alexandrians, and some from Cilicia and Asia, rose up and argued with Stephen.

But they were unable to cope with the wisdom and the **Spirit** with which he was speaking.

Acts 6:1-10

"You men who are stiff-necked and uncircumcised in heart and ears are always resisting the **Holy Spirit**; you are doing just as your fathers did. Which one of the prophets did your fathers not persecute?

"They killed those who had previously announced the coming of the Righteous One, whose betrayers and murderers you have now become; you who received the law as ordained by angels, and yet did not keep it."

Now when they heard this, they were cut to the quick, and they began gnashing their teeth at him.

But being full of the **Holy Spirit**, he gazed intently into heaven and saw the glory of God, and Jesus standing at the right hand of God; and he said, "Behold, I see the heavens opened up and the Son of Man standing at the right hand of God."

But they cried out with a loud voice, and covered their ears and rushed at him with one impulse.

When they had driven him out of the city, they began stoning him; and the witnesses laid aside their robes at the feet of a young man named Saul.

They went on stoning Stephen as he called on the Lord and said, "Lord Jesus, receive my spirit!"

Then falling on his knees, he cried out with a loud voice, "Lord, do not hold this sin against them!"

Having said this, he fell asleep.

Acts 7:51-60

When the apostles in Jerusalem heard that Samaria had received the word of God, they sent them Peter and John, who came down and prayed for them that they might receive the **Holy Spirit**. For He had not yet fallen upon any of them; they had simply been baptized in the name of the Lord Jesus.

Then they began laying their hands on them, and they were receiving the **Holy Spirit**.

Now when Simon saw that the **Spirit** was bestowed through the laying on of the apostles' hands, he offered them money, saying, "Give this authority to me as well, so that everyone on whom I lay my hands may receive the **Holy Spirit**."

But Peter said to him, "May your sil-ver perish with you, because you thought you could obtain the gift of God with money!

"You have no part or portion in this matter, for your heart is ˋnot right before God. Therefore repent of this wickedness of yours, and pray the Lord that, if possible, the intention of your heart may be forgiven you. For I see that you are in the gall of bitterness and in the bondage of iniquity."

But Simon answered and said, "Pray to the Lord for me yourselves, so that nothing of what you have said may come upon me."

So, when they had solemnly testified and spoken the word of the Lord, they started back to Jerusalem, and were preaching the gospel to many villages of the Samaritans.

But an angel of the Lord spoke to Philip saying, "Get up and go south to the road that descends from Jerusalem to Gaza." (This is a desert road.)

So he got up and went; and there was an Ethiopian eunuch, a court official of Candace, queen of the Ethiopians, who was in charge of all her treasure; and he had come to Jerusalem to worship, and he was returning and sitting in his chariot, and was reading the prophet Isaiah.

Then the **Spirit** said to Philip, "Go up and join this chariot."

Philip ran up and heard him reading Isaiah the prophet, and said, "Do you understand what you are reading?"

And he said, "Well, how could I, unless someone guides me?" And he invited Philip to come up and sit with him.

Now the passage of Scripture which he was reading was this: "He was led as a sheep to slaughter; and as a lamb before its shearer is silent, so He does not open His mouth. In humiliation His judgment was taken away; who will relate His generation? For His life is removed from the earth."

The eunuch answered Philip and said, "Please tell me, of whom does the prophet say this? Of himself or of someone else?"

Then Philip opened his mouth, and beginning from this Scripture he preached Jesus to him.

As they went along the road they came to some water; and the eunuch said, "Look! Water! What prevents me from being baptized?"

[And Philip said, "If you believe with all your heart, you may."

And he answered and said, "I believe that Jesus Christ is the Son of God."]

And he ordered the chariot to stop; and they both went down into the water, Philip as well as the eunuch, and he baptized him.

When they came up out of the water, the **Spirit of the Lord** snatched Philip away; and the eunuch no longer saw him, but went on his way rejoicing.

But Philip found himself at Azotus, and as he passed through he kept preaching the gospel to all the cities until he came to Caesarea.   *Acts 8:14-40*

There was a disciple at Damascus named Ananias; and the Lord said to him in a vision, "Ananias."

And he said, "Here I am, Lord."

And the Lord said to him, "Get up and go to the street called Straight, and inquire at the house of Judas for a man from Tarsus named Saul, for he is praying, and he has seen in a vision a man named Ananias come in and lay his hands on him, so that he might regain his sight."

But Ananias answered, "Lord, I have heard from many about this man, how much harm he did to Your saints at Jerusalem; and here he has authority from the chief priests to bind all who call on Your name."

But the Lord said to him, "Go, for he is a chosen instrument of Mine, to bear My name before the Gentiles and kings and the sons of Israel; for I will show him how much he must suffer for My name's sake."

So Ananias departed and entered the house, and after laying his hands on him said, "Brother Saul, the Lord Jesus, who appeared to you on the road by which you were coming, has sent me so that you may regain your sight and be filled with the **Holy Spirit**."

And immediately there fell from his eyes something like scales, and he regained his sight, and he got up and was baptized; and he took food and was strengthened.

Now for several days he was with the disciples who were at Damascus, and immediately he began to proclaim Jesus in the synagogues, saying, "He is the Son of God."   *Acts 9:10-20*

The church throughout all Judea and Galilee and Samaria enjoyed peace, being built up; and going on in the fear of the Lord and in the comfort of the **Holy Spirit**, it continued to increase.   *Acts 9:31*

While Peter was greatly perplexed in mind as to what the vision which he had seen might be, behold, the men who had been sent by Cornelius, having asked directions for Simon's house, appeared at the gate; and calling out, they were asking whether Simon, who was also called Peter, was staying there.

While Peter was reflecting on the vision, the **Spirit** said to him, "Behold, three men are looking for you. But get up, go downstairs and accompany them without misgivings, for I have sent them Myself."

Peter went down to the men and said, "Behold, I am the one you are looking for; what is the reason for which you have come?"

They said, "Cornelius, a centurion, a righteous and God-fearing man well spoken of by the entire nation of the Jews, was divinely directed by a holy angel to send for you to come to his house and hear a message from you."   *Acts 10:17-22*

Opening his mouth, Peter said: "I most certainly understand now that God is not one to show partiality, but in every nation the man who fears Him and does what is right is welcome to Him.

"The word which He sent to the sons of Israel, preaching peace through Jesus

Christ (He is Lord of all) - you yourselves know the thing which took place throughout all Judea, starting from Galilee, after the baptism which John proclaimed.

"You know of Jesus of Nazareth, how God anointed Him with the **Holy Spirit** and with power, and how He went about doing good and healing all who were oppressed by the devil, for God was with Him.

"We are witnesses of all the things He did both in the land of the Jews and in Jerusalem. They also put Him to death by hanging Him on a cross. " *Acts 10:34-39*

While Peter was still speaking these words, the **Holy Spirit** fell upon all those who were listening to the message.

All the circumcised believers who came with Peter were amazed, because the gift of the **Holy Spirit** had been poured out on the Gentiles also. For they were hearing them speaking with tongues and exalting God.

Then Peter answered, "Surely no one can refuse the water for these to be baptized who have received the **Holy Spirit** just as we did, can he?"

And he ordered them to be baptized in the name of Jesus Christ. Then they asked him to stay on for a few days.
Acts 10:44-48

"At that moment three men appeared at the house in which we were staying, having been sent to me from Caesarea. The **Spirit** told me to go with them without misgivings. These six brethren also went with me and we entered the man's house.

"And he reported to us how he had seen the angel standing in his house, and saying, 'Send to Joppa and have Simon, who is also called Peter, brought here; and he will speak words to you by which you will be saved, you and all your household.'

"And as I began to speak, the **Holy Spirit** fell upon them just as He did upon us at the beginning.

"And I remembered the word of the Lord, how He used to say, 'John baptized with water, but you will be baptized with the **Holy Spirit**.'

"Therefore if God gave to them the same gift as He gave to us also after believing in the Lord Jesus Christ, who was I that I could stand in God's way?"

When they heard this, they quieted down and glorified God, saying, "Well then, God has granted to the Gentiles also the repentance that leads to life."
Acts 11:11-18:5

The hand of the Lord was with them, and a large number who believed turned to the Lord. The news about them reached the ears of the church at Jerusalem, and they sent Barnabas off to Antioch.

Then when he arrived and witnessed the grace of God, he rejoiced and began to encourage them all with resolute heart to remain true to the Lord; for he was a good man, and full of the **Holy Spirit** and of faith. And considerable numbers were brought to the Lord.

And he left for Tarsus to look for Saul; and when he had found him, he brought him to Antioch. And for an entire year they met with the church and taught considerable numbers; and the disciples were first called Christians in Antioch.

Now at this time some prophets came down from Jerusalem to Antioch. One of them named Agabus stood up and began to indicate by the **Spirit** that there would certainly be a great famine all over the world. And this took place in the reign of Claudius.

And in the proportion that any of the disciples had means, each of them determined to send a contribution for the relief of the brethren living in Judea.

And this they did, sending it in charge of Barnabas and Saul to the elders.
Acts 11:21-30

There were at Antioch, in the church that was there, prophets and teachers: Barnabas, and Simeon who was called Niger, and Lucius of Cyrene, and Manaen who had been brought up with Herod the tetrarch, and Saul.

While they were ministering to the Lord and fasting, the **Holy Spirit** said, "Set apart for Me Barnabas and Saul for the work to which I have called them."

Then, when they had fasted and prayed and laid their hands on them, they sent them away.

So, being sent out by the **Holy Spirit**, they went down to Seleucia and from there they sailed to Cyprus.

When they reached Salamis, they began to proclaim the word of God in the synagogues of the Jews; and they also had John as their helper.

When they had gone through the whole island as far as Paphos, they found a magician, a Jewish false prophet whose name was Bar-Jesus, who was with the proconsul, Sergius Paulus, a man of intelligence.

This man summoned Barnabas and Saul and sought to hear the word of God. But Elymas the magician (for so his name is translated) was opposing them, seeking to turn the proconsul away from the faith.

But Saul, who was also known as Paul, filled with the **Holy Spirit**, fixed his gaze on him, and said, "You who are full of all deceit and fraud, you son of the devil, you enemy of all righteousness, will you not cease to make crooked the straight ways of the Lord?

"Now, behold, the hand of the Lord is upon you, and you will be blind and not see the sun for a time."

And immediately a mist and a darkness fell upon him, and he went about seeking those who would lead him by the hand.

Then the proconsul believed when he saw what had happened, being amazed at the teaching of the Lord. *Acts 13:1-12*

The Jews incited the devout women of prominence and the leading men of the city, and instigated a persecution against Paul and Barnabas, and drove them out of their district. But they shook off the dust of their feet in protest against them and went to Iconium.

And the disciples were continually filled with joy and with the **Holy Spirit**. *Acts 13:50-52*

When they arrived at Jerusalem, they were received by the church and the apostles and the elders, and they reported all that God had done with them.

But some of the sect of the Pharisees who had believed stood up, saying, "It is necessary to circumcise them and to direct them to observe the Law of Moses."

The apostles and the elders came together to look into this matter.

After there had been much debate, Peter stood up and said to them, "Brethren, you know that in the early days God made a choice among you, that by my mouth the Gentiles would hear the word of the gospel and believe.

"And God, who knows the heart, testified to them giving them the **Holy Spirit**, just as He also did to us; and He made no distinction between us and them, cleansing their hearts by faith." *Acts 15:4-9*

We have sent Judas and Silas, who themselves will also report the same things by word of mouth.

For it seemed good to the **Holy Spirit** and to us to lay upon you no greater burden than these essentials: that you abstain from things sacrificed to idols and from blood and from things strangled and from fornication; if you keep yourselves free from such things, you will do well. ~ *Acts 15:27-29*

While they were passing through the cities, they were delivering the decrees which had been decided upon by the apostles and elders who were in Jerusalem, for them to observe. So the churches were being strengthened in the faith, and were increasing in number daily.

They passed through the Phrygian and Galatian region, having been forbidden by the **Holy Spirit** to speak the word in Asia; and after they came to Mysia, they were trying to go into Bithynia, and the **Spirit** of Jesus did not permit them; and passing by Mysia, they came down to Troas. *Acts 16:4-8*

It happened that while Apollos was at Corinth, Paul passed through the upper country and came to Ephesus, and found some disciples.

He said to them, "Did you receive the **Holy Spirit** when you believed?"

And they said to him, "No, we have not even heard whether there is a **Holy Spirit**."

And he said, "Into what then were you baptized?"

And they said, "Into John's baptism."

Paul said, "John baptized with the baptism of repentance, telling the people to believe in Him who was coming after him, that is, in Jesus."

When they heard this, they were baptized in the name of the Lord Jesus.

And when Paul had laid his hands upon them, the **Holy Spirit** came on them, and they began speaking with tongues and prophesying. There were in all about twelve men.   *Acts 19:1-7*

The word of the Lord was growing mightily and prevailing.

Now after these things were finished, Paul purposed in the **Spirit** to go to Jerusalem after he had passed through Macedonia and Achaia, saying, "After I have been there, I must also see Rome."   *Acts 19:20-21*

Behold, bound by the **Spirit**, I am on my way to Jerusalem, not knowing what will happen to me there, except that the **Holy Spirit** solemnly testifies to me in every city, saying that bonds and afflictions await me.

But I do not consider my life of any account as dear to myself, so that I may finish my course and the ministry which I received from the Lord Jesus, to testify solemnly of the gospel of the grace of God.   *Acts 20:22-24*

Be on guard for yourselves and for all the flock, among which the **Holy Spirit** has made you overseers, to shepherd the church of God which He purchased with His own blood.   *Acts 20:28*

When we came in sight of Cyprus, leaving it on the left, we kept sailing to Syria and landed at Tyre; for there the ship was to unload its cargo.

After looking up the disciples, we stayed there seven days; and they kept telling Paul through the **Spirit** not to set foot in Jerusalem.

When our days there were ended, we left and started on our journey, while they all, with wives and children, escorted us until we were out of the city.

After kneeling down on the beach and praying, we said farewell to one another. Then we went on board the ship, and they returned home again.

When we had finished the voyage from Tyre, we arrived at Ptolemais, and after greeting the brethren, we stayed with them for a day.

On the next day we left and came to Caesarea, and entering the house of Philip the evangelist, who was one of the seven, we stayed with him. Now this man had four virgin daughters who were prophetesses.

As we were staying there for some days, a prophet named Agabus came down from Judea.

And coming to us, he took Paul's belt and bound his own feet and hands, and said, "This is what the **Holy Spirit** says: 'In this way the Jews at Jerusalem will bind the man who owns this belt and deliver him into the hands of the Gentiles.' "

When we had heard this, we as well as the local residents began begging him not to go up to Jerusalem.

Then Paul answered, "What are you doing, weeping and breaking my heart? For I am ready not only to be bound, but even to die at Jerusalem for the name of the Lord Jesus."

And since he would not be persuaded, we fell silent, remarking, "The will of the Lord be done!"   *Acts 21:3-14*

When they had set a day for Paul, they came to him at his lodging in large numbers; and he was explaining to them by solemnly testifying about the kingdom of God and trying to persuade them concerning Jesus, from both the Law of Moses and from the Prophets, from morning until evening.

Some were being persuaded by the things spoken, but others would not believe.

And when they did not agree with one another, they began leaving after Paul had spoken one parting word, "The **Holy Spirit** rightly spoke through Isaiah the prophet to your fathers, saying, 'Go to this people and say, "You will keep on hearing, but will not understand; and you will keep on seeing, but will not perceive; for the heart of this people has become dull, and with their ears they scarcely hear, and they have closed their eyes; otherwise they might see with their eyes, and hear with their ears, and understand with their heart and return, and I would heal them." '

"Therefore let it be known to you that this salvation of God has been sent to the Gentiles; they will also listen."

[When he had spoken these words, the Jews departed, having a great dispute among themselves.] *Acts 28:23-29*

Paul, a bond-servant of Christ Jesus, called as an apostle, set apart for the gospel of God, which He promised beforehand through His prophets in the Holy Scriptures, concerning His Son, who was born of a descendant of David according to the flesh, who was declared the Son of God with power by the resurrection from the dead, according to the **Spirit** of holiness, Jesus Christ our Lord, through whom we have received grace and apostleship to bring about the obedience of faith among all the Gentles for His name's sake, among whom you also are the called of Jesus Christ; to all who are beloved of God in Rome, called as saints: Grace to you and peace from God our Father and the Lord Jesus Christ.
Romans 1:1-7

He is not a Jew who is one outwardly, nor is circumcision that which is outward in the flesh.

But he is a Jew who is one inwardly; and circumcision is that which is of the heart, by the **Spirit**, not by the letter; and

his praise is not from men, but from God.
Romans 2:28-29

Having been justified by faith, we have peace with God through our Lord Jesus Christ, through whom also we have obtained our introduction by faith into this grace in which we stand; and we exult in hope of the glory of God.

And not only this, but we also exult in our tribulations, knowing that tribulation brings about perseverance; and perseverance, proven character; and proven character, hope; and hope does not disappoint, because the love of God has been poured out within our hearts through the **Holy Spirit** who was given to us. For while we were still helpless, at the right time Christ died for the ungodly.
Romans 5:1-6

My brethren, you also were made to die to the Law through the body of Christ, so that you might be joined to another, to Him who was raised from the dead, in order that we might bear fruit for God.

For while we were in the flesh, the sinful passions, which were aroused by the Law, were at work in the members of our body to bear fruit for death.

But now we have been released from the Law, having died to that by which we were bound, so that we serve in newness of the **Spirit** and not in oldness of the letter. *Romans 7:4-6*

There is now no condemnation for those who are in Christ Jesus. For the law of the **Spirit** of life in Christ Jesus has set you free from the law of sin and of death.

For what the Law could not do, weak as it was through the flesh, God did: sending His own Son in the likeness of sinful flesh and as an offering for sin, He condemned sin in the flesh, so that the requirement of the Law might be fulfilled in us, who do not walk according to the flesh but according to the **Spirit**.

For those who are according to the flesh set their minds on the things of the flesh, but those who are according to the **Spirit**, the things of the **Spirit**.

For the mind set on the flesh is death, but the mind set on the **Spirit** is life and peace, because the mind set on the flesh is hostile toward God; for it does not subject itself to the law of God, for it is not even able to do so, and those who are in the flesh cannot please God.

However, you are not in the flesh but in the **Spirit**, if indeed the **Spirit of God** dwells in you. But if anyone does not have the **Spirit** of Christ, he does not belong to Him.

If Christ is in you, though the body is dead because of sin, yet the **Spirit** is alive because of righteousness.

But if the **Spirit** of Him who raised Jesus from the dead dwells in you, He who raised Christ Jesus from the dead will also give life to your mortal bodies through His **Spirit** who dwells in you.

So then, brethren, we are under obligation, not to the flesh, to live according to the flesh - for if you are living according to the flesh, you must die; but if by the **Spirit** you are putting to death the deeds of the body, you will live.

For all who are being led by the **Spirit of God**, these are sons of God. For you have not received a spirit of slavery leading to fear again, but you have received a spirit of adoption as sons by which we cry out, "Abba! Father!"

The **Spirit** Himself testifies with our spirit that we are children of God, and if children, heirs also, heirs of God and fellow heirs with Christ, if indeed we suffer with Him so that we may also be glorified with Him. *Romans 8:1-17*

We know that the whole creation groans and suffers the pains of childbirth together until now.

And not only this, but also we ourselves, having the first fruits of the **Spirit**, even we ourselves groan within ourselves, waiting eagerly for our adoption as sons, the redemption of our body.

For in hope we have been saved, but hope that is seen is not hope; for who hopes for what he already sees? But if we hope for what we do not see, with perseverance we wait eagerly for it.

In the same way the **Spirit** also helps our weakness; for we do not know how to pray as we should, but the **Spirit** Himself intercedes for us with groanings too deep for words; and He who searches the hearts knows what the mind of the **Spirit** is, because He intercedes for the saints according to the will of God. *Romans 8:22-27*

I am telling the truth in Christ, I am not lying, my conscience testifies with me in the **Holy Spirit**, that I have great sorrow and unceasing grief in my heart.

For I could wish that I myself were accursed, separated from Christ for the sake of my brethren, my kinsmen according to the flesh, who are Israelites, to whom belongs the adoption as sons, and the glory and the covenants and the giving of the Law and the temple service and the promises, whose are the fathers, and from whom is the Christ according to the flesh, who is over all, God blessed forever. Amen. *Romans 9:1-5*

I know and am convinced in the Lord Jesus that nothing is unclean in itself; but to him who thinks anything to be unclean, to him it is unclean.

For if because of food your brother is hurt, you are no longer walking according to love. Do not destroy with your food him for whom Christ died.

Therefore do not let what is for you a good thing be spoken of as evil; for the kingdom of God is not eating and drinking, but righteousness and peace and joy in the **Holy Spirit**. For he who in this way serves Christ is acceptable to God and approved by men. *Romans 14:14-18*

May the God of hope fill you with all joy and peace in believing, so that you will abound in hope by the power of the **Holy Spirit**.

And concerning you, my brethren, I myself also am convinced that you yourselves are full of goodness, filled with all knowledge and able also to admonish one another.

But I have written very boldly to you

on some points so as to remind you again, because of the grace that was given me from God, to be a minister of Christ Jesus to the Gentiles, ministering as a priest the gospel of God, so that my offering of the Gentiles may become acceptable, sanctified by the **Holy Spirit**. Therefore in Christ Jesus I have found reason for boasting in things pertaining to God.

For I will not presume to speak of anything except what Christ has accomplished through me, resulting in the obedience of the Gentiles by word and deed, in the power of signs and wonders, in the power of the **Spirit**; so that from Jerusalem and round about as far as Illyricum I have fully preached the gospel of Christ.

And thus I aspired to preach the gospel, not where Christ was already named, so that I would not build on another man's foundation; but as it is written, "They who had no news of Him shall see, and they who have not heard shall understand."

Romans 15:13-21

I urge you, brethren, by our Lord Jesus Christ and by the love of the **Spirit**, to strive together with me in your prayers to God for me, that I may be rescued from those who are disobedient in Judea, and that my service for Jerusalem may prove acceptable to the saints; so that I may come to you in joy by the will of God and find refreshing rest in your company.

Now the God of peace be with you all. Amen. *Romans 15:30-33*

When I came to you, brethren, I did not come with superiority of speech or of wisdom, proclaiming to you the testimony of God. For I determined to know nothing among you except Jesus Christ, and Him crucified.

I was with you in weakness and in fear and in much trembling, and my message and my preaching were not in persuasive words of wisdom, but in demonstration of the **Spirit** and of power, so that your faith would not rest on the wisdom of men, but on the power of God.

Yet we do speak wisdom among those who are mature; a wisdom, however, not of this age nor of the rulers of this age, who are passing away; but we speak God's wisdom in a mystery, the hidden wisdom which God predestined before the ages to our glory; the wisdom which none of the rulers of this age has understood; for if they had understood it they would not have crucified the Lord of glory; but just as it is written, "Things which eye has not seen and ear has not heard, and which have not entered the heart of man, all that God has prepared for those who love Him."

For to us God revealed them through the **Spirit**; for the **Spirit** searches all things, even the depths of God. For who among men knows the thoughts of a man except the spirit of the man which is in him?

Even so the thoughts of God no one knows except the **Spirit of God**.

Now we have received, not the spirit of the world, but the **Spirit** who is from God, so that we may know the things freely given to us by God, which things we also speak, not in words taught by human wisdom, but in those taught by the **Spirit**, combining spiritual thoughts with spiritual words.

But a natural man does not accept the things of the **Spirit of God**, for they are foolishness to him; and he cannot understand them, because they are spiritually appraised.

But he who is spiritual appraises all things, yet he himself is appraised by no one. For who has known the mind of the Lord, that he will instruct Him? But we have the mind of Christ. *1 Corinthians 2:1-16*

Do you not know that you are a temple of God and that the **Spirit of God** dwells in you?

If any man destroys the temple of God, God will destroy him, for the temple of God is holy, and that is what you are.

1 Corinthians 3:16-17

Do you not know that the unrighteous will not inherit the kingdom of God?

Do not be deceived; neither fornicators, nor idolaters, nor adulterers, nor effeminate, nor homosexuals, nor thieves, nor the covetous, nor drunkards, nor revilers, nor swindlers, will inherit the kingdom of God.

Such were some of you; but you were washed, but you were sanctified, but you were justified in the name of the Lord Jesus Christ and in the **Spirit of** our **God**.

1 Corinthians 6:9-11

Do you not know that your bodies are members of Christ? Shall I then take away the members of Christ and make them members of a prostitute? May it never be!

Or do you not know that the one who joins himself to a prostitute is one body with her? For He says, "The two shall become one flesh."

But the one who joins himself to the Lord is one spirit with Him.

Flee immorality. Every other sin that a man commits is outside the body, but the immoral man sins against his own body.

Or do you not know that your body is a temple of the **Holy Spirit** who is in you, whom you have from God, and that you are not your own?

For you have been bought with a price: Therefore glorify God in your body.

1 Corinthians 6:15-20

A wife is bound as long as her husband lives; but if her husband is dead, she is free to be married to whom she wishes, only in the Lord.

But in my opinion she is happier if she remains as she is; and I think that I also have the **Spirit of God**.

1 Corinthians 7:39-40

Concerning Spiritual gifts, brethren, I do not want you to be unaware.

You know that when you were pagans, you were led astray to the mute idols, however you were led. Therefore I make known to you that no one speaking by the **Spirit of God** says, "Jesus is accursed"; and no one can say, "Jesus is Lord," except by the **Holy Spirit**.

Now there are varieties of gifts, but the same **Spirit**. And there are varieties of ministries, and the same Lord.

There are varieties of effects, but the same God who works all things in all persons.

But to each one is given the manifestation of the **Spirit** for the common good.

For to one is given the word of wisdom through the **Spirit**, and to another the word of knowledge according to the same **Spirit**; to another faith by the same **Spirit**, and to another gifts of healing by the one **Spirit**, and to another the effecting of miracles, and to another prophecy, and to another the distinguishing of **spirits**, to another various kinds of tongues, and to another the interpretation of tongues.

But one and the same **Spirit** works all these things, distributing to each one individually just as He wills. For even as the body is one and yet has many members, and all the members of the body, though they are many, are one body, so also is Christ.

For by one **Spirit** we were all baptized into one body, whether Jews or Greeks, whether slaves or free, and we were all made to drink of one **Spirit**. For the body is not one member, but many.

1 Corinthians 12:1-14

He who establishes us with you in Christ and anointed us is God, who also sealed us and gave us the **Spirit** in our hearts as a pledge.   *2 Corinthians 1:21-22*

Are we beginning to commend ourselves again? Or do we need, as some, letters of commendation to you or from you?

You are our letter, written in our hearts, known and read by all men; being manifested that you are a letter of Christ, cared for by us, written not with ink but with the **Spirit** of the living God, not on tablets of stone but on tablets of human hearts.

Such confidence we have through Christ toward God. Not that we are adequate in ourselves to consider anything as coming from ourselves, but our adequacy is from God, who also made us adequate as servants of a new covenant, not of the letter but of the **Spirit**; for the letter kills, but the **Spirit** gives life.

But if the ministry of death, in letters engraved on stones, came with glory, so that the sons of Israel could not look intently at the face of Moses because of the glory of his face, fading as it was, how will the ministry of the **Spirit** fail to be even more with glory?

For if the ministry of condemnation has glory, much more does the ministry of righteousness abound in glory.

2 Corinthians 3:1-9

The Lord is the **Spirit**, and where the **Spirit** of the Lord is, there is liberty.

But we all, with unveiled face, beholding as in a mirror the glory of the Lord, are being transformed into the same image from glory to glory, just as from the Lord, the **Spirit**.   *2 Corinthians 3:17-18*

Indeed while we are in this tent, we groan, being burdened, because we do not want to be unclothed but to be clothed, so that what is mortal will be swallowed up by life.

Now He who prepared us for this very purpose is God, who gave to us the **Spirit** as a pledge.

Therefore, being always of good courage, and knowing that while we are at home in the body we are absent from the Lord - for we walk by faith, not by sight - we are of good courage, I say, and prefer rather to be absent from the body and to be at home with the Lord.

Therefore we also have as our ambition, whether at home or absent, to be pleasing to Him.   *2 Corinthians 5:4-9*

He made Him who knew no sin to be sin on our behalf, so that we might become the righteousness of God in Him.

And working together with Him, we also urge you not to receive the grace of God in vain - for He says, "At the acceptable time I listened to you, and on the day of salvation I helped you."

Behold, now is "the acceptable time,"

behold, now is "the day of salvation" - giving no cause for offense in anything, so that the ministry will not be discredited, but in everything commending ourselves as servants of God, in much endurance, in afflict-ions, in hardships, in distresses, in beatings, in imprisonments, in tumults, in labors, in sleeplessness, in hunger, in purity, in knowledge, in patience, in kindness, in the **Holy Spirit**, in genuine love, in the word of truth, in the power of God; by the weapons of righteousness for the right hand and the left, by glory and dishonor, by evil report and good report; regarded as deceivers and yet true; as unknown yet well-known, as dying yet behold, we live; as punished yet not put to death, as sorrowful yet always rejoicing, as poor yet making many rich, as having nothing yet possessing all things.

2 Corinthians 5:21 - 6:10

Greet one another with a holy kiss. All the saints greet you.

The grace of the Lord Jesus Christ, and the love of God, and the fellowship of the **Holy Spirit**, be with you all.

2 Corinthians 13:12-14

You foolish Galatians, who has bewitched you, before whose eyes Jesus Christ was publicly portrayed as crucified?

This is the only thing I want to find out from you: Did you receive the **Spirit** by the works of the Law, or by hearing with faith? Are you so foolish?

Having begun by the **Spirit**, are you now being perfected by the flesh? Did you suffer so many things in vain - if indeed it was in vain?

So then, does He who provides you with the **Spirit** and works miracles among you, do it by the works of the Law, or by hearing with faith?

Even so Abraham believed God, and it was reckoned to him as righteousness.

Galatians 3:1-6

Christ redeemed us from the curse of the Law, having become a curse for us - for it is written, "Cursed is everyone who hangs on a tree" - in order that in Christ Jesus the blessing of Abraham might come to the Gentiles, so that we would receive the promise of the **Spirit** through faith.

Galatians 3:13-14

I say, as long as the heir is a child, he does not differ at all from a slave although he is owner of everything, but he is under guardians and managers until the date set by the father. So also we, while we were children, were held in bondage under the elemental things of the world.

But when the fullness of the time came, God sent forth His Son, born of a woman, born under the Law, so that He might redeem those who were under the Law, that we might receive the adoption as sons.

Because you are sons, God has sent forth the **Spirit** of His Son into our hearts, crying, "Abba! Father!"

Therefore you are no longer a slave, but a son; and if a son, then an heir through God. *Galatians 4:1-7*

You brethren, like Isaac, are children of promise. But as at that time he who was born according to the flesh persecuted him who was born according to the **Spirit**, so it is now also. *Galatians 4:28-29*

Behold I, Paul, say to you that if you receive circumcision, Christ will be of no benefit to you.

And I testify again to every man who receives circumcision, that he is under obligation to keep the whole Law. You have been severed from Christ, you who are seeking to be justified by law; you have fallen from grace.

For we through the **Spirit**, by faith, are waiting for the hope of righteousness. For in Christ Jesus neither circumcision nor uncircumcision means anything, but faith working through love. *Galatians 5:2-6*

Walk by the **Spirit**, and you will not carry out the desire of the flesh. For the flesh sets its desire against the **Spirit**, and the **Spirit** against the flesh; for these are in opposition to one another, so that you may not do the things that you please. But if you are led by the **Spirit**, you are

not under the Law.

Now the deeds of the flesh are evident, which are: immorality, impurity, sensuality, idolatry, sorcery, enmities, strife, jealousy, outbursts of anger, disputes, dissensions, factions, envying, drunkenness, carousing, and things like these, of which I forewarn you, just as I have forewarned you, that those who practice such things will not inherit the kingdom of God.

But the fruit of the **Spirit** is love, joy, peace, patience, kindness, goodness, faithfulness, gentleness, self-control; against such things there is no law.

Now those who belong to Christ Jesus have crucified the flesh with its passions and desires.

If we live by the **Spirit**, let us also walk by the **Spirit**. Let us not become boastful, challenging one another, envying one another.

Brethren, even if anyone is caught in any trespass, you who are spiritual, restore such a one in a spirit of gentleness; each one looking to yourself, so that you too will not be tempted.

Bear one another's burdens, and thereby fulfill the law of Christ.

Galatians 5:16 - 16:2

Do not be deceived, God is not mocked; for whatever a man sows, this he will also reap. For the one who sows to his own flesh will from the flesh reap corruption, but the one who sows to the **Spirit** will from the **Spirit** reap eternal life.

Let us not lose heart in doing good, for in due time we will reap if we do not grow weary. *Galatians 6:7-9*

In Him, you also, after listening to the message of truth, the gospel of your salvation - having also believed, you were sealed in Him with the **Holy Spirit** of promise, who is given as a pledge of our inheritance, with a view to the redemption of God's own possession, to the praise of His glory.

For this reason I too, having heard of the faith in the Lord Jesus which exists among you and your love for all the saints, do not cease giving thanks for you, while making mention of you in my prayers; that the God of our Lord Jesus Christ, the Father of glory, may give to you a spirit of wisdom and of revelation in the knowledge of Him. *Ephesians 1:13-17*

He came and preached peace to you who were far away, and peace to those who were near; for through Him we both have our access in one **Spirit** to the Father.

So then you are no longer strangers and aliens, but you are fellow citizens with the saints, and are of God's household, having been built on the foundation of the apostles and prophets, Christ Jesus Himself being the corner stone, in whom the whole building, being fitted together, is growing into a Holy temple in the Lord, in whom you also are being built together into a dwelling of God in the **Spirit**. *Ephesians 2:17-22*

When you read you can understand my insight into the mystery of Christ, which in other generations was not made known to the sons of men, as it has now been revealed to His Holy apostles and prophets in the **Spirit**; to be specific, that the Gentiles are fellow heirs and fellow members of the body, and fellow partakers of the promise in Christ Jesus through the gospel, of which I was made a minister, according to the gift of God's grace which was given to me according to the working of His power. *Ephesians 3:4-7*

I bow my knees before the Father, from whom every family in heaven and on earth derives its name, that He would grant you, according to the riches of His glory, to be strengthened with power through His **Spirit** in the inner man, so that Christ may dwell in your hearts through faith; and that you, being rooted and grounded in love, may be able to comprehend with all the saints what is the breadth and length and height and depth, and to know the love of Christ which surpasses knowledge, that you may be filled up to all the fullness of God.

Now to Him who is able to do far more abundantly beyond all that we ask or think, according to the power that works within us, to Him be the glory in the church and in Christ Jesus to all generations forever and ever. Amen.

Therefore I, the prisoner of the Lord, implore you to walk in a manner worthy of the calling with which you have been called, with all humility and gentleness, with patience, showing tolerance for one another in love, being diligent to preserve the unity of the **Spirit** in the bond of peace.

There is one body and one **Spirit**, just as also you were called in one hope of your calling; one Lord, one faith, one baptism, one God and Father of all who is over all and through all and in all.

But to each one of us grace was given according to the measure of Christ's gift. Therefore it says, "When He ascended on high, He led captive a host of captives, and He gave gifts to men." *Ephesians 3:14 - 4:8*

Let no unwholesome word proceed from your mouth, but only such a word as is good for edification according to the need of the moment, so that it will give grace to those who hear.

Do not grieve the **Holy Spirit of God**, by whom you were sealed for the day of redemption.

Let all bitterness and wrath and anger and clamor and slander be put away from you, along with all malice.

Be kind to one another, tenderhearted, forgiving each other, just as God in Christ also has forgiven you. *Ephesians 4:29-32*

Be careful how you walk, not as unwise men but as wise, making the most of your time, because the days are evil. So then do not be foolish, but understand what the will of the Lord is.

And do not get drunk with wine, for that is dissipation, but be filled with the **Spirit**, speaking to one another in Psalm and hymns and spiritual songs, singing and making melody with your heart to the Lord; always giving thanks for all things in the name of our Lord Jesus Christ to God, even the Father; and be subject to one another in the fear of Christ.

Ephesians 5:15-21

Take the helmet of salvation, and the sword of the **Spirit**, which is the word of God. With all prayer and petition pray at all times in the **Spirit**, and with this in view, be on the alert with all perseverance and petition for all the saints, and pray on my behalf, that utterance may be given to me in the opening of my mouth, to make known with boldness the mystery of the gospel, for which I am an ambassador in chains; that in proclaiming it I may speak boldly, as I ought to speak.

Ephesians 6:17-20

In every way, whether in pretense or in truth, Christ is proclaimed; and in this I rejoice.

Yes, and I will rejoice, for I know that this will turn out for my deliverance through your prayers and the provision of the **Spirit** of Jesus Christ, according to my earnest expectation and hope, that I will not be put to shame in anything, but that with all boldness, Christ will even now, as always, be exalted in my body, whether by life or by death. For to me, to live is Christ and to die is gain.

Philippians 1:18-21

If there is any encouragement in Christ, if there is any consolation of love, if there is any fellowship of the **Spirit**, if any affection and compassion, make my joy complete by being of the same mind, maintaining the same love, united in spirit, intent on one purpose.

Do nothing from selfishness or empty conceit, but with humility of mind regard one another as more important than yourselves; do not merely look out for your own personal interests, but also for the interests of others.

Philippians 2:1-4

Beware of the dogs, beware of the evil workers, beware of the false circumcision; for we are the true circumcision, who worship in the **Spirit of God** and glory in Christ Jesus and put no confidence in the flesh, ~

Philippians 3:2-3

Paul, an apostle of Jesus Christ by the will of God, and Timothy our brother, to the saints and faithful brethren in Christ who are at Colossae: Grace to you and peace from God our Father.

We give thanks to God, the Father of our Lord Jesus Christ, praying always for you, since we heard of your faith in Christ Jesus and the love which you have for all the saints; because of the hope laid up for you in heaven, of which you previously heard in the word of truth, the gospel which has come to you, just as in all the world also it is constantly bearing fruit and increasing, even as it has been doing in you also since the day you heard of it and understood the grace of God in truth; just as you learned it from Epaphras, our beloved fellow bond-servant, who is a faithful servant of Christ on our behalf, and he also informed us of your love in the **Spirit**.

For this reason also, since the day we heard of it, we have not ceased to pray for you and to ask that you may be filled with the knowledge of His will in all spiritual wisdom and understanding, so that you will walk in a manner worthy of the Lord, to please Him in all respects, bearing fruit in every good work and increasing in the knowledge of God; strengthened with all power, according to His glorious might, for the attaining of all steadfastness and patience; joyously giving thanks to the Father, who has qualified us to share in the inheritance of the saints in Light.

Colossians 1:1-12

Paul and Silvanus and Timothy, to the church of the Thessalonians in God the Father and the Lord Jesus Christ: Grace to you and peace.

We give thanks to God always for all of you, making mention of you in our prayers; constantly bearing in mind your work of faith and labor of love and steadfastness of hope in our Lord Jesus Christ in the presence of our God and Father, knowing, brethren beloved by God, His choice of you; for our gospel did not come to you in word only, but also in power and in the **Holy Spirit** and with full conviction; just as you know what kind of men we proved to be among you for your sake.

You also became imitators of us and of the Lord, having received the word in much tribulation with the joy of the **Holy Spirit**, so that you became an example to all the believers in Macedonia and in Achaia.

For the word of the Lord has sounded forth from you, not only in Macedonia and Achaia, but also in every place your faith toward God has gone forth, so that we have no need to say anything.

1 Thessalonians 1:1-8

Brethren, we request and exhort you in the Lord Jesus, that as you received from us instruction as to how you ought to walk and please God (just as you actually do walk), that you excel still more. For you know what commandments we gave you by the authority of the Lord Jesus.

For this is the will of God, your sanctification; that is, that you abstain from sexual immorality; that each of you know how to possess his own vessel in sanctification and honor, not in lustful passion, like the Gentiles who do not know God; and that no man transgress and defraud his brother in the matter because the Lord is the avenger in all these things, just as we also told you before and solemnly warned you.

For God has not called us for the purpose of impurity, but in sanctification. So, he who rejects this is not rejecting man but the God who gives His **Holy Spirit** to you. *1 Thessalonians 4:1-8*

Do not quench the **Spirit**; do not despise prophetic utterances. But examine everything carefully; hold fast to that which is good; abstain from every form of evil.

Now may the God of peace Himself sanctify you entirely; and may your spirit and soul and body be preserved complete, without blame at the coming of our Lord Jesus Christ. *1 Thessalonians 5:19-23*

We should always give thanks to God for you, brethren beloved by the Lord, because God has chosen you from the beginning for salvation through sanctification

by the **Spirit** and faith in the truth.

It was for this He called you through our gospel, that you may gain the glory of our Lord Jesus Christ.

2 Thessalonians 2:13-14

By common confession, great is the mystery of godliness: He who was revealed in the flesh, was vindicated in the **Spirit**, seen by angels, proclaimed among the nations, believed on in the world, taken up in glory.

But the **Spirit** explicitly says that in later times some will fall away from the faith, paying attention to deceitful spirits and doctrines of demons, by means of the hypocrisy of liars seared in their own conscience as with a branding iron, men who forbid marriage and advocate abstaining from foods which God has created to be gratefully shared in by those who believe and know the truth. *1 Timothy 3:16 - 4:3*

Retain the standard of sound words which you have heard from me, in the faith and love which are in Christ Jesus.

Guard, through the **Holy Spirit** who dwells in us, the treasure which has been entrusted to you. *2 Timothy 1:13-14*

Remind them to be subject to rulers, to authorities, to be obedient, to be ready for every good deed, to malign no one, to be peaceable, gentle, showing every consideration for all men.

For we also once were foolish ourselves, disobedient, deceived, enslaved to various lusts and pleasures, spending our life in malice and envy, hateful, hating one another.

But when the kindness of God our Savior and His love for mankind appeared, He saved us, not on the basis of deeds which we have done in righteousness, but according to His mercy, by the washing of regeneration and renewing by the **Holy Spirit**, whom He poured out upon us richly through Jesus Christ our Savior, so that being justified by His grace we would be made heirs according to the hope of eternal life.

This is a trustworthy statement; and concerning these things I want you to speak confidently, so that those who have believed God will be careful to engage in good deeds. These things are good and profitable for men.   *Titus 3:1-8*

For this reason we must pay much closer attention to what we have heard, so that we do not drift away from it.

For if the word spoken through angels proved unalterable, and every transgression and disobedience received a just penalty, how will we escape if we neglect so great a salvation?

After it was at the first spoken through the Lord, it was confirmed to us by those who heard, God also testifying with them, both by signs and wonders and by various miracles and by gifts of the **Holy Spirit** according to His own will.
                    Hebrews 2:1-4

Moses was faithful in all His house as a servant, for a testimony of those things which were to be spoken later; but Christ was faithful as a Son over His house - whose house we are, if we hold fast our confidence and the boast of our hope firm until the end.

Therefore, just as the **Holy Spirit** says, "Today if you hear His voice, do not harden your hearts as when they provoked Me, as in the day of trial in the wilderness, where your fathers tried Me by testing Me, and saw My works for forty years.

Therefore I was angry with this generation, and said, 'They always go astray in their heart, and they did not know My ways'; as I swore in My wrath, 'They shall not enter My rest.' "

Take care, brethren, that there not be in any one of you an evil, unbelieving heart that falls away from the living God.
                    Hebrews 3:5-12

Leaving the elementary teaching about the Christ, let us press on to maturity, not laying again a foundation of repentance from dead works and of faith toward God, of instruction about washings and laying on of hands, and the resurrection of the dead and eternal judgment. And this we will do, if God permits.

For in the case of those who have once been enlightened and have tasted of the heavenly gift and have been made partakers of the **Holy Spirit**, and have tasted the good word of God and the powers of the age to come, then have fallen away, it is impossible to renew them again to repentance, since they again crucify to themselves the Son of God and put Him to open shame.
                    Hebrews 6:1-6

When these things have been so prepared, the priests are continually entering the outer tabernacle performing the divine worship, but into the second, only the high priest enters once a year, not without taking blood, which he offers for himself and for the sins of the people committed in ignorance.

The **Holy Spirit** is signifying this, that the way into the Holy place has not yet been disclosed while the outer tabernacle is still standing, which is a symbol for the present time.

Accordingly both gifts and sacrifices are offered which cannot make the worshiper perfect in conscience, since they relate only to food and drink and various washings, regulations for the body imposed until a time of reformation.

But when Christ appeared as a high priest of the good things to come, He entered through the greater and more perfect tabernacle, not made with hands, that is to say, not of this creation; and not through the blood of goats and calves, but through His own blood, He entered the holy place once for all, having obtained eternal redemption.

For if the blood of goats and bulls and the ashes of a heifer sprinkling those who have been defiled sanctify for the cleansing of the flesh, how much more will the blood of Christ, who through the eternal **Spirit** offered Himself without blemish to God, cleanse your conscience from dead works to serve the living God?

For this reason He is the mediator of

a new covenant, so that, since a death has taken place for the redemption of the transgressions that were committed under the first covenant, those who have been called may receive the promise of the eternal inheritance. *Hebrews 9:6-15*

By one offering He has perfected for all time those who are sanctified.

And the **Holy Spirit** also testifies to us; for after saying, "This is the covenant that I will make with them after those days, says the Lord: I will put My laws upon their heart, and on their mind I will write them,"

He then says, "and their sins and their lawless deeds I will remember no more."

Now where there is forgiveness of these things, there is no longer any offering for sin. *Hebrews 10:14-18*

Anyone who has set aside the Law of Moses dies without mercy on the testimony of two or three witnesses.

How much severer punishment do you think he will deserve who has trampled under foot the Son of God, and has regarded as unclean the blood of the covenant by which he was sanctified, and has insulted the **Spirit** of grace? *Hebrews 10:28-29*

You adulteresses, do you not know that friendship with the world is hostility toward God? Therefore whoever wishes to be a friend of the world makes himself an enemy of God.

Or do you think that the Scripture speaks to no purpose: "He jealously desires the **Spirit** which He has made to dwell in us"? *James 4:4-5*

Peter, an apostle of Jesus Christ, to those who reside as aliens, scattered throughout Pontus, Galatia, Cappadocia, Asia, and Bithynia, who are chosen according to the foreknowledge of God the Father, by the sanctifying work of the **Spirit**, to obey Jesus Christ and be sprinkled with His blood: May grace and peace be yours in the fullest measure. *1 Peter 1:1-2*

As to this salvation, the prophets who prophesied of the grace that would come to you made careful searches and inquiries, seeking to know what person or time the **Spirit** of Christ within them was indicating as He predicted the sufferings of Christ and the glories to follow.

It was revealed to them that they were not serving themselves, but you, in these things which now have been announced to you through those who preached the gospel to you by the **Holy Spirit** sent from heaven - things into which angels long to look.

Therefore, prepare your minds for action, keep sober in spirit, fix your hope completely on the grace to be brought to you at the revelation of Jesus Christ. *1 Peter 1:10-13*

Beloved, do not be surprised at the fiery ordeal among you, which comes upon you for your testing, as though some strange thing were happening to you; but to the degree that you share the sufferings of Christ, keep on rejoicing, so that also at the revelation of His glory you may rejoice with exultation.

If you are reviled for the name of Christ, you are blessed, because the **Spirit** of glory and **of God** rests on you. *1 Peter 4:12-14*

We have the prophetic word made more sure, to which you do well to pay attention as to a lamp shining in a dark place, until the day dawns and the morning star arises in your hearts.

But know this first of all, that no prophecy of Scripture is a matter of one's own interpretation, for no prophecy was ever made by an act of human will, but men moved by the **Holy Spirit** spoke from God. *2 Peter 1:19-21*

Beloved, if our heart does not condemn us, we have confidence before God; and whatever we ask we receive from Him, because we keep His commandments and do the things that are pleasing in His sight.

This is His commandment, that we believe in the name of His Son Jesus Christ, and love one another, just as He commanded us.

The one who keeps His commandments abides in Him, and He in him. We know by this that He abides in us, by the **Spirit** whom He has given us.

Beloved, do not believe every spirit, but test the spirits to see whether they are from God, because many false prophets have gone out into the world.

By this you know the **Spirit of God**: Every spirit that confesses that Jesus Christ has come in the flesh is from God; and every spirit that does not confess Jesus is not from God; this is the spirit of the antichrist, of which you have heard that it is coming, and now it is already in the world.

You are from God, little children, and have overcome them; because greater is He who is in you than he who is in the world.

They are from the world; therefore they speak as from the world, and the world listens to them.

We are from God; he who knows God listens to us; he who is not from God does not listen to us. By this we know the spirit of truth and the spirit of error.

1 John 3:21 - 4:6

No one has seen God at any time; if we love one another, God abides in us, and His love is perfected in us.

By this we know that we abide in Him and He in us, because He has given us of His **Spirit**.   *1 John 4:12-13*

Whoever believes that Jesus is the Christ is born of God, and whoever loves the Father loves the child born of Him.

By this we know that we love the children of God, when we love God and observe His commandments.

For this is the love of God, that we keep His commandments; and His commandments are not burdensome. For whatever is born of God overcomes the world; and this is the victory that has overcome the world - our faith.

Who is the one who overcomes the world, but he who believes that Jesus is the Son of God?

This is the One who came by water and blood, Jesus Christ; not with the water only, but with the water and with the blood. It is the **Spirit** who testifies, because the **Spirit** is the truth.

For there are three that testify: The **Spirit** and the water and the blood; and the three are in agreement.   *1 John 5:1-8*

These are grumblers, finding fault, following after their own lusts; they speak arrogantly, flattering people for the sake of gaining an advantage.

But you, beloved, ought to remember the words that were spoken beforehand by the apostles of our Lord Jesus Christ, that they were saying to you, "In the last time there will be mockers, following after their own ungodly lusts."

These are the ones who cause divisions, worldly-minded, devoid of the **Spirit**.

But you, beloved, building yourselves up on your most Holy faith, praying in the **Holy Spirit**, keep yourselves in the love of God, waiting anxiously for the mercy of our Lord Jesus Christ to eternal life.

Jude 16-21

I, John, your brother and fellow partaker in the tribulation and kingdom and perseverance which are in Jesus, was on the island called Patmos because of the word of God and the testimony of Jesus.

I was in the **Spirit** on the Lord's day, and I heard behind me a loud voice like the sound of a trumpet, saying, "Write in a book what you see, and send it to the seven churches: to Ephesus and to Smyrna and to Pergamum and to Thyatira and to Sardis and to Philadelphia and to Laodicea."   *Revelation 1:9-11*

He who has an ear, let him hear what the **Spirit** says to the churches.

To him who overcomes, I will grant to eat of the tree of life which is in the Paradise of God.   *Revelation 2:7*

He who has an ear, let him hear what the **Spirit** says to the churches.

He who overcomes will not be hurt by the second death. *Revelation 2:11*

He who has an ear, let him hear what the **Spirit** says to the churches.

To him who overcomes, to him I will give some of the hidden manna, and I will give him a white stone, and a new name written on the stone which no one knows but he who receives it. *Revelation 2:17*

He who overcomes, and he who keeps My deeds until the end, to him I will give authority over the nations; and he shall rule them with a rod of iron, as the vessels of the potter are broken to pieces, as I also have received authority from My Father; and I will give him the morning star.

He who has an ear, let him hear what the **Spirit** says to the churches. *Revelation 2:26-29*

He who overcomes will thus be clothed in white garments; and I will not erase his name from the book of life, and I will confess his name before My Father and before His angels.

He who has an ear, let him hear what the **Spirit** says to the churches. *Revelation 3:5-6*

He who overcomes, I will make him a pillar in the temple of My God, and he will not go out from it anymore; and I will write on him the name of My God, and the name of the city of My God, the new Jerusalem, which comes down out of heaven from My God, and My new name.

He who has an ear, let him hear what the **Spirit** says to the churches. *Revelation 3:12-13*

He who overcomes, I will grant to him to sit down with Me on My throne, as I also overcame and sat down with My Father on His throne.

He who has an ear, let him hear what the **Spirit** says to the churches.

After these things I looked, and behold, a door standing open in heaven, and the first voice which I had heard, like the sound of a trumpet speaking with me, said, "Come up here, and I will show you what must take place after these things."

Immediately I was in the **Spirit**; and behold, a throne was standing in heaven, and One sitting on the throne. *Revelation 3:21 - 4:2*

I heard a voice from heaven, saying, "Write, 'Blessed are the dead who die in the Lord from now on!' "

"Yes," says the **Spirit**, "so that they may rest from their labors, for their deeds follow with them." *Revelation 14:13*

Then one of the seven angels who had the seven bowls came and spoke with me, saying, "Come here, I will show you the judgment of the great harlot who sits on many waters, with whom the kings of the earth committed acts of immorality, and those who dwell on the earth were made drunk with the wine of her immorality."

And he carried me away in the **Spirit** into a wilderness; and I saw a woman sitting on a scarlet beast, full of blasphemous names, having seven heads and ten horns.

The woman was clothed in purple and scarlet, and adorned with gold and precious stones and pearls, having in her hand a gold cup full of abominations and of the un-clean things of her immorality, and on her forehead a name was written, a mystery, "BABYLON THE GREAT, THE MOTHER OF HARLOTS AND OF THE ABOMINATIONS OF THE EARTH."

And I saw the woman drunk with the blood of the saints, and with the blood of the witnesses of Jesus. When I saw her, I wondered greatly.   *Revelation 17:1-6*

Then one of the seven angels who had the seven bowls full of the seven last plagues came and spoke with me, saying, "Come here, I will show you the bride, the wife of the Lamb."

And he carried me away in the **Spirit** to a great and high mountain, and showed me the holy city, Jerusalem, coming down out of heaven from God, having the glory of God. Her brilliance was like a very costly stone, as a stone of crystal-clear jasper.   *Revelation 21:9-11*

"I, Jesus, have sent My angel to testify to you these things for the churches. I am the root and the descendant of David, the bright morning star."

The **Spirit** and the bride say, "Come." And let the one who hears say, "Come."

And let the one who is thirsty come; let the one who wishes take the water of life without cost.   *Revelation 22:16-17*

SHEPHERD

/ SHEPHERD'S / SHEEPHERDERS / SHEPHERDS
/ SHEPHERDS' / SHEPHERDESS / SHEPHERDED

Definitions

Shepherd 1. A person who herds, tends, escorts or guards sheep.

    2. To tend or guard as a shepherd.

    3. To watch over, guide or lead.

    4. A person who protects, escorts, guides or watches over other people.

    5. One charged with the religious care and guidance of others; a cleric, priest or pastor etc.

    6. To give spiritual guidance.

OLD TESTAMENT

Jacob went on his journey, and came to the land of the sons of the east. He looked, and saw a well in the field, and behold, three flocks of sheep were lying there beside it, for from that well they watered the flocks.

Now the stone on the mouth of the well was large. When all the flocks were gathered there, they would then roll the stone from the mouth of the well and water the sheep, and put the stone back in its place on the mouth of the well.

Jacob said to them, "My brothers, where are you from?" And they said, "We are from Haran."

He said to them, "Do you know Laban the son of Nahor?" And they said, "We know him."

And he said to them, "Is it well with him?" And they said, "It is well, and here is Rachel his daughter coming with the sheep."

He said, "Behold, it is still high day; it is not time for the livestock to be gathered. Water the sheep, and go, pasture them." But they said, "We cannot, until all the flocks are gathered, and they roll the stone from the mouth of the well; then we water the sheep."

While he was still speaking with them, Rachel came with her father's sheep, for she was a **shepherdess**. When Jacob saw Rachel the daughter of Laban his mother's brother, and the sheep of Laban his mother's brother, Jacob went up and rolled the stone from the mouth of the well and watered the flock of Laban his mother's brother.

Then Jacob kissed Rachel, and lifted his voice and wept. Jacob told Rachel that he was a relative of her father and that he was Rebekah's son, and she ran and told her father.   *Genesis 29:1-12*

Israel said to Joseph, "Now let me die, since I have seen your face, that you are still alive." Joseph said to his brothers and to his father's household, "I will go up and tell Pharaoh, and will say to him, 'My brothers and my father's household, who were in the land of Canaan, have come to me; and the men are **shepherds,** for they have been keepers of livestock; and they have brought their flocks and their herds and all that they have.'

"When Pharaoh calls you and says, 'What is your occupation?' you shall say, 'Your servants have been keepers of livestock from our youth even until now, both we and our fathers,' that you may live in the land of Goshen; for every **shepherd** is loathsome to the Egyptians."

Then Joseph went in and told Pharaoh, and said, "My father and my brothers and their flocks and their herds and all that they have, have come out of the land of Canaan; and behold, they are in the land of Goshen."

He took five men from among his brothers and presented them to Pharaoh.

Then Pharaoh said to his brothers, "What is your occupation?" So they said to Pharaoh, "Your servants are **shepherds**, both we and our fathers."

They said to Pharaoh, "We have come to sojourn in the land, for there is no pasture for your servants' flocks, for the famine is severe in the land of Canaan. Now, therefore, please let your servants live in the land of Goshen."

Then Pharaoh said to Joseph, "Your father and your brothers have come to you. The land of Egypt is at your disposal; settle your father and your brothers in the best of the land, let them live in the land of Goshen; and if you know any capable men among them, then put them in charge of my livestock."

Genesis 46:30 - 47:6

The eyes of Israel were so dim from age that he could not see. Then Joseph brought them close to him, and he kissed them and embraced them. Israel said to Joseph, "I never expected to see your face, and behold, God has let me see your children as well."

Then Joseph took them from his knees, and bowed with his face to the ground.

Joseph took them both, Ephraim with his right hand toward Israel's left, and Manasseh with his left hand toward Israel's right, and brought them close to him. But Israel stretched out his right hand and laid it on the head of Ephraim, who was the younger, and his left hand on Manasseh's head, crossing his hands, although Manasseh was the first-born.

He blessed Joseph, and said, "The God before whom my fathers Abraham and Isaac walked, the God who has been my **shepherd** all my life to this day, the angel who has redeemed me from all evil, bless the lads; and may my name live on in them, and the names of my fathers Abraham and Isaac; and may they grow into a multitude in the midst of the earth."

Genesis 48:10-16

Joseph is a fruitful bough, a fruitful bough by a spring; its branches run over a wall. The archers bitterly attacked him, and shot at him and harassed him; but his bow remained firm, and his arms were agile, from the hands of the Mighty One of Jacob (from there is the **Shepherd**, the Stone of Israel), from the God of your father who helps you, and by the Almighty who blesses you with blessings of heaven above, blessings of the deep that lies beneath, blessings of the breasts and of the womb.   *Genesis 49:22-25*

The priest of Midian had seven daughters; and they came to draw water and filled the troughs to water their father's flock. Then the **shepherds** came and drove them away, but Moses stood up and helped them and watered their flock.

When they came to Reuel their father, he said, "Why have you come back so soon today?"

So they said, "An Egyptian delivered us from the hand of the **shepherds**, and what is more, he even drew the water for us and watered the flock."   *Exodus 2:16-19*

The Lord spoke to Moses and Aaron, saying, "How long shall I bear with this evil congregation who are grumbling against Me? I have heard the complaints of the sons of Israel, which they are making against Me.

"Say to them, 'As I live,' says the Lord, 'just as you have spoken in My hearing, so I will surely do to you; your corpses will fall in this wilderness, even all your numbered men, according to your complete number from twenty years old and upward, who have grumbled against Me. Surely you shall not come into the land in which I swore to settle you, except Caleb the son of Jephunneh and Joshua the son of Nun.

'Your children, however, whom you said would become a prey - I will bring them in, and they will know the land which you have rejected.

'But as for you, your corpses will fall in this wilderness. Your sons shall be **shepherds** for forty years in the wilderness, and they will suffer for your unfaithfulness, until your corpses lie in the wilderness.

'According to the number of days which you spied out the land, forty days, for every day you shall bear your guilt a year, even forty years, and you will know My opposition. I, the Lord, have spoken, surely this I will do to all this evil congregation who are gathered together against Me. In this wilderness they shall be destroyed, and there they will die.' "
Numbers 14:26-35

Moses spoke to the Lord, saying, "May the Lord, the God of the spirits of all flesh, appoint a man over the congregation, who will go out and come in before them, and who will lead them out and bring them in, so that the congregation of the Lord will not be like sheep which have no **shepherd**."

So the Lord said to Moses, "Take Joshua the son of Nun, a man in whom is the Spirit, and lay your hand on him; and have him stand before Eleazar the priest and before all the congregation, and commission him in their sight. You shall put some of your authority on him, in order that all the congregation of the sons of Israel may obey him." *Numbers 27:15-20*

Samuel did what the Lord said, and came to Bethlehem. And the elders of the city came trembling to meet him and said, "Do you come in peace?"

He said, "In peace; I have come to sacrifice to the Lord. Consecrate yourselves and come with me to the sacrifice." He also consecrated Jesse and his sons and invited them to the sacrifice.

When they entered, he looked at Eliab and thought, "Surely the Lord's anointed is before Him." But the Lord said to Samuel, "Do not look at his appearance or at the height of his stature, because I have rejected him; for God sees not as man sees, for man looks at the outward appearance, but the Lord looks at the heart."

Then Jesse called Abinadab and made him pass before Samuel. And he said, "The Lord has not chosen this one either." Next Jesse made Shammah pass by. And he said, "The Lord has not chosen this one either."

Thus Jesse made seven of his sons pass before Samuel. But Samuel said to Jesse, "The Lord has not chosen these."

And Samuel said to Jesse, "Are these all the children?" And he said, "There remains yet the youngest, and behold, he is tending the sheep." Then Samuel said to Jesse, "Send and bring him; for we will not sit down until he comes here." So he sent and brought him in.

Now he was ruddy, with beautiful eyes and a handsome appearance. And the Lord said, "Arise, anoint him; for this is he."

Then Samuel took the horn of oil and anointed him in the midst of his brothers; and the Spirit of the Lord came mightily upon David from that day forward. ~
1 Samuel 16:4-13

David said to Saul, "Let no man's heart fail on account of him; your servant will go and fight with this Philistine."

Then Saul said to David, "You are not able to go against this Philistine to fight with him; for you are but a youth while he has been a warrior from his youth."

But David said to Saul, "Your servant was tending his father's sheep. When a lion or a bear came and took a lamb from the flock, I went out after him and attacked him, and rescued it from his mouth; and when he rose up against me, I seized him by his beard and struck him and killed him. Your servant has killed both the lion and the bear; and this uncircumcised Philistine will be like one of them, since he has taunted the armies of the living God."

And David said, "The Lord who delivered me from the paw of the lion and from the paw of the bear, He will deliver me from the hand of this Philistine." And Saul said to David, "Go, and may the Lord be with you."

Then Saul clothed David with his garments and put a bronze helmet on his head, and he clothed him with armor. David girded his sword over his armor and tried to walk, for he had not tested them.

So David said to Saul, "I cannot go with these, for I have not tested them." And David took them off.

He took his stick in his hand and chose for himself five smooth stones from the brook, and put them in the **shepherd's** bag which he had, even in his pouch, and his sling was in his hand; and he approached the Philistine.

1 Samuel 17:32-40

One of the servants of Saul was there that day, detained before the Lord; and his name was Doeg the Edomite, the chief of Saul's **shepherds**. *1 Samuel 21:7*

There was a man in Maon whose business was in Carmel; and the man was very rich, and he had three thousand sheep and a thousand goats.

And it came about while he was shearing his sheep in Carmel (now the man's name was Nabal, and his wife's name was Abigail. And the woman was intelligent and beautiful in appearance, but the man was harsh and evil in his dealings, and he was a Calebite), that David heard in the wilderness that Nabal was shearing his sheep.

So David sent ten young men; and David said to the young men, "Go up to Carmel, visit Nabal and greet him in my name; and thus you shall say, 'Have a long life, peace be to you, and peace be to your house, and peace be to all that you have. Now I have heard that you have shearers; now your **shepherds** have been with us and we have not insulted them, nor have they missed anything all the days they were in Carmel.' "

1 Samuel 25:2-7

All the tribes of Israel came to David at Hebron and said, "Behold, we are your bone and your flesh. Previously, when Saul was king over us, you were the one who led Israel out and in. And the Lord said to you, 'You will **shepherd** My people Israel, and you will be a ruler over Israel.' "

So all the elders of Israel came to the king at Hebron, and King David made a covenant with them before the Lord at Hebron; then they anointed David king over Israel.

David was thirty years old when he became king, and he reigned forty years. At Hebron he reigned over Judah seven years and six months, and in Jerusalem he reigned thirty-three years over all Israel and Judah. *2 Samuel 5:1-5*

It came about when the king lived in his house, and the Lord had given him rest on every side from all his enemies, that the king said to Nathan the prophet, "See now, I dwell in a house of cedar, but the ark of God dwells within tent curtains."

Nathan said to the king, "Go, do all that is in your mind, for the Lord is with you."

But in the same night the word of the Lord came to Nathan, saying, "Go and say to My servant David, 'Thus says the Lord, "Are you the one who should build Me a house to dwell in? For I have not dwelt in a house since the day I brought up the sons of Israel from Egypt, even to this day; but I have been moving about in a tent, even in a tabernacle.

"Wherever I have gone with all the sons of Israel, did I speak a word with one of the tribes of Israel, which I commanded to **shepherd** My people Israel, saying, 'Why have you not built Me a house of cedar?'

"Now therefore, thus you shall say to My servant David, 'Thus says the Lord of hosts, "I took you from the pasture, from following the sheep, to be ruler over My people Israel. I have been with you wherever you have gone and have cut off all your enemies from before you; and I will make you a great name, like the names of the great men who are on the earth.'"'

2 Samuel 7:1-9

All the prophets were prophesying thus, saying, "Go up to Ramoth-gilead and prosper, for the Lord will give it into the hand of the king."

Then the messenger who went to summon Micaiah spoke to him saying, "Behold now, the words of the prophets are uniformly favorable to the king. Please let your word be like the word of one of them, and speak favorably."

But Micaiah said, "As the Lord lives, what the Lord says to me, that I shall speak."

When he came to the king, the king said to him, "Micaiah, shall we go to Ramoth-gilead to battle, or shall we refrain?" And he answered him, "Go up and succeed, and the Lord will give it into the hand of the king."

Then the king said to him, "How many times must I adjure you to speak to me nothing but the truth in the name of the Lord?"

So he said, "I saw all Israel scattered on the mountains, like sheep which have no **shepherd**. And the Lord said, 'These have no master. Let each of them return to his house in peace.' "

Then the king of Israel said to Jehoshaphat, "Did I not tell you that he would not prophesy good concerning me, but evil?" *1 Kings 22:12-18*

"Know then that there shall fall to the earth nothing of the word of the Lord, which the Lord spoke concerning the house of Ahab, for the Lord has done what He spoke through His servant Elijah."

So Jehu killed all who remained of the house of Ahab in Jezreel, and all his great men and his acquaintances and his priests, until he left him without a survivor. Then he arose and departed and went to Samaria.

On the way while he was at Beth-eked of the **shepherds**, Jehu met the relatives of Ahaziah king of Judah and said, "Who are you?"

And they answered, "We are the relatives of Ahaziah; and we have come down to greet the sons of the king and the sons of the queen mother."

He said, "Take them alive." So they took them alive and killed them at the pit of Beth-eked, forty-two men; and he left none of them. *2 Kings 10:10-14*

All Israel gathered to David at Hebron and said, "Behold, we are your bone and your flesh. In times past, even when Saul was king, you were the one who led out and brought in Israel; and the Lord your God said to you, 'You shall **shepherd** My people Israel, and you shall be prince over My people Israel.' "

So all the elders of Israel came to the king at Hebron, and David made a covenant with them in Hebron before the Lord; and they anointed David king over Israel, according to the word of the Lord through Samuel. *1 Chronicles 11:1-3*

Jehoshaphat his son then became king in his place, and made his position over Israel firm. He placed troops in all the fortified cities of Judah, and set garrisons in the land of Judah and in the cities of Ephraim which Asa his father had captured.

It came about the same night that the word of God came to Nathan, saying, "Go and tell David My servant, 'Thus says the Lord, "You shall not build a house for Me to dwell in; for I have not dwelt in a house since the day that I brought up Israel to this day, but I have gone from tent to tent and from one dwelling place to another.

"In all places where I have walked with all Israel, have I spoken a word with any of the judges of Israel, whom I commanded to **shepherd** My people, saying, 'Why have you not built for Me a house of cedar?'

"Now, therefore, thus shall you say to My servant David, 'Thus says the Lord of hosts, "I took you from the pasture, from following the sheep, to be leader over My people Israel. I have been with you wherever you have gone, and have cut off all your enemies from before you; and I will make you a name like the name of the great ones who are in the earth.""''

1 Chronicles 17:1-8

All the prophets were prophesying thus, saying, "Go up to Ramoth-gilead and succeed, for the Lord will give it into the hand of the king."

Then the messenger who went to summon Micaiah spoke to him saying, "Behold, the words of the prophets are uniformly favorable to the king. So please let your word be like one of them and speak favorably." But Micaiah said, "As the Lord lives, what my God says, that I will speak."

When he came to the king, the king said to him, "Micaiah, shall we go to Ramoth-gilead to battle, or shall I refrain?" He said, "Go up and succeed, for they will be given into your hand."

Then the king said to him, "How many times must I adjure you to speak to me nothing but the truth in the name of the Lord?"

So he said, "I saw all Israel scattered on the mountains, like sheep which have no **shepherd**; and the Lord said, 'These have no master. Let each of them return to his house in peace.' "

Then the king of Israel said to Jehoshaphat, "Did I not tell you that he would not prophesy good concerning me, but evil?" *2 Chronicles 18:11-17*

The Lord is my **shepherd**, I shall not want. He makes me lie down in green pastures; He leads me beside quiet waters. He restores my soul; He guides me in the paths of righteousness for His name's sake.

Even though I walk through the valley of the shadow of death, I fear no evil, for You are with me; Your rod and Your staff, they comfort me. *Psalm 23:1-4*

The Lord is my strength and my shield; my heart trusts in Him, and I am helped; therefore my heart exults, and with my song I shall thank Him. The Lord is their strength, and He is a saving defense to His anointed. Save Your people and

bless Your inheritance; be their **shepherd** also, and carry them forever. *Psalm 28:7-9*

Man in his pomp will not endure; he is like the beasts that perish. This is the way of those who are foolish, and of those after them who approve their words. As sheep they are appointed for Sheol; death shall be their **shepherd**; and the upright shall rule over them in the morning, and their form shall be for Sheol to consume so that they have no habitation.

But God will redeem my soul from the power of Sheol, for He will receive me. *Psalm 49:12-15*

The Lord awoke as if from sleep, like a warrior overcome by wine. He drove His adversaries backward; He put on them an everlasting reproach.

He also rejected the tent of Joseph, and did not choose the tribe of Ephraim, but chose the tribe of Judah, Mount Zion which He loved. And He built His sanctuary like the heights, like the earth which He has founded forever.

He also chose David His servant and took him from the sheepfolds; from the care of the ewes with suckling lambs He brought him to **shepherd** Jacob His people, and Israel His inheritance.

So he **shepherded** them according to the integrity of his heart, and guided them with his skillful hands. *Psalm 78:65-72*

Oh, give ear, **Shepherd** of Israel, you who lead Joseph like a flock; you who are enthroned above the cherubim, shine forth! Before Ephraim and Benjamin and Manasseh, stir up Your power and come to save us! O God, restore us and cause Your face to shine upon us, and we will be saved. *Psalm 80:1-3*

Come, let us worship and bow down, let us kneel before the Lord our Maker. For He is our God, and we are the people of His pasture and the sheep of His hand.

Today, if you would hear His voice, do not harden your hearts, as at Meribah, as in the day of Massah in the wilderness, "When your fathers tested Me, they tried

Me, though they had seen My work."

Psalm 95:6-9

"Vanity of vanities," says the Preacher, "all is vanity!"

In addition to being a wise man, the Preacher also taught the people knowledge; and he pondered, searched out and arranged many proverbs. The Preacher sought to find delightful words and to write words of truth correctly.

The words of wise men are like goads, and masters of these collections are like well-driven nails; they are given by one **Shepherd**. *Ecclesiastes 12:8-11*

Tell me, O you whom my soul loves, where do you pasture your flock, where do you make it lie down at noon? For why should I be like one who veils herself beside the flocks of your companions? If you yourself do not know, most beautiful among women, go forth on the trail of the flock and pasture your young goats by the tents of the **shepherds**.

Song of Solomon 1:7-8

Babylon, the beauty of kingdoms, the glory of the Chaldeans' pride, will be as when God overthrew Sodom and Gomorrah. It will never be inhabited or lived in from generation to generation; nor will the Arab pitch his tent there, nor will **shepherds** make their flocks lie down there. But desert creatures will lie down there, and their houses will be full of owls; ostriches also will live there, and shaggy goats will frolic there. *Isaiah 13:19-21*

The Egyptians are men and not God, and their horses are flesh and not spirit; so the Lord will stretch out His hand, and he who helps will stumble and he who is helped will fall, and all of them will come to an end together.

For thus says the Lord to me, "As the lion or the young lion growls over his prey, against which a band of **shepherds** is called out, and he will not be terrified at their voice nor disturbed at their noise, so will the Lord of hosts come down to wage war on Mount Zion and on its hill."

Like flying birds so the Lord of hosts will protect Jerusalem. He will protect and deliver it; He will pass over and rescue it. *Isaiah 31:3-5*

A writing of Hezekiah king of Judah after his illness and recovery: I said, "In the middle of my life I am to enter the gates of Sheol; I am to be deprived of the rest of my years."

I said, "I will not see the Lord, the Lord in the land of the living; I will look on man no more among the inhabitants of the world. Like a **shepherd's** tent my dwelling is pulled up and removed from me; as a weaver I rolled up my life. He cuts me off from the loom; from day until night You make an end of me."

Isaiah 38:9-12

Get yourself up on a high mountain, O Zion, bearer of good news, lift up your voice mightily, O Jerusalem, bearer of good news; lift it up, do not fear. Say to the cities of Judah, "Here is your God!"

Behold, the Lord God will come with might, with His arm ruling for Him. Behold, His reward is with Him and His recompense before Him.

Like a **shepherd** He will tend His flock, in His arm He will gather the lambs and carry them in His bosom; He will gently lead the nursing ewes. *Isaiah 40:9-11*

Thus says the Lord, your Redeemer, and the one who formed you from the womb, "I, the Lord, am the maker of all things, stretching out the heavens by Myself and spreading out the earth all alone, causing the omens of boasters to fail, making fools out of diviners, causing wise men to draw back and turning their knowledge into foolishness, confirming the word of His servant and performing the purpose of His messengers.

"It is I who says of Jerusalem, 'She shall be inhabited!' And of the cities of Judah, 'They shall be built.' And I will raise up her ruins again. It is I who says to the depth of the sea, 'Be dried up!' and I will make your rivers dry.

It is I who says of Cyrus, "He is My

shepherd! And he will perform all My desire."

And he declares of Jerusalem, "She will be built," and of the temple, "Your foundation will be laid."

Thus says the Lord to Cyrus His anointed, whom I have taken by the right hand, to subdue nations before him and to loose the loins of kings; to open doors before him so that gates will not be shut: "I will go before you and make the rough places smooth; I will shatter the doors of bronze and cut through their iron bars."

Isaiah 44:24 - 45:2

The Lord God, who gathers the dispersed of Israel, declares, "Yet others I will gather to them, to those already gathered. All you beasts of the field, all you beasts in the forest, come to eat. His watchmen are blind, all of them know nothing. All of them are mute dogs unable to bark, dreamers lying down, who love to slumber; and the dogs are greedy, they are not satisfied.

"And they are **shepherds** who have no understanding; they have all turned to their own way, each one to his unjust gain, to the last one. 'Come', they say, 'let us get wine, and let us drink heavily of strong drink; and tomorrow will be like today, only more so.' " *Isaiah 56:8-12*

He said, "Surely, they are My people, sons who will not deal falsely." So He became their Savior. In all their affliction He was afflicted, and the angel of His presence saved them; in His love and in His mercy He redeemed them, and He lifted them and carried them all the days of old. But they rebelled and grieved His Holy Spirit; therefore He turned Himself to become their enemy, He fought against them.

Then His people remembered the days of old, of Moses. Where is He who brought them up out of the sea with the **shepherds** of His flock? Where is He who put His Holy Spirit in the midst of them, who caused His glorious arm to go at the right hand of Moses, who divided the waters before them to make for Himself an everlasting name, who led them through the depths?

Like the horse in the wilderness, they did not stumble; as the cattle which go down into the valley, the Spirit of the Lord gave them rest. So You led Your people, to make for Yourself a glorious name.

Isaiah 63:8-14

The Lord said to me, "Faithless Israel has proved herself more righteous than treacherous Judah. Go and proclaim these words toward the north and say, 'Return, faithless Israel,' declares the Lord; 'I will not look upon you in anger. For I am gracious,' declares the Lord; 'I will not be angry forever. Only acknowledge your iniquity, that you have transgressed against the Lord your God and have scattered your favors to the strangers under every green tree, and you have not obeyed My voice,' declares the Lord.

'Return, O faithless sons,' declares the Lord; 'for I am a master to you, and I will take you one from a city and two from a family, and I will bring you to Zion. Then I will give you **shepherds** after My own heart, who will feed you on knowledge and understanding.' "

Jeremiah 3:11-15

Flee for safety, O sons of Benjamin, from the midst of Jerusalem! Now blow a trumpet in Tekoa and raise a signal over Beth-haccerem; for evil looks down from the north, and a great destruction. The comely and dainty one, the daughter of Zion, I will cut off. **Shepherds** and their flocks will come to her, they will pitch their tents around her, they will pasture each in his place. *Jeremiah 6:1-3*

Woe is me, because of my injury! My wound is incurable. But I said, "Truly this is a sickness, and I must bear it." My tent is destroyed, and all my ropes are broken; my sons have gone from me and are no more.

There is no one to stretch out my tent again or to set up my curtains. For the **shepherds** have become stupid and have not sought the Lord; therefore they have not prospered, and all their flock is scattered. *Jeremiah 10:19-21*

Many **shepherds** have ruined My vineyard, they have trampled down My field; they have made My pleasant field a desolate wilderness. It has been made a desolation, desolate, it mourns before Me; the whole land has been made desolate, because no man lays it to heart. *Jeremiah 12:10-11*

Heal me, O Lord, and I will be healed; save me and I will be saved, for You are my praise. Look, they keep saying to me, "Where is the word of the Lord? Let it come now!"

But as for me, I have not hurried away from being a **shepherd** after You, nor have I longed for the woeful day; You Yourself know that the utterance of my lips was in Your presence. Do not be a terror to me; You are my refuge in the day of disaster. *Jeremiah 17:14-17*

I spoke to you in your prosperity; but you said, "I will not listen!" This has been your practice from your youth, that you have not obeyed My voice.

The wind will sweep away all your **shepherds**, and your lovers will go into captivity; then you will surely be ashamed and humiliated because of all your wickedness. *Jeremiah 22:21-22*

"Woe to the **shepherds** who are destroying and scattering the sheep of My pasture!" declares the Lord. Therefore thus says the Lord God of Israel concerning the **shepherds** who are tending My people: "You have scattered My flock and driven them away, and have not attended to them; behold, I am about to attend to you for the evil of your deeds," declares the Lord.

"Then I Myself will gather the remnant of My flock out of all the countries where I have driven them and bring them back to their pasture, and they will be fruitful and multiply. I will also raise up **shepherds** over them and they will tend them; and

they will not be afraid any longer, nor be terrified, nor will any be missing," declares the Lord.

"Behold, the days are coming," declares the Lord, "when I will raise up for David a righteous Branch; and He will reign as king and act wisely and do justice and righteousness in the land. In His days Judah will be saved, and Israel will dwell securely; and this is His name by which He will be called, 'The Lord our righteousness.' " *Jeremiah 23:1-6*

Wail, you **shepherds**, and cry; and wallow in ashes, you masters of the flock; for the days of your slaughter and your dispersions have come, and you will fall like a choice vessel. Flight will perish from the **shepherds**, and escape from the masters of the flock.

Hear the sound of the cry of the **shepherds**, and the wailing of the masters of the flock! For the Lord is destroying their pasture, and the peaceful folds are made silent because of the fierce anger of the Lord.

He has left His hiding place like the lion; for their land has become a horror because of the fierceness of the oppressing sword and because of His fierce anger. *Jeremiah 25:34-38*

Hear the word of the Lord, O nations, and declare in the coastlands afar off, and say, "He who scattered Israel will gather him and keep him as a **shepherd** keeps his flock." For the Lord has ransomed Jacob and redeemed him from the hand of him who was stronger than he. *Jeremiah 31:10-11*

Thus says the Lord of hosts, "There will again be in this place which is waste, without man or beast, and in all its cities, a habitation of **shepherds** who rest their flocks. In the cities of the hill country, in the cities of the lowland, in the cities of the Negev, in the land of Benjamin, in the environs of Jerusalem and in the cities of Judah, the flocks will again pass under the hands of the one who numbers them," says the Lord.

"Behold, days are coming," declares the Lord, "when I will fulfill the good word which I have spoken concerning the house of Israel and the house of Judah."

Jeremiah 33:12-14

The word of the Lord came to Jeremiah in Tahpanhes, saying, "Take some large stones in your hands and hide them in the mortar in the brick terrace which is at the entrance of Pharaoh's palace in Tahpanhes, in the sight of some of the Jews; and say to them, 'Thus says the Lord of hosts, the God of Israel, "Behold, I am going to send and get Nebuchadnezzar the king of Babylon, My servant, and I am going to set his throne right over these stones that I have hidden; and he will spread his canopy over them.

"He will also come and strike the land of Egypt; those who are meant for death will be given over to death, and those for captivity to captivity, and those for the sword to the sword. And I shall set fire to the temples of the gods of Egypt, and he will burn them and take them captive.

"So he will wrap himself with the land of Egypt as a **shepherd** wraps himself with his garment, and he will depart from there safely. He will also shatter the obelisks of Heliopolis, which is in the land of Egypt; and the temples of the gods of Egypt he will burn with fire.""

Jeremiah 43:8-13

Behold, one will come up like a lion from the thickets of the Jordan against a perennially watered pasture; for in an instant I will make him run away from it, and whoever is chosen I shall appoint over it. For who is like Me, and who will summon Me into court? And who then is the **shepherd** who can stand against Me?

Therefore hear the plan of the Lord which He has planned against Edom, and His purposes which He has purposed against the inhabitants of Teman: surely they will drag them off, even the little ones of the flock; surely He will make their pasture desolate because of them.

Jeremiah 49:19-20

My people have become lost sheep; their **shepherds** have led them astray. They have made them turn aside on the mountains; they have gone along from mountain to hill and have forgotten their resting place.

All who came upon them have devoured them; and their adversaries have said, "We are not guilty, inasmuch as they have sinned against the Lord who is the habitation of righteousness, even the Lord, the hope of their fathers."

Jeremiah 50:6-7

Behold, one will come up like a lion from the thicket of the Jordan to a perennially watered pasture; for in an instant I will make them run away from it, and whoever is chosen I will appoint over it. For who is like Me, and who will summon Me into court? And who then is the **shepherd** who can stand before Me?

Therefore hear the plan of the Lord which He has planned against Babylon, and His purposes which He has purposed against the land of the Chaldeans: surely they will drag them off, even the little ones of the flock; surely He will make their pasture desolate because of them.

Jeremiah 50:44-45

He says, "You are My war-club, My weapon of war; and with you I shatter nations, and with you I destroy kingdoms. With you I shatter the horse and his rider, and with you I shatter the chariot and its rider, and with you I shatter the **shepherd** and his flock, and with you I shatter the farmer and his team, and with you I shatter governors and prefects."   *Jeremiah 51:20-23*

The word of the Lord came to me saying, "Son of man, prophesy against the **shepherds** of Israel. Prophesy and say to those **shepherds**, 'Thus says the Lord God, "Woe, **shepherds** of Israel who have been feeding themselves! Should not the **shepherds** feed the flock?

"You eat the fat and clothe yourselves with the wool, you slaughter the fat sheep without feeding the flock. Those who are sickly you have not strengthened, the diseased you have not healed, the broken you have not bound up, the scattered you have not brought back, nor have you sought for the lost; but with force and with severity you have dominated them.

"They were scattered for lack of a **shepherd**, and they became food for every beast of the field and were scattered. My flock wandered through all the mountains and on every high hill; My flock was scattered over all the surface of the earth, and there was no one to search or seek for them.

"Therefore, you **shepherds**, hear the word of the Lord: 'As I live,' declares the Lord God, 'surely because My flock has become a prey, My flock has even become food for all the beasts of the field for lack of a **shepherd**, and My **shepherds** did not search for My flock, but rather the **shepherds** fed themselves and did not feed My flock; therefore, you **shepherds**, hear the word of the Lord: "Thus says the Lord God, 'Behold, I am against the **shepherds**, and I will demand My sheep from them and make them cease from feeding sheep. So the **shepherds** will not feed themselves anymore, but I will deliver My flock from their mouth, so that they will not be food for them. ""'

'For thus says the Lord God, "Behold, I Myself will search for My sheep and seek them out. As a **shepherd** cares for his herd in the day when he is among his scattered sheep, so I will care for My sheep and will deliver them from all the places to which they were scattered on a cloudy and gloomy day.

"I will bring them out from the peoples and gather them from the countries and bring them to their own land; and I will feed them on the mountains of Israel, by the streams, and in all the inhabited places of the land.

"I will feed them in a good pasture, and their grazing ground will be on the mountain heights of Israel. There they will lie down on good grazing ground and feed in rich pasture on the mountains of Israel. I will feed My flock and I will lead them to rest," declares the Lord God. "I will seek the lost, bring back the scattered, bind up the broken and strengthen the sick; but the fat and the strong I will

destroy. I will feed them with judgment.

"As for you, My flock, thus says the Lord God, 'Behold, I will judge between one sheep and another, between the rams and the male goats. Is it too slight a thing for you that you should feed in the good pasture, that you must tread down with your feet the rest of your pastures? Or that you should drink of the clear waters, that you must foul the rest with your feet? As for My flock, they must eat what you tread down with your feet and drink what you foul with your feet!'

"Therefore, thus says the Lord God to them, 'Behold, I, even I, will judge between the fat sheep and the lean sheep. Because you push with side and with shoulder, and thrust at all the weak with your horns until you have scattered them abroad, therefore, I will deliver My flock, and they will no longer be a prey; and I will judge between one sheep and another.

'Then I will set over them one **shepherd**, My servant David, and he will feed them; he will feed them himself and be their **shepherd**. My servant David will be king over them, and they will all have one **shepherd**; and they will walk in My ordinances and keep My statutes and observe them.

'I will make a covenant of peace with them and eliminate harmful beasts from the land so that they may live securely in the wilderness and sleep in the woods. I will make them and the places around My hill a blessing.

'And I will cause showers to come down in their season; they will be showers of blessing. Also the tree of the field will yield its fruit and the earth will yield its increase, and they will be secure on their land.

'Then they will know that I am the Lord, when I have broken the bars of their yoke and have delivered them from the hand of those who enslaved them. They will no longer be a prey to the nations, and the beasts of the earth will not devour them; but they will live securely, and no one will make them afraid.

'I will establish for them a renowned

planting place, and they will not again be victims of famine in the land, and they will not endure the insults of the nations anymore. Then they will know that I, the Lord their God, am with them, and that they, the house of Israel, are My people,' declares the Lord God.

"As for you, My sheep, the sheep of My pasture, you are men, and I am your God," declares the Lord God.' "

Ezekiel 34:1-31

Say to them, "Thus says the Lord God, 'Behold, I will take the sons of Israel from among the nations where they have gone, and I will gather them from every side and bring them into their own land; and I will make them one nation in the land, on the mountains of Israel; and one king will be king for all of them; and they will no longer be two nations and no longer be divided into two kingdoms.

'They will no longer defile themselves with their idols, or with their detestable things, or with any of their transgressions; but I will deliver them from all their dwelling places in which they have sinned, and will cleanse them. And they will be My people, and I will be their God.

'My servant David will be king over them, and they will all have one **shepherd**; and they will walk in My ordinances and keep My statutes and observe them. They will live on the land that I gave to Jacob My servant, in which your fathers lived; and they will live on it, they, and their sons and their sons' sons, forever; and David My servant will be their prince forever.

'I will make a covenant of peace with them; it will be an everlasting covenant with them. And I will place them and multiply them, and will set My sanctuary in their midst forever. My dwelling place also will be with them; and I will be their God, and they will be My people. And the nations will know that I am the Lord who sanctifies Israel, when My sanctuary is in their midst forever.' "

Ezekiel 37:21-28

The words of Amos, who was among the **sheepherders** from Tekoa, which he

envisioned in visions concerning Israel in the days of Uzziah king of Judah, and in the days of Jeroboam son of Joash, king of Israel, two years before the earthquake.

He said, "The Lord roars from Zion and from Jerusalem He utters His voice; and the **shepherds'** pasture grounds mourn, and the summit of Carmel dries up."

Amos 1:1-2

Thus says the Lord, "Just as the **shepherd** snatches from the lion's mouth a couple of legs or a piece of an ear, so will the sons of Israel dwelling in Samaria be snatched away - with the corner of a bed and the cover of a couch!"

Amos 3:12

Muster yourselves in troops, daughter of troops; they have laid siege against us; with a rod they will smite the judge of Israel on the cheek. But as for you, Bethlehem Ephrathah, too little to be among the clans of Judah, from you One will go forth for Me to be ruler in Israel. His goings forth are from long ago, from the days of eternity.

Therefore He will give them up until the time when she who is in labor has borne a child. Then the remainder of His brethren will return to the sons of Israel. And He will arise and **shepherd** His flock in the strength of the Lord, in the majesty of the name of the Lord His God. And they will remain, because at that time He will be great to the ends of the earth.

This One will be our peace. When the Assyrian invades our land, when he tramples on our citadels, then we will raise against him seven **shepherds** and eight leaders of men. They will **shepherd** the land of Assyria with the sword, the land of Nimrod at its entrances; and He will deliver us from the Assyrian when he attacks our land and when he tramples our territory.

Micah 5:1-6

Shepherd Your people with Your scepter, the flock of Your possession which dwells by itself in the woodland, in the midst of a fruitful field. Let them feed in Bashan and Gilead as in the days of old. As in the days when you came out from the land of Egypt, I will show you miracles.

Nations will see and be ashamed of all their might. They will put their hand on their mouth, their ears will be deaf.

Micah 7:14-16

Your **shepherds** are sleeping, O king of Assyria; your nobles are lying down. Your people are scattered on the mountains and there is no one to regather them.   *Nahum 3:18*

Woe to the inhabitants of the seacoast, the nation of the Cherethites! The word of the Lord is against you, O Canaan, land of the Philistines; and I will destroy you so that there will be no inhabitant.

So the seacoast will be pastures, with caves for **shepherds** and folds for flocks. And the coast will be for the remnant of the house of Judah, they will pasture on it. In the houses of Ashkelon they will lie down at evening; for the Lord their God will care for them and restore their fortune.   *Zephaniah 2:5-7*

Ask rain from the Lord at the time of the spring rain - the Lord who makes the storm clouds; and He will give them showers of rain, vegetation in the field to each man. For the teraphim speak iniquity, and the diviners see lying visions and tell false dreams; they comfort in vain. Therefore the people wander like sheep, they are afflicted, because there is no **shepherd**.

My anger is kindled against the **shepherds**, and I will punish the male goats; for the Lord of hosts has visited His flock, the house of Judah, and will make them like His majestic horse in battle.

Zechariah 10:1-3

Open your doors, O Lebanon, that a fire may feed on your cedars. Wail, O cypress, for the cedar has fallen, because the glorious trees have been destroyed; wail, O oaks of Bashan, for the impenetrable forest has come down. There is a sound of the **shepherds'** wail, for their glory is ruined; there is a sound of the young lions' roar, for the pride of the Jordan is ruined.

Thus says the Lord my God, "Pasture the flock doomed to slaughter. Those who buy them slay them and go unpunished, and each of those who sell them says, 'Blessed be the Lord, for I have become rich!'

"And their own **shepherds** have no pity on them. For I will no longer have pity on the inhabitants of the land," declares the Lord; "but behold, I will cause the men to fall, each into another's power and into the power of his king; and they will strike the land, and I will not deliver them from their power."

So I pastured the flock doomed to slaughter, hence the afflicted of the flock. And I took for myself two staffs: the one I called Favor and the other I called Union; so I pastured the flock. Then I annihilated the three **shepherds** in one month, for my soul was impatient with them, and their soul also was weary of me.

Then I said, "I will not pasture you. What is to die, let it die, and what is to be annihilated, let it be annihilated; and let those who are left eat one another's flesh."

I took my staff Favor and cut it in pieces, to break my covenant which I had made with all the peoples. So it was broken on that day, and thus the afflicted of the flock who were watching me realized that it was the word of the Lord. I said to them, "If it is good in your sight, give me my wages; but if not, never mind!" So they weighed out thirty shekels of silver as my wages.

Then the Lord said to me, "Throw it to the potter, that magnificent price at which I was valued by them." So I took the thirty shekels of silver and threw them to the potter in the house of the Lord. Then I cut in pieces my second staff Union, to break the brotherhood between Judah and Israel.

The Lord said to me, "Take again for yourself the equipment of a foolish **shepherd**. For behold, I am going to raise up a **shepherd** in the land who will not care for the perishing, seek the scattered, heal the broken, or sustain the one standing, but will devour the flesh of the fat sheep and tear off their hoofs.

"Woe to the worthless **shepherd** who leaves the flock! A sword will be on his arm and on his right eye! His arm will be totally withered and his right eye will be blind." *Zechariah 11:1-17*

"Awake, O sword, against My **Shepherd**, and against the man, My Associate," declares the Lord of hosts. "Strike the **Shepherd** that the sheep may be scattered; and I will turn My hand against the little ones. It will come about in all the land," declares the Lord, "that two parts in it will be cut off and perish; but the third will be left in it.

"And I will bring the third part through the fire, refine them as silver is refined, and test them as gold is tested.

"They will call on My name, and I will answer them; I will say, 'They are My people,' and they will say, 'The Lord is my God.' " *Zechariah 13:7-9*

NEW TESTAMENT

After Jesus was born in Bethlehem of Judea in the days of Herod the king, magi from the east arrived in Jerusalem, saying, "Where is He who has been born King of the Jews? For we saw His star in the east and have come to worship Him."

When Herod the king heard this, he was troubled, and all Jerusalem with him. Gathering together all the chief priests and scribes of the people, he inquired of them where the Messiah was to be born.

They said to him, "In Bethlehem of Judea; for this is what has been written by the prophet: 'And you, Bethlehem, land of Judah, are by no means least among the leaders of Judah; for out of you shall come forth a Ruler who will **shepherd** My people Israel.' " *Matthew 2:1-6*

Jesus was going through all the cities and villages, teaching in their synagogues and proclaiming the gospel of the kingdom, and healing every kind of disease and every kind of sickness.

Seeing the people, He felt compassion for them, because they were distressed and dispirited like sheep without a **shepherd**.

Then He said to His disciples, "The harvest is plentiful, but the workers are few. Therefore beseech the Lord of the harvest to send out workers into His harvest."

Jesus summoned His twelve disciples and gave them authority over unclean spirits, to cast them out, and to heal every kind of disease and every kind of sickness. *Matthew 9:35 - 10:1*

When the Son of Man comes in His glory, and all the angels with Him, then He will sit on His glorious throne. All the nations will be gathered before Him; and He will separate them from one another, as the **shepherd** separates the sheep from the goats; and He will put the sheep on His right, and the goats on the left.

Then the King will say to those on His right, "Come, you who are blessed of My

Father, inherit the kingdom prepared for you from the foundation of the world." Then the King will say to those on His right, "Come, you who are blessed of My Father, inherit the kingdom prepared for you from the foundation of the world.

"For I was hungry, and you gave Me something to eat; I was thirsty, and you gave Me something to drink; I was a stranger, and you invited Me in; naked, and you clothed Me; I was sick, and you visited Me; I was in prison, and you came to Me."

Then the righteous will answer Him, "Lord, when did we see You hungry, and feed You, or thirsty, and give You something to drink? And when did we see You a stranger, and invite You in, or naked, and clothe You? When did we see You sick, or in prison, and come to You?"

The King will answer and say to them, "Truly I say to you, to the extent that you did it to one of these brothers of Mine, even the least of them, you did it to Me."

Then He will also say to those on His left, "Depart from Me, accursed ones, into the eternal fire which has been prepared for the devil and his angels; for I was hungry, and you gave Me nothing to eat; I was thirsty, and you gave Me nothing to drink; I was a stranger, and you did not invite Me in; naked, and you did not clothe Me; sick, and in prison, and you did not visit Me."

Then they themselves also will answer, "Lord, when did we see You hungry, or thirsty, or a stranger, or naked, or sick, or in prison, and did not take care of You?"

Then He will answer them, "Truly I say to you, to the extent that you did not do it to one of the least of these, you did not do it to Me." These will go away into eternal punishment, but the righteous into eternal life. *Matthew 25:31-46*

Jesus said to them, "You will all fall away because of Me this night, for it is written, 'I will strike down the **shepherd**, and the sheep of the flock shall be scattered.' But after I have been raised, I will go ahead of

you to Galilee." *Matthew 26:31-32*

When Jesus went ashore, He saw a large crowd, and He felt compassion for them because they were like sheep without a **shepherd**; and He began to teach them many things. *Mark 6:34*

Jesus said to them, "You will all fall away, because it is written, 'I will strike down the **shepherd**, and the sheep shall be scattered.'

"But after I have been raised, I will go ahead of you to Galilee." *Mark 14:27-28*

In the same region there were some **shepherds** staying out in the fields and keeping watch over their flock by night. And an angel of the Lord suddenly stood before them, and the glory of the Lord shone around them; and they were terribly frightened.

But the angel said to them, "Do not be afraid; for behold, I bring you good news of great joy which will be for all the people; for today in the city of David there has been born for you a Savior, who is Christ the Lord. This will be a sign for you: you will find a baby wrapped in cloths and lying in a manger."

And suddenly there appeared with the angel a multitude of the heavenly host praising God and saying, "Glory to God in the highest, and on earth peace among men with whom He is pleased."

When the angels had gone away from them into heaven, the **shepherds** began saying to one another, "Let us go straight to Bethlehem then, and see this thing that has happened which the Lord has made known to us."

So they came in a hurry and found their way to Mary and Joseph, and the baby as He lay in the manger. When they had seen this, they made known the statement which had been told them about this Child. And all who heard it wondered at the things which were told them by the **shepherds**. But Mary treasured all these things, pondering them in her heart.

The **shepherds** went back, glorifying and praising God for all that they had heard and seen, just as had been told them. *Luke 2:8-20*

Which of you, having a slave plowing or tending sheep, will say to him when he has come in from the field, "Come immediately and sit down to eat"? But will he not say to him, "Prepare something for me to eat, and properly clothe yourself and serve me while I eat and drink; and afterward you may eat and drink"? He does not thank the slave because he did the things which were commanded, does he?

So you too, when you do all the things which are commanded you, say, "We are unworthy slaves; we have done only that which we ought to have done." *Luke 17:7-10*

"Truly, truly, I say to you, he who does not enter by the door into the fold of the sheep, but climbs up some other way, he is a thief and a robber. But he who enters by the door is a **shepherd** of the sheep. To him the doorkeeper opens, and the sheep hear his voice, and he calls his own sheep by name and leads them out.

"When he puts forth all his own, he goes ahead of them, and the sheep follow him because they know his voice. A stranger they simply will not follow, but will flee from him, because they do not know the voice of strangers." This figure of speech Jesus spoke to them, but they did not understand what those things were which He had been saying to them.

So Jesus said to them again, "Truly, truly, I say to you, I am the door of the sheep. All who came before Me are thieves and robbers, but the sheep did not hear them. I am the door; if anyone enters through Me, he will be saved, and will go in and out and find pasture.

"The thief comes only to steal and kill and destroy; I came that they may have life, and have it abundantly. I am the good **shepherd**; the good **shepherd** lays down His life for the sheep.

"He who is a hired hand, and not a **shepherd**, who is not the owner of the sheep, sees the wolf coming, and leaves the sheep and flees, and the wolf snatches them and scatters them. He flees because he is a hired hand and is not concerned about the sheep.

"I am the good **shepherd**, and I know My own and My own know Me, even as the Father knows Me and I know the Father; and I lay down My life for the sheep.

"I have other sheep, which are not of this fold; I must bring them also, and they will hear My voice; and they will become one flock with one **shepherd**." *John 10:1-16*

At that time the Feast of the Dedication took place at Jerusalem; it was winter, and Jesus was walking in the temple in the portico of Solomon. The Jews then gathered around Him, and were saying to Him, "How long will You keep us in suspense? If You are the Christ, tell us plainly."

Jesus answered them, "I told you, and you do not believe; the works that I do in My Father's name, these testify of Me. But you do not believe because you are not of My sheep. My sheep hear My voice, and I know them, and they follow Me; and I give eternal life to them, and they will never perish; and no one will snatch them out of My hand.

"My Father, who has given them to Me, is greater than all; and no one is able to snatch them out of the Father's hand. I and the Father are one."

The Jews picked up stones again to stone Him. *John 10:24-31*

When they had finished breakfast, Jesus said to Simon Peter, "Simon, son of John, do you love Me more than these?"

He said to Him, "Yes, Lord; You know that I love You." He said to him, "Tend My lambs."

He said to him again a second time, "Simon, son of John, do you love Me?" He said to Him, "Yes, Lord; You know that I love You." He said to him, "**Shepherd** My sheep."

He said to him the third time, "Simon, son of John, do you love Me?"

Peter was grieved because He said to him the third time, "Do you love Me?" And he said to Him, "Lord, You know all things; You know that I love You."

Jesus said to him, "Tend My sheep. Truly, truly, I say to you, when you were younger, you used to gird yourself and walk wherever you wished; but when you grow old, you will stretch out your hands and someone else will gird you, and bring you where you do not wish to go."

John 21:15-18

Be on guard for yourselves and for all the flock, among which the Holy Spirit has made you overseers, to **shepherd** the church of God which He purchased with His own blood. I know that after my departure savage wolves will come in among you, not sparing the flock; and from among your own selves men will arise, speaking perverse things, to draw away the disciples after them.

Acts 20:28-30

Now the God of peace, who brought up from the dead the great **Shepherd** of the sheep through the blood of the eternal covenant, even Jesus our Lord, equip you in every good thing to do His will, working in us that which is pleasing in His sight, through Jesus Christ, to whom be the glory forever and ever. Amen.

Hebrews 13:20-21

What credit is there if, when you sin and are harshly treated, you endure it with patience? But if when you do what is right and suffer for it you patiently endure it, this finds favor with God. For you have been called for this purpose, since Christ also suffered for you, leaving you an example for you to follow in His steps, who committed no sin, nor was any deceit found in His mouth; and while being reviled, He did not revile in return; while suffering, He uttered no threats, but kept entrusting Himself to Him who judges righteously; and He Himself bore our sins in His body on the cross, so that we might die to sin and live to righteousness; for by His wounds you were healed. For you were continually straying like sheep, but now you have returned to the **Shepherd** and Guardian of your souls. *1 Peter 2:20-25*

I exhort the elders among you, as your fellow elder and witness of the sufferings of Christ, and a partaker also of the glory that is to be revealed, **shepherd** the flock of God among you, exercising oversight not under compulsion, but voluntarily, according to the will of God; and not for sordid gain, but with eagerness; nor yet as lording it over those allotted to your charge, but proving to be examples to the flock.

And when the Chief **Shepherd** appears, you will receive the unfading crown of glory. *1 Peter 5:1-4*

All the angels were standing around the throne and around the elders and the four living creatures; and they fell on their faces before the throne and worshiped God, saying, "Amen, blessing and glory and wisdom and thanksgiving and honor and power and might, be to our God forever and ever. Amen."

Then one of the elders answered, saying to me, "These who are clothed in the white robes, who are they, and where have they come from?" I said to him, "My lord, you know."

And he said to me, "These are the ones who come out of the great tribulation, and they have washed their robes and made them white in the blood of the Lamb. For this reason, they are before the throne of God; and they serve Him day and night in His temple; and He who sits on the throne will spread His tabernacle over them.

"They will hunger no longer, nor thirst anymore; nor will the sun beat down on them, nor any heat; for the Lamb in the center of the throne will be their **shepherd**, and will guide them to springs of the water of life; and God will wipe every tear from their eyes." *Revelation 7:11-17*

CRUCIFY

/ CRUCIFIED / CRUCIFIXION

Definitions

Crucify   1. To put to death by nailing or binding the hands and feet to a cross.

2. To treat cruelly, persecute, torment or torture.

3. To punish or criticize severely.

4. To subdue or repress passion, lust, sin, etc.

Crucifixion   1. The act of crucifying or the state of being crucified.

2. The death of Jesus upon the cross, a picture or representation of this.

3. Severe or unjust punishment, suffering or torture.

NEW TESTAMENT

As Jesus was about to go up to Jerusalem, He took the twelve disciples aside by themselves, and on the way He said to them, "Behold, we are going up to Jerusalem; and the Son of Man will be delivered to the chief priests and scribes, and they will condemn Him to death, and will hand Him over to the Gentiles to mock and scourge and **crucify** Him, and on the third day He will be raised up."

Matthew 20:17-19

Woe to you, scribes and Pharisees, hypocrites! For you build the tombs of the prophets and adorn the monuments of the righteous, and say, "If we had been living in the days of our fathers, we would not have been partners with them in shedding the blood of the prophets."

So you testify against yourselves, that you are sons of those who murdered the prophets.

Fill up, then, the measure of the guilt of your fathers. You serpents, you brood of vipers, how will you escape the sentence of hell?

Therefore, behold, I am sending you prophets and wise men and scribes; some of them you will kill and **crucify**, and some of them you will scourge in your synagogues, and persecute from city to city, so that upon you may fall the guilt of all the righteous blood shed on earth, from the blood of righteous Abel to the blood of Zechariah, the son of Berechiah, whom you murdered between the temple and the altar.

Truly I say to you, all these things will come upon this generation.

Matthew 23:29-36

When Jesus had finished all these words, He said to His disciples, "You know that after two days the Passover is coming, and the Son of Man is to be handed over for **crucifixion**."

Then the chief priests and the elders of the people were gathered together in the court of the high priest, named Caiaphas; and they plotted together to seize Jesus by stealth and kill Him.

But they were saying, "Not during the festival, otherwise a riot might occur among the people."   *Matthew 26:1-5*

Jesus stood before the governor, and the governor questioned Him, saying, "Are You the King of the Jews?" And Jesus said to him, "It is as you say."

And while He was being accused by the chief priests and elders, He did not answer.

Then Pilate said to Him, "Do You not hear how many things they testify against You?"

And He did not answer him with regard to even a single charge, so the governor was quite amazed.

Now at the feast the governor was accustomed to release for the people any one prisoner whom they wanted. At that time they were holding a notorious prisoner, called Barabbas.

So when the people gathered together, Pilate said to them, "Whom do you want me to release for you? Barabbas, or Jesus who is called Christ?" For he knew that because of envy they had handed Him over.

While he was sitting on the judgment seat, his wife sent him a message, saying, "Have nothing to do with that righteous Man; for last night I suffered greatly in a dream because of Him."

But the chief priests and the elders persuaded the crowds to ask for Barabbas and to put Jesus to death.

But the governor said to them, "Which of the two do you want me to release for you?" And they said, "Barabbas."

Pilate said to them, "Then what shall I do with Jesus who is called Christ?"

They all said, "**Crucify** Him!"

And he said, "Why, what evil has He done?" But they kept shouting all the more, saying, "**Crucify** Him!"

When Pilate saw that he was accomplishing nothing, but rather that a riot was starting, he took water and washed his hands in front of the crowd, saying, "I am innocent of this man's blood; see to that yourselves."

And all the people said, "His blood shall be on us and on our children!"

Then he released Barabbas for them; but after having Jesus scourged, he handed Him over to be **crucified**.

Then the soldiers of the governor took Jesus into the Praetorium and gathered the whole Roman cohort around Him.

They stripped Him and put a scarlet robe on Him. And after twisting together a crown of thorns, they put it on His head, and a reed in His right hand; and they knelt down before Him and mocked Him, saying, "Hail, King of the Jews!"

They spat on Him, and took the reed and began to beat Him on the head. After they had mocked Him, they took the scarlet robe off Him and put His own garments back on Him, and led Him away to **crucify** Him.

As they were coming out, they found a man of Cyrene named Simon, whom they pressed into service to bear His cross.

And when they came to a place called Golgotha, which means Place of a Skull, they gave Him wine to drink mixed with gall; and after tasting it, He was unwilling to drink.

And when they had **crucified** Him, they divided up His garments among themselves by casting lots. And sitting down, they began to keep watch over Him there.

And above His head they put up the charge against Him which read, "THIS IS JESUS THE KING OF THE JEWS."

At that time two robbers were **crucified** with Him, one on the right and one on the left.

And those passing by were hurling abuse at Him, wagging their heads and saying, "You who are going to destroy the temple and rebuild it in three days, save Yourself! If You are the Son of God, come down from the cross."

In the same way the chief priests also, along with the scribes and elders, were mocking Him and saying, "He saved others; He cannot save Himself. He is the King of Israel; let Him now come down from the cross, and we will believe in Him. He trusts in God; let God rescue Him now, if He delights in Him; for He said, 'I am the Son of God.' "

The robbers who had been **crucified** with Him were also insulting Him with the same words.

Now from the sixth hour darkness fell upon all the land until the ninth hour. About the ninth hour Jesus cried out with a loud voice, saying, "Eli, Eli, lama sabachthani?" that is, "My God, My God, why have You forsaken Me?"

And some of those who were standing there, when they heard it, began saying, "This man is calling for Elijah."

Immediately one of them ran, and taking a sponge, he filled it with sour wine and put it on a reed, and gave Him a drink. But the rest of them said, "Let us see whether Elijah will come to save Him."

And Jesus cried out again with a loud voice, and yielded up His spirit. And behold, the veil of the temple was torn in two from top to bottom; and the earth shook and the rocks were split.

The tombs were opened, and many bodies of the saints who had fallen asleep were raised; and coming out of the tombs after His resurrection they entered the holy city and appeared to many.

Now the centurion, and those who were with him keeping guard over Jesus, when they saw the earthquake and the things that were happening, became very frightened and said, "Truly this was the Son of God!"

Many women were there looking on from a distance, who had followed Jesus from Galilee while ministering to Him. Among them was Mary Magdalene, and Mary the mother of James and Joseph, and the mother of the sons of Zebedee.

When it was evening, there came a rich man from Arimathea, named Joseph, who himself had also become a disciple of Jesus. This man went to Pilate and asked for the body of Jesus. Then Pilate ordered it to be given to him.

And Joseph took the body and wrapped it in a clean linen cloth, and laid it in his own new tomb, which he had hewn out in the rock; and he rolled a large stone against the entrance of the tomb and went away.

And Mary Magdalene was there, and the other Mary, sitting opposite the grave.

Matthew 27:11-61

After the Sabbath, as it began to dawn toward the first day of the week, Mary Magdalene and the other Mary came to look at the grave.

And behold, a severe earthquake had occurred, for an angel of the Lord descended from heaven and came and rolled away the stone and sat upon it. And his appearance was like lightning, and his clothing as white as snow. The guards shook for fear of him and became like dead men.

The angel said to the women, "Do not be afraid; for I know that you are looking for Jesus who has been **crucified**. He is not here, for He has risen, just as He said. Come, see the place where He was lying.

"Go quickly and tell His disciples that He has risen from the dead; and behold, He is going ahead of you into Galilee, there you will see Him; behold, I have told you. Go quickly and tell His disciples that He has risen from the dead; and behold, He is going ahead of you into Galilee, there you will see Him; behold, I have told you." *Matthew 28:1-7*

Early in the morning the chief priests with the elders and scribes and the whole Council, immediately held a consultation; and binding Jesus, they led Him away and delivered Him to Pilate. Pilate questioned Him, "Are You the King of the Jews?"

And He answered him, "It is as you say."

The chief priests began to accuse Him harshly. Then Pilate questioned Him again, saying, "Do You not answer? See how many charges they bring against You!"

But Jesus made no further answer; so Pilate was amazed.

Now at the feast he used to release for them any one prisoner whom they requested. The man named Barabbas had been imprisoned with the insurrectionists who had committed murder in the insurrection.

The crowd went up and began asking him to do as he had been accustomed to do for them.

Pilate answered them, saying, "Do you want me to release for you the King of the Jews?" For he was aware that the chief priests had handed Him over because of envy.

But the chief priests stirred up the crowd to ask him to release Barabbas for them instead.

Answering again, Pilate said to them, "Then what shall I do with Him whom you call the King of the Jews?" They shouted back, "**Crucify** Him!"

But Pilate said to them, "Why, what evil has He done?" But they shouted all the more, "**Crucify** Him!"

Wishing to satisfy the crowd, Pilate released Barabbas for them, and after having Jesus scourged, he handed Him over to be **crucified**. The soldiers took Him away into the palace (that is, the Praetorium), and they called together the whole Roman cohort.

They dressed Him up in purple, and after twisting a crown of thorns, they put it on Him; and they began to acclaim Him, "Hail, King of the Jews!"

They kept beating His head with a reed, and spitting on Him, and kneeling and bowing before Him.

After they had mocked Him, they took the purple robe off Him and put His own garments on Him. And they led Him out to **crucify** Him.

They pressed into service a passerby coming from the country, Simon of Cyrene (the father of Alexander and Rufus), to bear His cross.

Then they brought Him to the place Golgotha, which is translated, Place of a Skull.

They tried to give Him wine mixed with myrrh; but He did not take it. And they **crucified** Him, and divided up His garments among themselves, casting lots for them to decide what each man should take. It was the third hour when they **crucified** Him.

The inscription of the charge against Him read, "THE KING OF THE JEWS."

They **crucified** two robbers with Him, one on His right and one on His left. [And the Scripture was fulfilled which says, "And He was numbered with transgressors."]

Those passing by were hurling abuse at Him, wagging their heads, and saying, "Ha! You who are going to destroy the temple and rebuild it in three days, save Yourself, and come down from the cross!"

In the same way the chief priests also, along with the scribes, were mocking Him among themselves and saying, "He saved others; He cannot save Himself. Let this Christ, the King of Israel, now come down from the cross, so that we may see and believe!"

Those who were **crucified** with Him were also insulting Him.

When the sixth hour came, darkness fell over the whole land until the ninth hour.

At the ninth hour Jesus cried out with a loud voice, "Eloi, Eloi, lama sabachthani?" which is translated, "My God, My God, why have You forsaken Me?" When some of the bystanders heard it, they began saying, "Behold, He is calling for Elijah."

Someone ran and filled a sponge with sour wine, put it on a reed, and gave Him a drink, saying, "Let us see whether Elijah will come to take Him down."

And Jesus uttered a loud cry, and breathed His last. And the veil of the temple was torn in two from top to bottom. When the centurion, who was standing right in front of Him, saw the way He breathed His last, he said, "Truly this man was the Son of God!" *Mark 15:1-39*

When the Sabbath was over, Mary Magdalene, and Mary the mother of James, and Salome, bought spices, so that they might come and anoint Him. Very early on the first day of the week, they came to the tomb when the sun had risen.

They were saying to one another, "Who will roll away the stone for us from the entrance of the tomb?" Looking up, they saw that the stone had been rolled away, although it was extremely large.

Entering the tomb, they saw a young man sitting at the right, wearing a white robe; and they were amazed.

And he said to them, "Do not be amazed; you are looking for Jesus the

Nazarene, who has been **crucified**. He has risen; He is not here; behold, here is the place where they laid Him.

"But go, tell His disciples and Peter, 'He is going ahead of you to Galilee; there you will see Him, just as He told you.' "

Mark 16:1-7

Pilate summoned the chief priests and the rulers and the people, and said to them, "You brought this man to me as one who incites the people to rebellion, and behold, having examined Him before you, I have found no guilt in this man regarding the charges which you make against Him. No, nor has Herod, for he sent Him back to us; and behold, nothing deserving death has been done by Him. Therefore I will punish Him and release Him." [Now he was obliged to release to them at the feast one prisoner.]

But they cried out all together, saying, "Away with this man, and release for us Barabbas!" (He was one who had been thrown into prison for an insurrection made in the city, and for murder.)

Pilate, wanting to release Jesus, addressed them again, but they kept on calling out, saying, "**Crucify, crucify** Him!"

And he said to them the third time, "Why, what evil has this man done? I have found in Him no guilt demanding death; therefore I will punish Him and release Him."

But they were insistent, with loud voices asking that He be **crucified**. And their voices began to prevail. And Pilate pronounced sentence that their demand be granted.

And he released the man they were asking for who had been thrown into prison for insurrection and murder, but he delivered Jesus to their will.

When they led Him away, they seized a man, Simon of Cyrene, coming in from the country, and placed on him the cross to carry behind Jesus.

And following Him was a large crowd of the people, and of women who were mourning and lamenting Him.

But Jesus turning to them said, "Daughters of Jerusalem, stop weeping for Me, but weep for yourselves and for your children.

"For behold, the days are coming when they will say, 'Blessed are the barren, and the wombs that never bore, and the breasts that never nursed.'

"Then they will begin to say to the mountains, 'Fall on us,' and to the hills, 'Cover us.' For if they do these things when the tree is green, what will happen when it is dry?"

Two others also, who were criminals, were being led away to be put to death with Him.

When they came to the place called The Skull, there they **crucified** Him and the criminals, one on the right and the other on the left.

But Jesus was saying, "Father, forgive them; for they do not know what they are doing." And they cast lots, dividing up His garments among themselves.

And the people stood by, looking on. And even the rulers were sneering at Him, saying, "He saved others; let Him save Himself if this is the Christ of God, His Chosen One."

The soldiers also mocked Him, coming up to Him, offering Him sour wine, and saying, "If You are the King of the Jews, save Yourself!"

Now there was also an inscription above Him, "THIS IS THE KING OF THE JEWS."

One of the criminals who were hanged there was hurling abuse at Him, saying, "Are You not the Christ? Save Yourself and us!"

But the other answered, and rebuking him said, "Do you not even fear God, since you are under the same sentence of condemnation? And we indeed are suffering justly, for we are receiving what we deserve for our deeds; but this man has done nothing wrong."

And he was saying, "Jesus, remember me when You come in Your kingdom!"

And He said to him, "Truly I say to you, today you shall be with Me in Paradise."

It was now about the sixth hour, and darkness fell over the whole land until the ninth hour, because the sun was obscured; and the veil of the temple was torn in two.

And Jesus, crying out with a loud voice, said, "Father, into Your hands I commit My spirit." Having said this, He breathed His last.

Now when the centurion saw what had happened, he began praising God, saying, "Certainly this man was innocent."

And all the crowds who came together for this spectacle, when they observed what had happened, began to return, beating their breasts.

And all His acquaintances and the women who accompanied Him from Galilee were standing at a distance, seeing these things.   *Luke 23:13-49*

On the first day of the week, at early dawn, they came to the tomb bringing the spices which they had prepared. And they found the stone rolled away from the tomb, but when they entered, they did not find the body of the Lord Jesus.

While they were perplexed about this, behold, two men suddenly stood near them in dazzling clothing; and as the women were terrified and bowed their faces to the ground, the men said to them, "Why do you seek the living One among the dead? He is not here, but He has risen.

"Remember how He spoke to you while He was still in Galilee, saying that the Son of Man must be delivered into the hands of sinful men, and be **crucified**, and the third day rise again."

And they remembered His words, and returned from the tomb and reported all these things to the eleven and to all the rest.   *Luke 24:1-9*

Two of them were going that very day to a village named Emmaus, which was about seven miles from Jerusalem. And they were talking with each other about all these things which had taken place.

While they were talking and discussing, Jesus Himself approached and began traveling with them. But their eyes were prevented from recognizing Him.

And He said to them, "What are these words that you are exchanging with one another as you are walking?" And they stood still, looking sad.

One of them, named Cleopas, answered and said to Him, "Are You the only one visiting Jerusalem and unaware of the things which have happened here in these days?"

And He said to them, "What things?"

And they said to Him, "The things about Jesus the Nazarene, who was a prophet mighty in deed and word in the sight of God and all the people, and how the chief priests and our rulers delivered Him to the sentence of death, and **crucified** Him. But we were hoping that it was He who was going to redeem Israel.

"Indeed, besides all this, it is the third day since these things happened."   *Luke 24:13-21*

They led Jesus from Caiaphas into the Praetorium, and it was early; and they themselves did not enter into the Praetorium so that they would not be defiled, but might eat the Passover. Therefore Pilate went out to them and said, "What accusation do you bring against this Man?"

They answered and said to him, "If this Man were not an evildoer, we would not have delivered Him to you."

So Pilate said to them, "Take Him yourselves, and judge Him according to your law." The Jews said to him, "We are not permitted to put anyone to death," to fulfill the word of Jesus which He spoke, signifying by what kind of death He was about to die.

Therefore Pilate entered again into the Praetorium, and summoned Jesus and said to Him, "Are You the King of the Jews?" Jesus answered, "Are you saying this on your own initiative, or did others tell you about Me?"

Pilate answered, "I am not a Jew, am I? Your own nation and the chief priests delivered You to me; what have You done?"

Jesus answered, "My kingdom is not of this world. If My kingdom were of this world, then My servants would be fighting so that I would not be handed over to the Jews; but as it is, My kingdom is not of this realm."

Therefore Pilate said to Him, "So You are a king?" Jesus answered, "You say correctly that I am a king. For this I have been born, and for this I have come into the world, to testify to the truth. Everyone who is of the truth hears My voice."

Pilate said to Him, "What is truth?" And when he had said this, he went out again to the Jews and said to them, "I find no guilt in Him.

"But you have a custom that I release someone for you at the Passover; do you wish then that I release for you the King of the Jews?"

So they cried out again, saying, "Not this Man, but Barabbas." Now Barabbas was a robber.

Pilate then took Jesus and scourged Him. And the soldiers twisted together a crown of thorns and put it on His head, and put a purple robe on Him; and they began to come up to Him and say, "Hail, King of the Jews!" and to give Him slaps in the face.

Pilate came out again and said to them, "Behold, I am bringing Him out to you so that you may know that I find no guilt in Him." Jesus then came out, wearing the crown of thorns and the purple robe. Pilate said to them, "Behold, the Man!"

So when the chief priests and the officers saw Him, they cried out saying, "**Crucify, crucify!**" Pilate said to them, "Take Him yourselves and **crucify** Him, for I find no guilt in Him."

The Jews answered him, "We have a law, and by that law He ought to die because He made Himself out to be the Son of God."

Therefore when Pilate heard this statement, he was even more afraid; and he entered into the Praetorium again and said to Jesus, "Where are You from?" But Jesus gave him no answer.

So Pilate said to Him, "You do not speak to me? Do You not know that I have authority to release You, and I have authority to **crucify** You?"

Jesus answered, "You would have no authority over Me, unless it had been given you from above; for this reason he who delivered Me to you has the greater sin."

As a result of this Pilate made efforts to release Him, but the Jews cried out saying, "If you release this man, you are no friend of Caesar; everyone who makes himself out to be a king opposes Caesar."

Therefore when Pilate heard these words, he brought Jesus out, and sat down on the judgment seat at a place called The Pavement, but in Hebrew, Gabbatha.

Now it was the day of preparation for the Passover; it was about the sixth hour. And he said to the Jews, "Behold, your King!"

So they cried out, "Away with Him, away with Him, **crucify** Him!" Pilate said to them, "Shall I **crucify** your King?"

The chief priests answered, "We have no king but Caesar."

So he then handed Him over to them to be **crucified**.

They took Jesus, therefore, and He went out, bearing His own cross, to the place called the Place of a Skull, which is called in Hebrew, Golgotha. There they **crucified** Him, and with Him two other men, one on either side, and Jesus in between.

Pilate also wrote an inscription and put it on the cross. It was written, "JESUS THE NAZARENE, THE KING OF THE JEWS."

Therefore many of the Jews read this inscription, for the place where Jesus was **crucified** was near the city; and it was written in Hebrew, Latin and in Greek.

So the chief priests of the Jews were saying to Pilate, "Do not write, 'The King of the Jews'; but that He said, 'I am King of the Jews.' "

Pilate answered, "What I have written I have written."

Then the soldiers, when they had **crucified** Jesus, took His outer garments and made four parts, a part to every soldier and also the tunic; now the tunic was seamless, woven in one piece. So they said to one another, "Let us not tear it, but cast lots for it, to decide whose it shall be"; this was to fulfill the Scripture: "They divided My outer garments among them, and for My clothing they cast lots." Therefore the soldiers did these things.

But standing by the cross of Jesus were His mother, and His mother's sister, Mary the wife of Clopas, and Mary Magdalene. When Jesus then saw His mother, and the disciple whom He loved standing nearby, He said to His mother, "Woman, behold, your son!"

Then He said to the disciple, "Behold, your mother!" From that hour the disciple took her into his own household.

After this, Jesus, knowing that all things had already been accomplished, to fulfill the Scripture, said, "I am thirsty."

A jar full of sour wine was standing there; so they put a sponge full of the sour wine upon a branch of hyssop and brought it up to His mouth.

Therefore when Jesus had received the sour wine, He said, "It is finished!" And He bowed His head and gave up His spirit.

Then the Jews, because it was the day of preparation, so that the bodies would not remain on the cross on the Sabbath (for that Sabbath was a high day), asked Pilate that their legs might be broken, and that they might be taken away.

So the soldiers came, and broke the legs of the first man and of the other who was **crucified** with Him; but coming to Jesus, when they saw that He was already dead, they did not break His legs. But one of the soldiers pierced His side with a spear, and immediately blood and water came out.

And he who has seen has testified, and his testimony is true; and he knows that he is telling the truth, so that you also may believe. For these things came to pass to fulfill the Scripture, "Not a bone of Him shall be broken." And again another Scripture says, "They shall look on Him whom they pierced."

After these things Joseph of Arimathea, being a disciple of Jesus, but a secret one for fear of the Jews, asked Pilate that he might take away the body of Jesus; and Pilate granted permission. So he came and took away His body.

Nicodemus, who had first come to Him by night, also came, bringing a mixture of myrrh and aloes, about a hundred pounds weight. So they took the body of Jesus and bound it in linen wrappings with the spices, as is the burial custom of the Jews.

Now in the place where He was **crucified** there was a garden, and in the garden a new tomb in which no one had yet been laid. Therefore because of the Jewish day of preparation, since the tomb was nearby, they laid Jesus there.

John 18:28 - 19:42

"This Jesus God raised up again, to which we are all witnesses. Therefore having been exalted to the right hand of God, and having received from the Father the promise of the Holy Spirit, He has poured forth this which you both see and hear.

"For it was not David who ascended into heaven, but he himself says: 'The Lord said to my Lord, "Sit at My right hand, until I make Your enemies a footstool for Your feet." ' Therefore let all the house of Israel know for certain that God has made Him both Lord and Christ - this Jesus whom you **crucified**."

Now when they heard this, they were pierced to the heart, and said to Peter and the rest of the apostles, "Brethren, what shall we do?"

Peter said to them, "Repent, and each of you be baptized in the name of Jesus Christ for the forgiveness of your sins; and you will receive the gift of the Holy Spirit. For the promise is for you and your children and for all who are far off, as many as the Lord our God will call to Himself."

And with many other words he solemnly testified and kept on exhorting them, saying, "Be saved from this perverse generation!"   *Acts 2:32-40*

Peter, filled with the Holy Spirit, said to them, "Rulers and elders of the people, if we are on trial today for a benefit done to a sick man, as to how this man has been made well, let it be known to all of you and to all the people of Israel, that by the name of Jesus Christ the Nazarene, whom you **crucified**, whom God raised from the dead - by this name this man stands here before you in good health.

"He is the stone which was rejected by you, the builders, but which became the chief corner stone. And there is salvation in no one else; for there is no other name under heaven that has been given among men by which we must be saved."
                    Acts 4:8-12

The Law came in so that the transgression would increase; but where sin increased, grace abounded all the more, so that, as sin reigned in death, even so grace would reign through righteousness to eternal life through Jesus Christ our Lord.

What shall we say then? Are we to continue in sin so that grace may increase? May it never be! How shall we who died to sin still live in it? Or do you not know that all of us who have been baptized into Christ Jesus have been baptized into His death?

Therefore we have been buried with Him through baptism into death, so that as Christ was raised from the dead through the glory of the Father, so we too might walk in newness of life. For if we have become united with Him in the likeness of His death, certainly we shall also be in the likeness of His resurrection, knowing this, that our old self was **crucified** with Him, in order that our body of sin might be done away with, so that we would no longer be slaves to sin; for he who has died is freed from sin.

Now if we have died with Christ, we believe that we shall also live with Him,

knowing that Christ, having been raised from the dead, is never to die again; death no longer is master over Him. For the death that He died, He died to sin once for all; but the life that He lives, He lives to God.

Even so consider yourselves to be dead to sin, but alive to God in Christ Jesus.   *Romans 5:20 - 6:10*

I exhort you, brethren, by the name of our Lord Jesus Christ, that you all agree and that there be no divisions among you, but that you be made complete in the same mind and in the same judgment. For I have been informed concerning you, my brethren, by Chloe's people, that there are quarrels among you.

Now I mean this, that each one of you is saying, "I am of Paul," and "I of Apollos," and "I of Cephas," and "I of Christ." Has Christ been divided? Paul was not **crucified** for you, was he? Or were you baptized in the name of Paul?

"I thank God that I baptized none of you except Crispus and Gaius, so that no one would say you were baptized in my name.   *1 Corinthians 1:10-15*

Where is the wise man? Where is the scribe? Where is the debater of this age? Has not God made foolish the wisdom of the world? For since in the wisdom of God the world through its wisdom did not come to know God, God was well-pleased through the foolishness of the message preached to save those who believe.

For indeed Jews ask for signs and Greeks search for wisdom; but we preach Christ **crucified**, to Jews a stumbling block and to Gentiles foolishness, but to those who are the called, both Jews and Greeks, Christ the power of God and the wisdom of God. Because the foolishness of God is wiser than men, and the weakness of God is stronger than men.
                    1 Corinthians 1:20-25

When I came to you, brethren, I did not come with superiority of speech or of wisdom, proclaiming to you the testimony of God. For I determined to know nothing among you except Jesus Christ, and Him **crucified**. I was with you in weakness and in fear and in much trembling, and my message and my preaching were not in persuasive words of wisdom, but in demonstration of the Spirit and of power, so that your faith would not rest on the wisdom of men, but on the power of God.

Yet we do speak wisdom among those who are mature; a wisdom, however, not of this age nor of the rulers of this age, who are passing away; but we speak God's wisdom in a mystery, the hidden wisdom which God predestined before the ages to our glory; the wisdom which none of the rulers of this age has understood; for if they had understood it they would not have **crucified** the Lord of glory; but just as it is written, "Things which eye has not seen and ear has not heard, and which have not entered the heart of man, all that God has prepared for those who love Him." *1 Corinthians 2:1-9*

Indeed He was **crucified** because of weakness, yet He lives because of the power of God. For we also are weak in Him, yet we will live with Him because of the power of God directed toward you.
2 Corinthians 13:4

We are Jews by nature and not sinners from among the Gentiles; nevertheless knowing that a man is not justified by the works of the Law but through faith in Christ Jesus, even we have believed in Christ Jesus, so that we may be justified by faith in Christ and not by the works of the Law; since by the works of the Law no flesh will be justified.

But if, while seeking to be justified in Christ, we ourselves have also been found sinners, is Christ then a minister of sin? May it never be! For if I rebuild what I have once destroyed, I prove myself to be a transgressor.

For through the Law I died to the Law, so that I might live to God. I have been **crucified** with Christ; and it is no longer I who live, but Christ lives in me; and the life which I now live in the flesh I

live by faith in the Son of God, who loved me and gave Himself up for me. I do not nullify the grace of God, for if righteousness comes through the Law, then Christ died needlessly.

You foolish Galatians, who has bewitched you, before whose eyes Jesus Christ was publicly portrayed as **crucified**? This is the only thing I want to find out from you: Did you receive the Spirit by the works of the Law, or by hearing with faith? Are you so foolish? Having begun by the Spirit, are you now being perfected by the flesh? *Galatians 2:15 - 3:3*

I say, walk by the Spirit, and you will not carry out the desire of the flesh. For the flesh sets its desire against the Spirit, and the Spirit against the flesh; for these are in opposition to one another, so that you may not do the things that you please. But if you are led by the Spirit, you are not under the Law.

Now the deeds of the flesh are evident, which are: immorality, impurity, sensuality, idolatry, sorcery, enmities, strife, jealousy, outbursts of anger, disputes, dissensions, factions, envying, drunkenness, carousing, and things like these, of which I forewarn you, just as I have forewarned you, that those who practice such things will not inherit the kingdom of God.

But the fruit of the Spirit is love, joy, peace, patience, kindness, goodness, faithfulness, gentleness, self-control; against such things there is no law. Now those who belong to Christ Jesus have **crucified** the flesh with its passions and desires. If we live by the Spirit, let us also walk by the Spirit. *Galatians 5:16-25*

May it never be that I would boast, except in the cross of our Lord Jesus Christ, through which the world has been **crucified** to me, and I to the world.
Galatians 6:14

In the case of those who have once been enlightened and have tasted of the heavenly gift and have been made partakers of the Holy Spirit, and have tasted the good word of God and the powers of the age to come, and then have fallen away, it is impossible to renew them again to repentance, since they again **crucify** to themselves the Son of God and put Him to open shame.   *Hebrews 6:4-6*

I will grant authority to my two witnesses, and they will prophesy for twelve hundred and sixty days, clothed in sackcloth. These are the two olive trees and the two lampstands that stand before the Lord of the earth. And if anyone wants to harm them, fire flows out of their mouth and devours their enemies; so if anyone wants to harm them, he must be killed in this way.

These have the power to shut up the sky, so that rain will not fall during the days of their prophesying; and they have power over the waters to turn them into blood, and to strike the earth with every plague, as often as they desire.

When they have finished their testimony, the beast that comes up out of the abyss will make war with them, and overcome them and kill them. And their dead bodies will lie in the street of the great city which mystically is called Sodom and Egypt, where also their Lord was **crucified**.   *Revelation 11:3-8*

RESURRECTION

+ RESTORED TO LIFE + RAISE* / RAISING* / RAISES* /
RAISED* / RISE* / RISING* / ARISE* / RISEN* / ROSE*
+ REVIVED*

*These terms are often accompanied by "**dead**" &/or "**again**".*

Definitions

Resurrection   1. The act of rising from the dead to life; restoration to life.

2. The rising of Christ after his death and burial.

3. The rising of the dead on Judgment Day.

4. The state of those risen from the dead.

5. A rising again, as from decay or disease; a revival.

Revived   To be restored to life or consciousness.

OLD TESTAMENT

It came about that the son of the woman, the mistress of the house, became sick; and his sickness was so severe that there was no breath left in him.

So she said to Elijah, "What do I have to do with you, O man of God? You have come to me to bring my iniquity to remembrance and to put my son to death!"

He said to her, "Give me your son."

Then he took him from her bosom and carried him up to the upper room where he was living, and laid him on his own bed.

He called to the Lord and said, "O Lord my God, have You also brought calamity to the widow with whom I am staying, by causing her son to die?"

Then he stretched himself upon the child three times, and called to the Lord and said, "O Lord my God, I pray You, let this child's life return to him."

The Lord heard the voice of Elijah, and the life of the child returned to him and he **revived**.

Elijah took the child and brought him down from the upper room into the house and gave him to his mother; and Elijah said, "See, your son is alive."

Then the woman said to Elijah, "Now I know that you are a man of God and that the word of the Lord in your mouth is truth."   *1 Kings 17:17-24*

When she came to the man of God to the hill, she caught hold of his feet. And Gehazi came near to push her away; but the man of God said, "Let her alone, for her soul is troubled within her; and the Lord has hidden it from me and has not told me."

Then she said, "Did I ask for a son from my lord? Did I not say, 'Do not deceive me'?"

Then he said to Gehazi, "Gird up your loins and take my staff in your hand, and go your way; if you meet any man, do not salute him, and if anyone salutes you, do not answer him; and lay my staff on the lad's face."

The mother of the lad said, "As the Lord lives and as you yourself live, I will not leave you." And he arose and followed her.

Then Gehazi passed on before them and laid the staff on the lad's face, but there was no sound or response.

So he returned to meet him and told him, "The lad has not awakened."

When Elisha came into the house,

behold the lad was dead and laid on his bed. So he entered and shut the door behind them both and prayed to the Lord.

And he went up and lay on the child, and put his mouth on his mouth and his eyes on his eyes and his hands on his hands, and he stretched himself on him; and the flesh of the child became warm.

Then he returned and walked in the house once back and forth, and went up and stretched himself on him; and the lad sneezed seven times and the lad opened his eyes.

He called Gehazi and said, "Call this Shunammite." So he called her.

And when she came in to him, he said, "Take up your son."

Then she went in and fell at his feet and bowed herself to the ground, and she took up her son and went out.

2 Kings 4:27-37

Elisha spoke to the woman whose son he had **restored to life**, saying, "Arise and go with your household, and sojourn wherever you can sojourn; for the Lord has called for a famine, and it will even come on the land for seven years."

So the woman arose and did according to the word of the man of God, and she went with her household and sojourned in the land of the Philistines seven years.

At the end of seven years, the woman returned from the land of the Philistines; and she went out to appeal to the king for her house and for her field.

Now the king was talking with Gehazi, the servant of the man of God, saying, "Please relate to me all the great things that Elisha has done."

As he was relating to the king how he had **restored to life** the one who was dead, behold, the woman whose son he had **restored to life** appealed to the king for her house and for her field.

And Gehazi said, "My lord, O king, this is the woman and this is her son, whom Elisha **restored to life**."

When the king asked the woman, she related it to him. So the king appointed for her a certain officer, saying, "Restore all that was hers and all the produce of the field from the day that she left the land even until now."

2 Kings 8:1-6

Elisha died, and they buried him. Now the bands of the Moabites would invade the land in the spring of the year.

As they were burying a man, behold, they saw a marauding band; and they cast the man into the grave of Elisha.

And when the man touched the bones of Elisha he **revived** and stood up on his feet.

2 Kings 13:20-21

The hand of the Lord was upon me, and He brought me out by the Spirit of the Lord and set me down in the middle of the valley; and it was full of bones. He caused me to pass among them round about, and behold, there were very many on the surface of the valley; and lo, they were very dry.

He said to me, "Son of man, can these bones live?"

And I answered, "O Lord God, You know."

Again He said to me, "Prophesy over these bones and say to them, 'O dry bones, hear the word of the Lord.'

"Thus says the Lord God to these bones, 'Behold, I will cause breath to enter you that you may come to life. I will put sinews on you, make flesh grow back on you, cover you with skin and put breath in you that you may come alive; and you will know that I am the Lord.' "

So I prophesied as I was commanded; and as I prophesied, there was a noise, and behold, a rattling; and the bones came together, bone to its bone.

And I looked, and behold, sinews were on them, and flesh grew and skin covered them; but there was no breath in them.

Then He said to me, "Prophesy to the breath, prophesy, son of man, and say to the breath, 'Thus says the Lord God, "Come from the four winds, O breath, and breathe on these slain, that they come to life."'"

So I prophesied as He commanded me, and the breath came into them, and they came to life and stood on their feet, an exceedingly great army.

Then He said to me, "Son of man, these bones are the whole house of Israel; behold, they say, 'Our bones are dried up and our hope has perished. We are completely cut off.'

"Therefore prophesy and say to them, 'Thus says the Lord God, "Behold, I will open your graves and cause you to come up out of your graves, My people; and I will bring you into the land of Israel. Then you will know that I am the Lord, when I have opened your graves and caused you to come up out of your graves, My people.

"I will put My Spirit within you and you will come to life, and I will place you on your own land.

Then you will know that I, the Lord, have spoken and done it" declares the Lord." *Ezekiel 37:1-14*

At that time Michael, the great prince who stands guard over the sons of your people, will arise.

And there will be a time of distress such as never occurred since there was a nation until that time; and at that time your people, everyone who is found written in the book, will be rescued.

Many of those who sleep in the dust of the ground will awake, these to everlasting life, but the others to disgrace and everlasting contempt.

Those who have insight will shine brightly like the brightness of the expanse of heaven, and those who lead the many to righteousness, like the stars forever and ever. *Daniel 12:1-3*

I heard but could not understand; so I said, "My lord, what will be the outcome of these events?"

He said, "Go your way, Daniel, for these words are concealed and sealed up until the end time.

"Many will be purged, purified and refined, but the wicked will act wickedly; and none of the wicked will understand, but those who have insight will understand.

"From the time that the regular sacrifice is abolished and the abomination of desolation is set up, there will be 1,290 days. How blessed is he who keeps waiting and attains to the 1,335 days!

"But as for you, go your way to the end; then you will enter into rest and **rise again** for your allotted portion at the end of the age." *Daniel 12:8-13*

Come, let us return to the Lord. For He has torn us, but He will heal us; He has wounded us, but He will bandage us.

He will revive us after two days; He will **raise** us up on the third day, that we may live before Him. *Hosea 6:1-2*

NEW TESTAMENT

While He was saying these things to them, a synagogue official came and bowed down before Him, and said, "My daughter has just died; but come and lay Your hand on her, and she will live."

Jesus got up and began to follow him, and so did His disciples. ...

... When Jesus came into the official's house, and saw the flute-players and the crowd in noisy disorder, He said, "Leave; for the girl has not died, but is asleep." And they began laughing at Him.

But when the crowd had been sent out, He entered and took her by the hand, and the girl got up.

This news spread throughout all that land.   *Matthew 9:18-20...24-26*

These twelve Jesus sent out after instructing them: "Do not go in the way of the Gentiles, and do not enter any city of the Samaritans; but rather go to the lost sheep of the house of Israel.

And as you go, preach, saying, 'The kingdom of heaven is at hand.'

"Heal the sick, **raise the dead**, cleanse the lepers, cast out demons.

"Freely you received, freely give."
      Matthew 10:5-8

When John, while imprisoned, heard of the works of Christ, he sent word by his disciples and said to Him, "Are You the Expected One, or shall we look for someone else?"

Jesus answered and said to them, "Go and report to John what you hear and see: the blind receive sight and the lame walk, the lepers are cleansed and the deaf hear, the **dead** are **raised** up, and the poor have the gospel preached to them.

"And blessed is he who does not take offense at Me."   *Matthew 11:2-6*

On that day some Sadducees (who say there is no **resurrection**) came to Jesus and questioned Him, asking, "Teacher,

Moses said, 'If a man dies having no children, his brother as next of kin shall marry his wife, and raise up children for his brother'.

"Now there were seven brothers with us; and the first married and died, and having no children left his wife to his brother; so also the second, and the third, down to the seventh. Last of all, the woman died. In the **resurrection**, therefore, whose wife of the seven will she be? For they all had married her."

But Jesus answered and said to them, "You are mistaken, not understanding the Scriptures nor the power of God. For in the **resurrection** they neither marry nor are given in marriage, but are like angels in heaven.

"But regarding the **resurrection** of the dead, have you not read what was spoken to you by God: 'I am the God of Abraham, and the God of Isaac, and the God of Jacob'? He is not the God of the dead but of the living."

When the crowds heard this, they were astonished at His teaching.
      Matthew 22:23-33

Jesus cried out again with a loud voice, and yielded up His spirit.

And behold, the veil of the temple was torn in two from top to bottom; and the earth shook and the rocks were split.

The tombs were opened, and many bodies of the saints who had fallen asleep were **raised**; and coming out of the tombs after His **resurrection** they entered the holy city and appeared to many.

Now the centurion, and those who were with him keeping guard over Jesus, when they saw the earthquake and the things that were happening, became very frightened and said, "Truly this was the Son of God!"   *Matthew 27:50-54*

When Jesus had crossed over again in the boat to the other side, a large crowd gathered around Him; and so He stayed by the seashore.

One of the synagogue officials named Jairus came up, and on seeing Him, fell at His feet and implored Him earnestly, saying, "My little daughter is at the point of death; please come and lay Your hands on her, so that she will get well and live."

And He went off with him; and a large crowd was following Him and pressing in on Him. ...

... While He was still speaking, they came from the house of the synagogue official, saying, "Your daughter has died; why trouble the Teacher anymore?"

But Jesus, overhearing what was being spoken, said to the synagogue official, "Do not be afraid any longer, only believe."

And He allowed no one to accompany Him, except Peter and James and John the brother of James.

They came to the house of the synagogue official; and He saw a commotion, and people loudly weeping and wailing.

And entering in, He said to them, "Why make a commotion and weep? The child has not died, but is asleep." They began laughing at Him.

But putting them all out, He took along the child's father and mother and His own companions, and entered the room where the child was.

Taking the child by the hand, He said to her, "Talitha kum!" (which translated means, "Little girl, I say to you, get up!").

Immediately the girl got up and began to walk, for she was twelve years old. And immediately they were completely astounded.

And He gave them strict orders that no one should know about this, and He said that something should be given her to eat. *Mark 5:21-24...35-43*

Six days later, Jesus took with Him Peter and James and John, and brought them up on a high mountain by themselves.

And He was transfigured before them; and His garments became radiant and exceedingly white, as no launderer on earth can whiten them.

Elijah appeared to them along with Moses; and they were talking with Jesus.

Peter said to Jesus, "Rabbi, it is good for us to be here; let us make three tabernacles, one for You, and one for Moses,

and one for Elijah." For he did not know what to answer; for they became terrified.

Then a cloud formed, overshadowing them, and a voice came out of the cloud, "This is My beloved Son, listen to Him!"

All at once they looked around and saw no one with them anymore, except Jesus alone.

As they were coming down from the mountain, He gave them orders not to relate to anyone what they had seen, until the Son of Man **rose from the dead**.

They seized upon that statement, discussing with one another what **rising from the dead** meant.

They asked Him, saying, "Why is it that the scribes say that Elijah must come first?"

And He said to them, "Elijah does first come and restore all things. And yet how is it written of the Son of Man that He will suffer many things and be treated with contempt?

"But I say to you that Elijah has indeed come, and they did to him whatever they wished, just as it is written of him."

Mark 9:2-13

Some Sadducees (who say that there is no **resurrection**) came to Jesus, and began questioning Him, saying, "Teacher, Moses wrote for us that if a man's brother dies and leaves behind a wife and leaves no child, his brother should marry the wife and raise up children to his brother.

"There were seven brothers; and the first took a wife, and died leaving no children. The second one married her, and died leaving behind no children; and the third likewise; and so all seven left no children. Last of all the woman died also.

"In the **resurrection**, when they **rise again**, which one's wife will she be? For all seven had married her."

Jesus said to them, "Is this not the reason you are mistaken, that you do not understand the Scriptures or the power of God? For when they **rise from the dead**, they neither marry nor are given in marriage, but are like angels in heaven.

"But regarding the fact that the **dead rise again**, have you not read in the book of Moses, in the passage about the burning bush, how God spoke to him, saying, 'I am the God of Abraham, and the God of Isaac, and the God of Jacob'? He is not the God of the dead, but of the living; you are greatly mistaken."   *Mark 12:18-27*

He went to a city called Nain; and His disciples were going along with Him, accompanied by a large crowd.

Now as He approached the gate of the city, a dead man was being carried out, the only son of his mother, and she was a widow; and a sizeable crowd from the city was with her.

When the Lord saw her, He felt compassion for her, and said to her, "Do not weep." And He came up and touched the coffin; and the bearers came to a halt.

And He said, "Young man, I say to you, **arise!**"

The dead man sat up and began to speak. And Jesus gave him back to his mother.

Fear gripped them all, and they began glorifying God, saying, "A great prophet has arisen among us!" and, "God has visited His people!"

This report concerning Him went out all over Judea and in all the surrounding district. The disciples of John reported to him about all these things.

Summoning two of his disciples, John sent them to the Lord, saying, "Are You the Expected One, or do we look for someone else?"

When the men came to Him, they said, "John the Baptist has sent us to You, to ask, 'Are You the Expected One, or do we look for someone else?' "

At that very time He cured many people of diseases and afflictions and evil spirits; and He gave sight to many who were blind.

And He answered and said to them, "Go and report to John what you have seen and heard: the blind receive sight, the lame walk, the lepers are cleansed, and the deaf hear, the **dead are raised** up, the poor have the gospel preached to them.

"Blessed is he who does not take offense at Me."   *Luke 7:11-23*

There came a man named Jairus, and he was an official of the synagogue; and he fell at Jesus' feet, and began to implore Him to come to his house; for he had an only daughter, about twelve years old, and she was dying. But as He went, the crowds were pressing against Him. ...

... While He was still speaking, someone came from the house of the synagogue official, saying, "Your daughter has died; do not trouble the Teacher anymore."

But when Jesus heard this, He answered him, "Do not be afraid any longer; only believe, and she will be made well."

When He came to the house, He did not allow anyone to enter with Him, except Peter and John and James, and the girl's father and mother.

Now they were all weeping and lamenting for her; but He said, "Stop weeping, for she has not died, but is asleep." And they began laughing at Him, knowing that she had died.

He, however, took her by the hand and called, saying, "Child, **arise!**"

And her spirit returned, and she got up immediately; and He gave orders for something to be given her to eat.

Her parents were amazed; but He instructed them to tell no one what had happened.   *Luke 8:41-42...49-56*

He also went on to say to the one who had invited Him, "When you give a luncheon or a dinner, do not invite your friends or your brothers or your relatives or rich neighbors, otherwise they may also invite you in return and that will be your repayment.

"But when you give a reception, invite the poor, the crippled, the lame, the blind, and you will be blessed, since they do not have the means to repay you; for you will be repaid at the **resurrection** of the righteous."

When one of those who were reclining at the table with Him heard this, he said to Him, "Blessed is everyone who will eat bread in the kingdom of God!"

Luke 14:12-15

There came to Him some of the Sadducees (who say that there is no **resurrection**), and they questioned Him, saying, "Teacher, Moses wrote for us that if a man's brother dies, having a wife, and he is childless, his brother should marry the wife and raise up children to his brother.

"Now there were seven brothers; and the first took a wife and died childless; and the second and the third married her; and in the same way all seven died, leaving no children. Finally the woman died also.

"In the **resurrection** therefore, which one's wife will she be? For all seven had married her."

Jesus said to them, "The sons of this age marry and are given in marriage, but those who are considered worthy to attain to that age and the **resurrection** from the dead, neither marry nor are given in marriage; for they cannot even die anymore, because they are like angels, and are sons of God, being sons of the **resurrection**.

"But that the **dead are raised**, even Moses showed, in the passage about the burning bush, where he calls the Lord the God of Abraham, and the God of Isaac, and the God of Jacob. Now He is not the God of the dead but of the living; for all live to Him."

Some of the scribes answered and said, "Teacher, You have spoken well." For they did not have courage to question Him any longer about anything.

Luke 20:27-40

The Passover of the Jews was near, and Jesus went up to Jerusalem.

And He found in the temple those who were selling oxen and sheep and doves, and the money changers seated at their tables.

And He made a scourge of cords, and drove them all out of the temple, with the sheep and the oxen; and He poured out the coins of the money changers and overturned their tables; and to those who were selling the doves He said, "Take these things away; stop making My Father's house a place of business."

His disciples remembered that it was written, "Zeal for Your house will consume me."

The Jews then said to Him, "What sign do You show us as your authority for doing these things?"

Jesus answered them, "Destroy this temple, and in three days I will raise it up."

The Jews then said, "It took forty-six years to build this temple, and will You raise it up in three days?" But He was speaking of the temple of His body.

So when He was **raised from the dead**, His disciples remembered that He said this; and they believed the Scripture and the word which Jesus had spoken.

John 2:13-22

Jesus answered and was saying to them, "Truly, truly, I say to you, the Son can do nothing of Himself, unless it is something He sees the Father doing; for whatever the Father does, these things the Son also does in like manner.

"For the Father loves the Son, and shows Him all things that He Himself is doing; and the Father will show Him greater works than these, so that you will marvel.

"For just as the Father **raises the dead** and gives them life, even so the Son also gives life to whom He wishes.

"For not even the Father judges anyone, but He has given all judgment to the Son, so that all will honor the Son even as they honor the Father. He who does not honor the Son does not honor the Father who sent Him.

"Truly, truly, I say to you, he who hears My word, and believes Him who sent Me, has eternal life, and does not come into judgment, but has passed out of death into life.

"Truly, truly, I say to you, an hour is coming and now is, when the dead will hear the voice of the Son of God, and those who hear will live.

"For just as the Father has life in Himself, even so He gave to the Son also to have life in Himself; and He gave Him authority to execute judgment, because He is the Son of Man.

"Do not marvel at this; for an hour is coming, in which all who are in the tombs will hear His voice, and will come forth; those who did the good deeds to a **resurrection** of life, those who committed the evil deeds to a **resurrection** of judgment."   *John 5:19-29*

Martha then said to Jesus, "Lord, if You had been here, my brother would not have died. Even now I know that whatever You ask of God, God will give You."

Jesus said to her, "Your brother will **rise again**."

Martha said to Him, "I know that he will **rise again** in the **resurrection** on the last day."

Jesus said to her, "I am the **resurrection** and the life; he who believes in Me will live even if he dies, and everyone who lives and believes in Me will never die. Do you believe this?"

She said to Him, "Yes, Lord; I have believed that You are the Christ, the Son of God, even He who comes into the world."   *John 11:21-27*

Jesus had not yet come into the village, but was still in the place where Martha met Him.

Therefore, when Mary came where Jesus was, she saw Him, and fell at His feet, saying to Him, "Lord, if You had been here, my brother would not have died."

When Jesus therefore saw her weeping, and the Jews who came with her also weeping, He was deeply moved in spirit and was troubled, and said, "Where have you laid him?"

They said to Him, "Lord, come and see."

Jesus wept. So the Jews were saying, "See how He loved him!"

But some of them said, "Could not this man, who opened the eyes of the blind man, have kept this man also from dying?"

So Jesus, again being deeply moved within, came to the tomb. Now it was a cave, and a stone was lying against it.

Jesus said, "Remove the stone."

Martha, the sister of the deceased, said to Him, "Lord, by this time there will be a stench, for he has been dead four days."

Jesus said to her, "Did I not say to you that if you believe, you will see the glory of God?" So they removed the stone.

Then Jesus raised His eyes, and said, "Father, I thank You that You have heard Me. I knew that You always hear Me; but because of the people standing around I said it, so that they may believe that You sent Me."

When He had said these things, He cried out with a loud voice, "Lazarus, come forth."

The man who had died came forth, bound hand and foot with wrappings, and his face was wrapped around with a cloth.

Jesus said to them, "Unbind him, and let him go."

Therefore many of the Jews who came to Mary, and saw what He had done, believed in Him.   *John 11:30-45*

Jesus, six days before the Passover, came to Bethany where Lazarus was, whom Jesus had **raised from the dead**.

So they made Him a supper there, and Martha was serving; but Lazarus was one of those reclining at the table with Him.   *John 12:1-2*

The large crowd of the Jews then learned that He was there; and they came, not for Jesus' sake only, but that they might also see Lazarus, whom He **raised from the dead**.

But the chief priests planned to put Lazarus to death also; because on account of him many of the Jews were going away and were believing in Jesus.

On the next day the large crowd who had come to the feast, when they heard that Jesus was coming to Jerusalem, took the branches of the palm trees and went out to meet Him, and began to shout, "Hosanna! Blessed is He who comes in the name of the Lord, even the King of Israel."

Jesus, finding a young donkey, sat on it; as it is written, "Fear not, daughter of Zion; behold, your King is coming, seated on a donkey's colt."

These things His disciples did not understand at the first; but when Jesus was glorified, then they remembered that these things were written of Him, and that they had done these things to Him.

So the people, who were with Him when He called Lazarus out of the tomb and **raised** him **from the dead**, continued to testify about Him. For this reason also the people went and met Him, because they heard that He had performed this sign. *John 12:9-18*

After these things Jesus manifested Himself again to the disciples at the Sea of Tiberias, and He manifested Himself in this way.

Simon Peter, and Thomas called Didymus, and Nathanael of Cana in Galilee, and the sons of Zebedee, and two others of His disciples were together.

Simon Peter said to them, "I am going fishing."

They said to him, "We will also come with you." They went out and got into the boat; and that night they caught nothing.

But when the day was now breaking, Jesus stood on the beach; yet the disciples did not know that it was Jesus.

So Jesus said to them, "Children, you do not have any fish, do you?"

They answered Him, "No."

And He said to them, "Cast the net on the right-hand side of the boat and you will find a catch."

So they cast, and then they were not able to haul it in because of the great number of fish. Therefore that disciple whom Jesus loved said to Peter, "It is the Lord."

So when Simon Peter heard that it was the Lord, he put his outer garment on (for he was stripped for work), and threw himself into the sea.

But the other disciples came in the little boat, for they were not far from the land, but about one hundred yards away, dragging the net full of fish.

So when they got out on the land, they saw a charcoal fire already laid and fish placed on it, and bread.

Jesus said to them, "Bring some of the fish which you have now caught."

Simon Peter went up and drew the net to land, full of large fish, a hundred and fifty-three; and although there were so many, the net was not torn.

Jesus said to them, "Come and have breakfast."

None of the disciples ventured to question Him, "Who are You?" knowing that it was the Lord.

Jesus came and took the bread and gave it to them, and the fish likewise.

This is now the third time that Jesus was manifested to the disciples, after He was **raised from the dead**. *John 21:1-14*

It is necessary that of the men who have accompanied us all the time that the Lord Jesus went in and out among us - beginning with the baptism of John until the day that He was taken up from us - one of these must become a witness with us of His **resurrection**.

So they put forward two men, Joseph called Barsabbas (who was also called Justus), and Matthias. *Acts 1:21-23*

Men of Israel, listen to these words: Jesus the Nazarene, a man attested to you by God with miracles and wonders and signs which God performed through Him in your midst, just as you yourselves know - this Man, delivered over by the predetermined plan and foreknowledge of God, you nailed to a cross by the hands of godless men and put Him to death.

But God **raised** Him up **again**, putting an end to the agony of death, since it was impossible for Him to be held in its power.

For David says of Him, "I saw the Lord always in my presence; for He is at my right hand, so that I will not be shaken. Therefore my heart was glad and my tongue exulted; moreover my flesh also will live in hope; because You will not abandon my soul to Hades, nor allow Your Holy One to undergo decay.

"You have made known to me the ways of life; You will make me full of gladness with Your presence."

Brethren, I may confidently say to you regarding the patriarch David that he both died and was buried, and his tomb is with us to this day.

And so, because he was a prophet and knew that God had sworn to him with an oath to seat one of his descendants on his throne, he looked ahead and spoke of the **resurrection** of the Christ, that He was neither abandoned to Hades, nor did His flesh suffer decay. This Jesus God **raised** up **again**, to which we are all witnesses.

Therefore having been exalted to the right hand of God, and having received from the Father the promise of the Holy Spirit, He has poured forth this which you both see and hear.   *Acts 2:22-33*

The God of Abraham, Isaac and Jacob, the God of our fathers, has glorified His servant Jesus, the one whom you delivered and disowned in the presence of Pilate, when he had decided to release Him.

But you disowned the Holy and Righteous One and asked for a murderer to be granted to you, but put to death the Prince of life, the one whom God **raised from the dead**, a fact to which we are witnesses.   *Acts 3:13-15*

As they were speaking to the people, the priests and the captain of the temple guard and the Sadducees came up to them, being greatly disturbed because they were teaching the people and proclaiming in Jesus the **resurrection** from the dead.

And they laid hands on them and put them in jail until the next day, for it was already evening.

But many of those who had heard the message believed; and the number of the men came to be about five thousand.
     Acts 4:1-4

Peter, filled with the Holy Spirit, said to them, "Rulers and elders of the people, if we are on trial today for a benefit done to a sick man, as to how this man has been made well, let it be known to all of you and to all the people of Israel, that by the name of Jesus Christ the Nazarene, whom you crucified, whom God **raised from the dead** - by this name this man stands here before you in good health."
     Acts 4:8-10

The congregation of those who believed were of one heart and soul; and not one of them claimed that anything belonging to him was his own, but all things were common property to them.

And with great power the apostles were giving testimony to the **resurrection** of the Lord Jesus, and abundant grace was upon them all.   *Acts 4:32-33*

In Joppa there was a disciple named Tabitha (which translated in Greek is called Dorcas); this woman was abounding with deeds of kindness and charity which she continually did.

And it happened at that time that she fell sick and died; and when they had washed her body, they laid it in an upper room.

Since Lydda was near Joppa, the disciples, having heard that Peter was there, sent two men to him, imploring him, "Do not delay in coming to us." So Peter arose and went with them.

When he arrived, they brought him into the upper room; and all the widows stood beside him, weeping and showing all the tunics and garments that Dorcas used to make while she was with them.

But Peter sent them all out and knelt down and prayed, and turning to the body, he said, "Tabitha, **arise**."

And she opened her eyes, and when she saw Peter, she sat up.

And he gave her his hand and raised her up; and calling the saints and widows, he presented her alive.

It became known all over Joppa, and many believed in the Lord.   *Acts 9:36-42*

Brethren, sons of Abraham's family, and those among you who fear God, to us the message of this salvation has been sent. For those who live in Jerusalem, and their rulers, recognizing neither Him nor the utterances of the prophets which are read every Sabbath, fulfilled these by condemning Him. And though they found no ground for putting Him to death, they asked Pilate that He be executed.

When they had carried out all that was written concerning Him, they took Him down from the cross and laid Him in a tomb.

But God **raised** Him **from the dead**; and for many days He appeared to those who came up with Him from Galilee to Jerusalem, the very ones who are now His witnesses to the people.

And we preach to you the good news of the promise made to the fathers, that God has fulfilled this promise to our children in that He **raised** up Jesus, as it is also written in the second Psalm, "You are My Son; today I have begotten You."

As for the fact that He **raised** Him up **from the dead**, no longer to return to decay, He has spoken in this way: "I will give you the holy and sure blessings of David."

Therefore He also says in another Psalm, "You will not allow Your Holy One to undergo decay."

For David, after he had served the purpose of God in his own generation, fell asleep, and was laid among his fathers and underwent decay; but He whom God **raised** did not undergo decay.

Therefore let it be known to you, brethren, that through Him forgiveness of sins is proclaimed to you, and through Him everyone who believes is freed from all things, from which you could not be freed through the Law of Moses.

Acts 13:26-39

While Paul was waiting for them at Athens, his spirit was being provoked within him as he was observing the city full of idols.

So he was reasoning in the synagogue with the Jews and the God-fearing Gentiles, and in the market place every day with those who happened to be present. And also some of the Epicurean and Stoic philosophers were conversing with him.

Some were saying, "What would this idle babbler wish to say?"

Others, "He seems to be a proclaimer of strange deities," - because he was preaching Jesus and the **resurrection**.

And they took him and brought him to the Areopagus, saying, "May we know what this new teaching is which you are proclaiming? For you are bringing some strange things to our ears; so we want to know what these things mean."

(Now all the Athenians and the strangers visiting there used to spend their time in nothing other than telling or hearing something new.) *Acts 17:16-21*

Being the children of God, we ought not to think that the Divine Nature is like gold or silver or stone, an image formed by the art and thought of man.

Therefore having overlooked the times of ignorance, God is now declaring to men that all people everywhere should repent, because He has fixed a day in which He will judge the world in righteousness through a Man whom He has appointed, having furnished proof to all men by **raising** Him **from the dead**.

Now when they heard of the **resurrection** of the dead, some began to sneer, but others said, "We shall hear you again concerning this."

So Paul went out of their midst.

But some men joined him and believed, among whom also were Dionysius the Areopagite and a woman named Damaris and others with them.

Acts 17:29-34

Perceiving that one group were Sadducees and the other Pharisees, Paul began crying out in the Council, "Brethren, I am a Pharisee, a son of Pharisees; I am on trial for the hope and **resurrection** of the dead!"

As he said this, there occurred a dissension between the Pharisees and Sadducees, and the assembly was divided. For the Sadducees say that there is no **resurrection**, nor an angel, nor a spirit, but the Pharisees acknowledge them all.

And there occurred a great uproar; and some of the scribes of the Pharisaic party stood up and began to argue heatedly, saying, "We find nothing wrong with this man; suppose a spirit or an angel has spoken to him?" *Acts 23:6-9*

When the governor had nodded for him to speak, Paul responded: "Knowing that for many years you have been a judge to this nation, I cheerfully make my defense, since you can take note of the fact that no more than twelve days ago I went up to Jerusalem to worship.

Neither in the temple, nor in the synagogues, nor in the city itself did they find me carrying on a discussion with anyone or causing a riot. Nor can they prove to you the charges of which they now accuse me.

"But this I admit to you, that according to the Way which they call a sect I do serve the God of our fathers, believing everything that is in accordance with the Law and that is written in the Prophets; having a hope in God, which these men cherish themselves, that there shall certainly be a **resurrection** of both the righteous and the wicked.

In view of this, I also do my best to maintain always a blameless conscience both before God and before men.

"Now after several years I came to bring alms to my nation and to present offerings; in which they found me occupied in the temple, having been purified, without any crowd or uproar.

But there were some Jews from Asia - who ought to have been present before you and to make accusation, if they should have anything against me. Or else let these men themselves tell what misdeed they found when I stood before the Council, other than for this one statement which I shouted out while standing among them, 'For the **resurrection** of the dead I am on trial before you today.' " *Acts 24:10-21*

I am standing trial for the hope of the promise made by God to our fathers; the promise to which our twelve tribes hope to attain, as they earnestly serve God night and day. And for this hope, O King, I am being accused by Jews.

Why is it considered incredible among you people if God does **raise the dead**? *Acts 26:6-8*

"King Agrippa, I did not prove disobedient to the heavenly vision, but kept declaring both to those of Damascus first, and also at Jerusalem and then throughout all the region of Judea, and even to the Gentiles, that they should repent and turn to God, performing deeds appropriate to repentance. For this reason some Jews seized me in the temple and tried to put me to death.

"So, having obtained help from God, I stand to this day testifying both to small and great, stating nothing but what the Prophets and Moses said was going to take place; that the Christ was to suffer, and that by reason of His **resurrection** from the dead He would be the first to proclaim light both to the Jewish people and to the Gentiles."

While Paul was saying this in his defense, Festus said in a loud voice, "Paul, you are out of your mind! Your great learning is driving you mad."

But Paul said, "I am not out of my mind, most excellent Festus, but I utter words of sober truth." *Acts 26:19-25*

Paul, a bond-servant of Christ Jesus, called as an apostle, set apart for the gospel of God, He promised beforehand through His prophets in the holy Scriptures, concerning His Son, who was born of a descendant of David according to the flesh, who was declared the Son of God with power by the **resurrection** from the dead, according to the Spirit of holiness, Jesus Christ our Lord, through whom we have received grace and apostleship to bring about the obedience of faith among all the Gentiles for His name's sake, among whom you also are the called of Jesus Christ; to all who are beloved of

God in Rome, called as saints: Grace to you and peace from God our Father and the Lord Jesus Christ.   *Romans 1:1-7*

For this reason it is by faith, in order that it may be in accordance with grace, so that the promise will be guaranteed to all the descendants, not only to those who are of the Law, but also to those who are of the faith of Abraham, who is the father of us all, (as it is written, "A father of many nations have I made you") in the presence of Him whom he believed, even God, who gives life to the dead and calls into being that which does not exist. In hope against hope he believed, so that he might become a father of many nations according to that which had been spoken, "So shall your descendants be."

Without becoming weak in faith he contemplated his own body, now as good as dead since he was about a hundred years old, and the deadness of Sarah's womb; yet, with respect to the promise of God, he did not waver in unbelief but grew strong in faith, giving glory to God, and being fully assured that what God had promised, He was able also to perform.

Therefore it was also credited to him as righteousness. Now not for his sake only was it written that it was credited to him, but for our sake also, to whom it will be credited, as those who believe in Him who **raised** Jesus our Lord **from the dead**, He who was delivered over because of our transgressions, and was **raised** because of our justification.

Therefore, having been justified by faith, we have peace with God through our Lord Jesus Christ, through whom also we have obtained our introduction by faith into this grace in which we stand; and we exult in hope of the glory of God.
          Romans 4:16 - 5:2

The Law came in so that the transgression would increase; but where sin increased, grace abounded all the more, so that, as sin reigned in death, even so grace would reign through righteousness to eternal life through Jesus Christ our Lord.

What shall we say then? Are we to continue in sin so that grace may increase? May it never be! How shall we who died to sin still live in it?

Or do you not know that all of us who have been baptized into Christ Jesus have been baptized into His death?

Therefore we have been buried with Him through baptism into death, so that as Christ was **raised from the dead** through the glory of the Father, so we too might walk in newness of life.

For if we have become united with Him in the likeness of His death, certainly we shall also be in the likeness of His **resurrection**, knowing this, that our old self was crucified with Him, in order that our body of sin might be done away with, so that we would no longer be slaves to sin; for he who has died is freed from sin.

Now if we have died with Christ, we believe that we shall also live with Him, knowing that Christ, having been **raised from the dead**, is never to die again; death no longer is master over Him. For the death that He died, He died to sin once for all; but the life that He lives, He lives to God.

Even so consider yourselves to be dead to sin, but alive to God in Christ Jesus.

Therefore do not let sin reign in your mortal body so that you obey its lusts, and do not go on presenting the members of your body to sin as instruments of unrighteousness; but present yourselves to God as those alive from the dead, and your members as instruments of righteousness to God.   *Romans 5:20 - 6:13*

Having been freed from sin and enslaved to God, you derive your benefit, resulting in sanctification, and the outcome, eternal life. For the wages of sin is death, but the free gift of God is eternal life in Christ Jesus our Lord.

Or do you not know, brethren (for I am speaking to those who know the law), that the law has jurisdiction over a person as long as he lives? For the married woman is bound by law to her husband while he is living; but if her husband dies, she is released from the law concerning the husband.

So then, if while her husband is living she is joined to another man, she shall be called an adulteress; but if her husband dies, she is free from the law, so that she is not an adulteress though she is joined to another man.

Therefore, my brethren, you also were made to die to the Law through the body of Christ, so that you might be joined to another, to Him who was **raised from the dead**, in order that we might bear fruit for God.

For while we were in the flesh, the sinful passions, which were aroused by the Law, were at work in the members of our body to bear fruit for death.

But now we have been released from the Law, having died to that by which we were bound, so that we serve in newness of the Spirit and not in oldness of the letter. *Romans 6:22 - 7:6*

Those who are according to the flesh set their minds on the things of the flesh, but those who are according to the Spirit, the things of the Spirit.

For the mind set on the flesh is death, but the mind set on the Spirit is life and peace, because the mind set on the flesh is hostile toward God; for it does not subject itself to the law of God, for it is not even able to do so, and those who are in the flesh cannot please God.

However, you are not in the flesh but in the Spirit, if indeed the Spirit of God dwells in you. But if anyone does not have the Spirit of Christ, he does not belong to Him.

If Christ is in you, though the body is dead because of sin, yet the spirit is alive because of righteousness. But if the Spirit of Him who **raised** Jesus **from the dead** dwells in you, He who **raised** Christ Jesus **from the dead** will also give life to your mortal bodies through His Spirit who dwells in you.

So then, brethren, we are under obligation, not to the flesh, to live according to the flesh - for if you are living according to the flesh, you must die; but if by the Spirit you are putting to death the deeds of the body, you will live. For all who are being led by the Spirit of God, these are sons of God. *Romans 8:5-14*

What then shall we say to these things? If God is for us, who is against us?

He who did not spare His own Son, but delivered Him over for us all, how will He not also with Him freely give us all things?

Who will bring a charge against God's elect? God is the one who justifies; who is the one who condemns?

Christ Jesus is He who died, yes, rather who was **raised**, who is at the right hand of God, who also intercedes for us. *Romans 8:31-34*

Christ is the end of the law for righteousness to everyone who believes. For Moses writes that the man who practices the righteousness which is based on law shall live by that righteousness.

But the righteousness based on faith speaks as follows: "Do not say in your heart, 'Who will ascend into heaven?' (that is, to bring Christ down), or 'Who will descend into the abyss?' (that is, to bring Christ up from the dead)."

But what does it say? "The word is near you, in your mouth and in your heart" - that is, the word of faith which we are preaching, that if you confess with your mouth Jesus as Lord, and believe in your heart that God **raised** Him **from the dead**, you will be saved; for with the heart a person believes, resulting in righteousness, and with the mouth he confesses, resulting in salvation.

For the Scripture says, "Whoever believes in Him will not be disappointed." *Romans 10:4-11*

What then? What Israel is seeking, it has not obtained, but those who were chosen obtained it, and the rest were hardened; just as it is written, "God gave them a spirit of stupor, eyes to see not and ears to hear not, down to this very day."

And David says, "Let their table become a snare and a trap, and a stumbling block and a retribution to them. Let their eyes be darkened to see not, and bend their backs forever."

I say then, they did not stumble so as to fall, did they? May it never be! But by their transgression salvation has come to the Gentiles, to make them jealous.

Now if their transgression is riches for the world and their failure is riches for the Gentiles, how much more will their fulfillment be!

But I am speaking to you who are Gentiles. Inasmuch then as I am an apostle of Gentiles, I magnify my ministry, if somehow I might move to jealousy my fellow countrymen and save some of them.

For if their rejection is the reconciliation of the world, what will their acceptance be but life from the dead?

Romans 11:13-15

Food is for the stomach and the stomach is for food, but God will do away with both of them. Yet the body is not for immorality, but for the Lord, and the Lord is for the body.

Now God has not only **raised** the Lord, but will also **raise** us up through His power.   *1 Corinthians 6:13-14*

If Christ is preached, that He has been **raised from the dead**, how do some among you say that there is no **resurrection** of the dead?

But if there is no **resurrection** of the dead, not even Christ has been **raised**; and if Christ has not been **raised**, then our preaching is vain, your faith also is vain.

Moreover we are even found to be false witnesses of God, because we testified against God that He **raised** Christ, whom He did not **raise**, if in fact the dead are not **raised**.

For if the dead are not **raised**, not even Christ has been **raised**; if Christ has not been **raised**, your faith is worthless; you are still in your sins. Then those also who have fallen asleep in Christ have perished.

If we have hoped in Christ in this life only, we are of all men most to be pitied. But now Christ has been **raised from the dead**, the first fruits of those who are asleep.

For since by a man came death, by a man also came the **resurrection** of the dead. For as in Adam all die, so also in Christ all will be made alive.

But each in his own order: Christ the first fruits, after that those who are Christ's at His coming, then comes the end, when He hands over the kingdom to the God and Father, when He has abolished all rule and all authority and power.

The last enemy that will be abolished is death. For He has put all things in subjection under His feet.

But when He says, "All things are put in subjection," it is evident that He is excepted who put all things in subjection to Him.

When all things are subjected to Him, then the Son Himself also will be subjected to the One who subjected all things to Him, so that God may be all in all. Otherwise, what will those do who are baptized for the dead? If the **dead** are not **raised** at all, why then are they baptized for them? Why are we also in danger every hour?

I affirm, brethren, by the boasting in you which I have in Christ Jesus our Lord, I die daily. If from human motives I fought with wild beasts at Ephesus, what does it profit me?

If the **dead** are not **raised**, let us eat and drink, for tomorrow we die. Do not be deceived: "Bad company corrupts good morals."

Become sober-minded as you ought, and stop sinning; for some have no knowledge of God. I speak this to your shame. For He must reign until He has put all His enemies under His feet.

But someone will say, "How are the **dead raised**? And with what kind of body do they come?"

You fool! That which you sow does not come to life unless it dies; and that which you sow, you do not sow the body which is to be, but a bare grain, perhaps of wheat or of something else. But God gives it a body just as He wished, and to each of the seeds a body of its own.

All flesh is not the same flesh, but there is one flesh of men, and another flesh of beasts, and another flesh of birds, and another of fish.

There are also heavenly bodies and earthly bodies, but the glory of the heavenly is one, and the glory of the earthly is another. There is one glory of the sun, and another glory of the moon, and another glory of the stars; for star differs from star in glory.

So also is the **resurrection** of the **dead**. It is sown a perishable body, it is **raised** an imperishable body; it is sown in dishonor, it is **raised** in glory; it is sown in weakness, it is **raised** in power; it is sown a natural body, it is **raised** a spiritual body.

If there is a natural body, there is also a spiritual body. So also it is written, "The first man, Adam, became a living soul." The last Adam became a life-giving spirit.

However, the spiritual is not first, but the natural; then the spiritual. The first man is from the earth, earthy; the second man is from heaven. As is the earthy, so also are those who are earthy; and as is the heavenly, so also are those who are heavenly.

Just as we have borne the image of the earthy, we will also bear the image of the heavenly.

Now I say this, brethren, that flesh and blood cannot inherit the kingdom of God; nor does the perishable inherit the imperishable.

Behold, I tell you a mystery; we will not all sleep, but we will all be changed, in a moment, in the twinkling of an eye, at the last trumpet; for the trumpet will sound, and the **dead** will be **raised** imperishable, and we will be changed. For this perishable must put on the imperishable, and this mortal must put on immortality.

But when this perishable will have put on the imperishable, and this mortal will have put on immortality, then will come about the saying that is written, "Death is swallowed up in victory. O death, where is your victory? O death, where is your sting?"

The sting of death is sin, and the power of sin is the law; but thanks be to God, who gives us the victory through our Lord Jesus Christ.

Therefore, my beloved brethren, be steadfast, immovable, always abounding in the work of the Lord, knowing that your toil is not in vain in the Lord.

1 Corinthians 15:12-58

We do not want you to be unaware, brethren, of our affliction which came to us in Asia, that we were burdened excessively, beyond our strength, so that we despaired even of life; indeed, we had the sentence of death within ourselves so that we would not trust in ourselves, but in God who **raises the dead**; who delivered us from so great a peril of death, and will deliver us, He on whom we have set our hope.

And He will yet deliver us, you also joining in helping us through your prayers, so that thanks may be given by many persons on our behalf for the favor bestowed on us through the prayers of many. *2 Corinthians 1:8-11*

The love of Christ controls us, having concluded this, that one died for all, therefore all died; and He died for all, so that they who live might no longer live for themselves, but for Him who died and **rose again** on their behalf.

Therefore from now on we recognize no one according to the flesh; even though we have known Christ according to the flesh, yet now we know Him in this way no longer.

Therefore if anyone is in Christ, he is a new creature; the old things passed away; behold, new things have come.

2 Corinthians 5:14-17

Paul, an apostle (not sent from men nor through the agency of man, but through Jesus Christ and God the Father, who **raised** Him **from the dead**), and all the brethren who are with me, to the churches of Galatia: Grace to you and peace from God our Father and the Lord Jesus Christ, who gave Himself for our sins so that He might rescue us from this present evil age, according to the will of our God and Father, to whom be the glory forevermore. Amen. *Galatians 1:1-5*

I pray that the eyes of your heart may be enlightened, so that you will know what is the hope of His calling, what are the riches of the glory of His inheritance in the saints, and what is the surpassing greatness of His power toward us who believe.

These are in accordance with the working of the strength of His might which He brought about in Christ, when He **raised** Him **from the dead** and seated Him at His right hand in the heavenly places, far above all rule and authority and power and dominion, and every name that is named, not only in this age but also in the one to come.

And He put all things in subjection under His feet, and gave Him as head over all things to the church, which is His body, the fullness of Him who fills all in all.

And you were dead in your trespasses and sins, in which you formerly walked according to the course of this world, according to the prince of the power of the air, of the spirit that is now working in the sons of disobedience.

Among them we too all formerly lived in the lusts of our flesh, indulging the desires of the flesh and of the mind, and were by nature children of wrath, even as the rest.

But God, being rich in mercy, because of His great love with which He loved us, even when we were dead in our transgressions, made us alive together with Christ (by grace you have been saved), and **raised** us up with Him, and seated us with Him in the heavenly places in Christ Jesus, so that in the ages to come He might show the surpassing riches of His grace in kindness toward us in Christ Jesus.

For by grace you have been saved through faith; and that not of yourselves, it is the gift of God; not as a result of works, so that no one may boast.

For we are His workmanship, created in Christ Jesus for good works, which God prepared beforehand so that we would walk in them. *Ephesians 1:18 - 2:10*

Do not participate in the unfruitful deeds of darkness, but instead even expose them; for it is disgraceful even to speak of the things which are done by them in secret.

But all things become visible when they are exposed by the light, for everything that becomes visible is light.

For this reason it says, "Awake, sleeper, and **arise from the dead**, and Christ will shine on you."

Therefore be careful how you walk, not as unwise men but as wise, making the most of your time, because the days are evil. So then do not be foolish, but understand what the will of the Lord is. *Ephesians 5:11-17*

Whatever things were gain to me, those things I have counted as loss for the sake of Christ.

More than that, I count all things to be loss in view of the surpassing value of knowing Christ Jesus my Lord, for whom I have suffered the loss of all things, and count them but rubbish so that I may gain Christ, and may be found in Him, not having a righteousness of my own derived from the Law, but that which is through faith in Christ, the righteousness which comes from God on the basis of faith, that I may know Him and the power of His **resurrection** and the fellowship of His sufferings, being conformed to His death; in order that I may attain to the **resurrection** from the dead.

Not that I have already obtained it or have already become perfect, but I press on so that I may lay hold of that for which also I was laid hold of by Christ Jesus.

Brethren, I do not regard myself as having laid hold of it yet; but one thing I do: Forgetting what lies behind and reaching forward to what lies ahead, I press on toward the goal for the prize of the upward call of God in Christ Jesus.

Let us therefore, as many as are perfect, have this attitude; and if in anything you have a different attitude, God will reveal that also to you; however, let us keep living by that same standard to which we have attained.   *Philippians 3:7-16*

See to it that no one takes you captive through philosophy and empty deception, according to the tradition of men, according to the elementary principles of the world, rather than according to Christ.

For in Him all the fullness of Deity dwells in bodily form, and in Him you have been made complete, and He is the head over all rule and authority; and in Him you were also circumcised with a circumcision made without hands, in the removal of the body of the flesh by the circumcision of Christ; having been buried with Him in baptism, in which you were also **raised** up with Him through faith in the working of God, who **raised** Him **from the dead**.

When you were dead in your transgressions and the uncircumcision of your flesh, He made you alive together with Him, having forgiven us all our transgressions, having canceled out the certificate of debt consisting of decrees against us, which was hostile to us; and He has taken it out of the way, having nailed it to the cross.   *Colossians 2:8-14*

The word of the Lord has sounded forth from you, not only in Macedonia and Achaia, but also in every place your faith toward God has gone forth, so that we have no need to say anything.

For they themselves report about us what kind of a reception we had with you, and how you turned to God from idols to serve a living and true God, and to wait for His Son from heaven, whom He **raised from the dead**, that is Jesus, who rescues us from the wrath to come.
     1 Thessalonians 1:8-10

We do not want you to be uninformed, brethren, about those who are asleep, so that you will not grieve as do the rest who have no hope.

For if we believe that Jesus died and **rose again**, even so God will bring with Him those who have fallen asleep in Jesus. For this we say to you by the word of the Lord, that we who are alive and remain until the coming of the Lord, will not precede those who have fallen asleep.

For the Lord Himself will descend from heaven with a shout, with the voice of the archangel and with the trumpet of God, and the **dead** in Christ will **rise** first.

Then we who are alive and remain will be caught up together with them in the clouds to meet the Lord in the air, and so we shall always be with the Lord.

Therefore comfort one another with these words.   *1 Thessalonians 4:13-18*

Consider what I say, for the Lord will give you understanding in everything.

Remember Jesus Christ, **risen from the dead**, descendant of David, according to my gospel, for which I suffer hardship even to imprisonment as a criminal; but the word of God is not imprisoned.

For this reason I endure all things for the sake of those who are chosen, so that they also may obtain the salvation which is in Christ Jesus and with it eternal glory.

It is a trustworthy statement: for if we died with Him, we will also live with Him; if we endure, we will also reign with Him; if we deny Him, He also will deny us; if we are faithless, He remains faithful, for He cannot deny Himself.

Remind them of these things, and solemnly charge them in the presence of God not to wrangle about words, which is useless and leads to the ruin of the hearers.

Be diligent to present yourself approved to God as a workman who does not need to be ashamed, accurately handling the word of truth.

But avoid worldly and empty chatter, for it will lead to further ungodliness, and their talk will spread like gangrene.

Among them are Hymenaeus and Philetus, men who have gone astray from the truth saying that the **resurrection** has already taken place, and they upset the faith of some.

Nevertheless, the firm foundation of God stands, having this seal, "The Lord knows those who are His," and, "Everyone who names the name of the Lord is to abstain from wickedness."

2 Timothy 2:7-19

Leaving the elementary teaching about the Christ, let us press on to maturity, not laying again a foundation of repentance from dead works and of faith toward God, of instruction about washings and laying on of hands, and the **resurrection** of the dead and eternal judgment. And this we will do, if God permits.

For in the case of those who have once been enlightened and have tasted of the heavenly gift and have been made partakers of the Holy Spirit, and have tasted the good word of God and the powers of the age to come, and then have fallen away, it is impossible to renew them again to repentance, since they again crucify to themselves the Son of God and put Him to open shame.

Hebrews 6:1-6

By faith Abraham, when he was tested, offered up Isaac, and he who had received the promises was offering up his only begotten son; it was he to whom it was said, "In Isaac your descendants shall be called."

He considered that God is able to **raise** people even **from the dead**, from which he also received him back as a type.

Hebrews 11:17-19

What more shall I say? For time will fail me if I tell of Gideon, Barak, Samson, Jephthah, of David and Samuel and the prophets, who by faith conquered kingdoms, performed acts of righteousness, obtained promises, shut the mouths of lions, quenched the power of fire, escaped the edge of the sword, from weakness were made strong, became mighty in war, put foreign armies to flight.

Women received back their dead by **resurrection**; and others were tortured, not accepting their release, so that they might obtain a better **resurrection**; and others experienced mockings and scourgings, yes, also chains and imprisonment. They were stoned, they were sawn in two, they were tempted, they were put to death with the sword; they went about in sheepskins, in goatskins, being destitute, afflicted, ill-treated (men of whom the world was not worthy), wandering in deserts and mountains and caves and holes in the ground.

Hebrews 11:32-38

Blessed be the God and Father of our Lord Jesus Christ, who according to His great mercy has caused us to be born again to a living hope through the **resurrection** of Jesus Christ from the dead, to obtain an inheritance which is imperishable and undefiled and will not fade away, reserved in heaven for you, who are protected by the power of God through faith for a salvation ready to be revealed in the last time.

In this you greatly rejoice, even though now for a little while, if necessary, you have been distressed by various trials, so that the proof of your faith, being more precious than gold which is perishable, even though tested by fire, may be found to result in praise and glory and honor at the revelation of Jesus Christ; and though you have not seen Him, you love Him, and though you do not see Him now, but believe in Him, you greatly rejoice with joy inexpressible and full of glory, obtaining as the outcome of your faith the salvation of your souls.

1 Peter 1:3-9

If you address as Father the One who impartially judges according to each one's work, conduct yourselves in fear during the time of your stay on earth; knowing that you were not redeemed with perishable things like silver or gold from your futile way of life inherited from your forefathers, but with precious blood, as of a lamb unblemished and spotless, the blood of Christ.

For He was foreknown before the foundation of the world, but has appeared in these last times for the sake of you who through Him are believers in God, who **raised** Him **from the dead** and gave Him glory, so that your faith and hope are in God.

Since you have in obedience to the truth purified your souls for a sincere love of the brethren, fervently love one another from the heart, for you have been born again not of seed which is perishable but imperishable, that is, through the living and enduring word of God.

For, "All flesh is like grass, and all its glory like the flower of grass. The grass withers, and the flower falls off, but the word of the Lord endures forever."

And this is the word which was preached to you.   *1 Peter 1:17-25*

Christ also died for sins once for all, the just for the unjust, so that He might bring us to God, having been put to death in the flesh, but made alive in the spirit; in which also He went and made proclamation to the spirits now in prison, who once were disobedient, when the patience of God kept waiting in the days of Noah, during the construction of the ark, in which a few, that is, eight persons, were brought safely through the water.

Corresponding to that, baptism now saves you - not the removal of dirt from the flesh, but an appeal to God for a good conscience - through the **resurrection** of Jesus Christ, who is at the right hand of God, having gone into heaven, after angels and authorities and powers had been subjected to Him.   *1 Peter 3:18-22*

I saw an angel coming down from heaven, holding the key of the abyss and a great chain in his hand.

And he laid hold of the dragon, the serpent of old, who is the devil and Satan, and bound him for a thousand years; and he threw him into the abyss, and shut it and sealed it over him, so that he would not deceive the nations any longer, until the thousand years were completed; after these things he must be released for a short time.

Then I saw thrones, and they sat on them, and judgment was given to them.

And I saw the souls of those who had been beheaded because of their testimony of Jesus and because of the word of God, and those who had not worshiped the beast or his image, and had not received the mark on their forehead and on their hand; and they came to life and reigned with Christ for a thousand years.

The rest of the dead did not come to life until the thousand years were completed. This is the first **resurrection**.

Blessed and holy is the one who has a part in the first **resurrection**; over these the second death has no power, but they will be priests of God and of Christ and will reign with Him for a thousand years.

Revelation 20:1-6

~ End of Scriptures ~

IMPROVING THE SOLA SCRIPTURA TOPICAL BIBLE
SEVEN SYMBOLS SERIES

This edition of the **Sola Scriptura Topical Bible**: *Seven Symbols of Jesus* is as complete and accurate as possible at the time of its publication, but there is always room for improvement.

Sola Scriptura, and the works that are based upon its text, is open to comment, review and criticism. As the many eyes and minds of the group are better than a few, it is hoped that people from around the world would share their input to help further refine future editions this work. As such, everyone is encouraged to submit their comments, corrections and suggestions, using the form at: solascriptura.ca/outreach/

All input to help improve this topical Bible is greatly appreciated,
and may enhance future editions of this work! Thank You!

If you enjoyed reading this book, please help spread The Word, by leaving an honest and positive review at:

amazon.com/dp/198827186X

goodreads.com/book/show/69241395-sola-scriptura-topical-bible

Other editions of this publication,
Sola Scriptura Topical Bible: *Seven Symbols of Jesus*

Kindle: ISBN 978-1-77885-021-9   ePub: ISBN 978-1-77885-022-6
PDF: ISBN 978-1-77885-023-3   Hard Cover: ISBN 978-1-77885-020-2

Available at: solascriptura.ca   *See more* **Seven Symbols** *on the following page.*

Editions of: **Sola Scriptura Topical Bible**: *Top 20 Spiritual Symbols*

1. Angel	8. Demon	15. Pray
2. Baptism	9. Devil / Satan	16. Resurrection
3. Believe	10. Faith	17. Salvation
4. Christ + Messiah	11. Gospel	18. Son of God
5. Church	12. Hell	19. Son of Man
6. Commandments	13. Holy Spirit / Spirit	20. Tithe
7. Covenant	14. Kingdom	

Kindle: ISBN 978-1-988271-14-9   ePub: ISBN 978-1-988271-13-2
PDF: ISBN 978-1-988271-12-5
Hard Cover: ISBN 978-1-988271-87-3   Paperback: ISBN 978-1-988271-86-6

Available at: solascriptura.ca

Look for these other Titles in the **SEVEN SYMBOLS** Series:

The CHURCH	SALVATION	HEALING
Church	Salvation	Healing
Kingdom	Redemption	Miracle
Baptism	Atonement	Pray
Gospel	Repentance	Faith
Salvation	Forgive	Holy Spirit
Apostle	Believe	Blind
Saint	Faith	Fasting

GOD	EVIL	MARRIAGE
Eternal	The Devil	Marriage
Highest Heaven	Demons	Wedding
Holy Spirit	The Anti-Christ	Bride + Groom
Glory	Hell	Husband
Father	Hades / Sheol	Harlot
Angels	Idolatry	Adultery
Wisdom	Blasphemy	Divorce

THE LAW	JUDAISM	NATURE
Covenant	Commandment	Mountain
Commandment	Circumcise	Drought
Justice	Sabbath	Earthquake
Discipline	Tithe	Storm
Prison	Jubilee	Flood
Confess	High Priest	Cloud
Test	Feast	Rainbow

Available at: solascriptura.ca

Other publications by Daniel John:

Five Column: *Four Gospel Harmony & Word-For-Word Merger* ISBN 978-1-9882710-1-9

The Synoptic Gospel: *The Story of The Life of Jesus* ISBN 978-1-988271-44-6

The Red Letter Gospel: *All The Words of Jesus Christ in Red* ISBN 978-1-988271-08-8

are available at: synopticgospel.com

www.ingramcontent.com/pod-product-compliance
Lightning Source LLC
LaVergne TN
LVHW051520080426
835509LV00017B/2129